The New Writers of the South

The New Writers of the South

A FICTION ANTHOLOGY

Edited by Charles East

The University of Georgia Press

ATHENS AND LONDON

Designed by Kathi L. Dailey
Set in 11 on 13 Mergenthaler Electra
with W. A. Dwiggins ornament

Typeset by The Composing Room of Michigan
Printed and bound by Cushing-Malloy

The paper in this book meets the guidelines for
permanence and durability of the Committee on
Production Guidelines for Book Longevity of the Council
on Library Resources.

Printed in the United States of America

91   90   89   88   87   5   4   3   2

Library of Congress Cataloging in Publication Data

The New writers of the South.

1. American fiction—Southern States. 2. American
fiction—20th century. 3. Southern States—Fiction.
I. East, Charles.
PS551.N5   1987   813'.54'080975   86-19518
ISBN 0-8203-0923-0 (alk. paper)
ISBN 0-8203-0924-9 (pbk.: alk. paper)

British Library Cataloging in Publication Data available.

For Sarah

Contents

CONTENTS

Acknowledgments

I would first of all like to thank those who helped by suggesting writers—and specific stories or novels by those writers—they thought I ought to consider. Without this kind of input, my job would have been much more difficult than it was. I want especially to thank Bob Summer for the help he gave me from the beginning of the project. Bob's vantage point as a contributing editor of *Publishers Weekly* and free-lance book reviewer, and particularly his familiarity with Southern publishing, enabled him to spot writers that I might otherwise have overlooked, and his suggestions and comments were invaluable to me. In several instances where I had trouble finding a copy of a book that I wanted to see, he promptly came to my rescue.

I would also like to acknowledge the debt that I owe the distinguished Southern scholar Lewis P. Simpson, in whose classes and seminars I long ago came to appreciate the richness of Southern literature. I am grateful to him not only for the encouragement that he gave, but for reading an early draft of the introduction and pointing out ways in which I might improve it. This book gives me the occasion to acknowledge a friendship that has meant a great deal to me over a period of a quarter of a century.

When I approached the University of Georgia Press with the idea of a book, Malcolm Call, Karen Orchard, and Douglas Armato responded enthusiastically, and during the time that I worked on the anthology they were unfailingly helpful. I would also like to express my gratitude to Kathi Dailey, who designed the book—and did such a fine job of it.

Finally, the Press and I would like to acknowledge the authors and publishers who gave us permission to include the stories or excerpts from novels that appear in this volume. They are as follows:

Excerpt from *Appalachee Red* by Raymond Andrews. Published by the Dial Press. Copyright © 1978 by Raymond Andrews. Reprinted by permission of the author.

"Monkey Park" by Madison Smartt Bell first appeared in the *Hudson Review*. Copyright © 1985 by Madison Smartt Bell. Reprinted by permission of John Farquharson Ltd.

"A Long Time Coming, A Long Time Gone" appeared in *All Set About with Fever Trees and Other Stories* by Pam Durban. Published by David R. Godine, Publisher. Copyright © 1985 by Pam Durban. Reprinted by permission of the publisher.

Excerpt from *Raney* by Clyde Edgerton. Published by Algonquin Books. Copyright © 1985 by Clyde Edgerton. Reprinted by permission of the publisher.

"Sweethearts" by Richard Ford first appeared in *Esquire*. Copyright © 1986 by Richard Ford. Reprinted by permission of the author.

"There's a Garden of Eden" appeared in *In the Land of Dreamy Dreams* by Ellen Gilchrist. Published by the University of Arkansas Press and later by Little, Brown and Company. Copyright © 1981 by Ellen Gilchrist. Reprinted by permission of Little, Brown and Company.

Excerpt from *The Dixie Association* by Donald Hays. Published by Simon & Schuster, Inc. Copyright © 1984 by Donald Hays. Reprinted by permission of the publisher.

"How Far She Went" appeared in *How Far She Went* by Mary Hood. Published by the University of Georgia Press. Copyright © 1984 by Mary Hood. Reprinted by permission of the publisher.

Excerpt from *Dreams of Sleep* by Josephine Humphreys. Published by the Viking Press. Copyright © 1984 by Josephine Humphreys. Reprinted by permission of Viking Penguin, Inc.

Excerpt from *Come Back, Lolly Ray* by Beverly Lowry. Published by Doubleday & Company, Inc. Copyright © 1976, 1977 by Beverly Lowry. Reprinted by permission of the author.

Excerpt from *July 7th* by Jill McCorkle. Published by Algonquin Books. Copyright © 1984 by Algonquin Books. Reprinted by permission of the publisher.

"Drawing Names" appeared in *Shiloh and Other Stories* by Bobbie Ann Mason. Published by Harper & Row, Publishers, Inc. Copyright © 1982 by Bobbie Ann Mason. Reprinted by permission of the publisher.

"Storyteller" by Lewis Nordan first appeared in *Harper's* and later in *Welcome to the Arrow-Catcher Fair,* published by the Louisiana State University Press. Copyright © 1983 by Lewis Nordan. Reprinted by permission of the author.

Excerpt from *A Short History of a Small Place* by T. R. Pearson. Published by the Linden Press, a division of Simon & Schuster, Inc. Copyright © 1985 by T. R. Pearson. Reprinted by permission of the publisher.

Excerpt from *Machine Dreams* by Jayne Anne Phillips. Published by E. P. Dutton/Seymour Lawrence, a division of New American Library. Copyright © 1984 by Jayne Anne Phillips. Reprinted by permission of the publisher.

Excerpt from *Edisto* by Padgett Powell. Published by Farrar, Straus & Giroux, Inc. Copyright © 1983, 1984 by Padgett Powell. Reprinted by permission of the publisher.

Excerpt from *Here to Get My Baby Out of Jail* by Louise Shivers. Published by Random House, Inc. Copyright © 1983 by Louise Shivers. Reprinted by permission of the publisher.

Excerpt from *Canaan* by Charlie Smith. Published by Simon & Schuster, Inc. Copyright © 1984 by Charlie Smith. Reprinted by permission of the publisher.

Excerpt from *North Gladiola* by James Wilcox. Published by Harper & Row, Publishers, Inc. Copyright © 1985 by James Wilcox. Reprinted by permission of the publisher.

"Country Blues for Melissa" first appeared in *From the Bottom Up* by Leigh Allison Wilson. Published by the University of Georgia Press. Copyright © 1983 by Leigh Allison Wilson. Reprinted by permission of the publisher.

Introduction

Putting together an anthology of fiction from the new writers of the South at once presents the problem of defining not only what is "new" but what criteria are to be used in sorting out several categories of writers who could conceivably be called Southern. Must a Southern writer have been born in the South? Have grown up there? What of the writers—frequently writer-teachers—who came into the South at twenty-five or thirty but who prior to that lived elsewhere? Or the reverse: those Southerners who left the South, many of them to teach in Northern colleges? Must a Southern writer write about the South? Is there any longer a South to write about—that is, a South with a regional identity of its own, distinct from the rest of the country?

These are the questions that I wrestled with as I worked on this anthology, and I might say they are some of the same questions that, as a Southerner, I have turned around in my head for most of my life. I am aware that others may very well argue for a different reading. The South, which John Donald Wade called "one of the great abstractions of our race," continues to baffle and elude us.

The new writers of the South are, first of all, as I define them, new in the sense that none had come onto the literary scene before the second half of the seventies. Most of those whose work appears in this volume (sixteen of the twenty) did not in fact publish first books of fiction until after 1980. Second, they are writers who spent all or a substantial part of their early lives in one or more of the states that I consider Southern: Mississippi, Louisiana, Arkansas, Texas (East Texas, at least, is Southern), Alabama, Georgia, Florida, Tennessee, Kentucky, North Carolina, South Carolina, Virginia, Maryland, and West Virginia. Notions of precisely which states make up the South of course differ. Some would include Delaware or Oklahoma, or even Missouri. But the South that called itself South—the old slaveholding South for whom "Dixie" was, as late as the sixties, an anthem— moves toward something else along its borders. (*Harper's* inclusion of New Mexico writer Lee K. Abbott in a 1986 gathering of "Southern writers" illustrates the problem. Abbott, clearly uncomfortable, wriggles out of it by calling himself a "*Southwestern* writer.")

My decision to confine the anthology to the period 1975- 1985—to writers whose first books (novels or short story collections) appeared in those years—is obviously an arbitrary one: writing neither sets its time by clocks nor keeps track of itself on a calendar. Writers like Richard Ford, whose first book came out in 1976, and Beverly Lowry, 1977, may by now seem too familiar to be called new. But to draw the line at, say, 1980 seemed to me too nearsighted a reading. Unfortunately the line I have drawn excludes a number of writers whose work I admire but whose first books were published in the early seventies—Barry Hannah, Gail Godwin, and Alice Walker, for instance. I have also, with some reluctance, excluded writers who have published stories but not yet published either a collection of short fiction or a novel.

The definition of "Southern writer" that I settled upon—a writer who grew up in the South, no matter where he or she was born or where he or she lives now—is simply the one that makes the most sense to me. As it happens, all of the writers included in this volume were born in the South, but they need not have been in order to meet my criteria. It is the years between the age that can be summoned up in memory (three or four, or, some say, two) and the age at which one goes out into the world that are perhaps the most important ones for the writer. These are the years in which he grows up listening to the sound of voices, surrounded by the quirks and myths and lies that will shape his view of human history and that, though he does not know it yet, will in some mysterious way infuse his characters. Flannery O'Connor told a friend that what growing up in the South provided was "the texture and the idiom and so forth." So much depends, she said, on "what you have an ear for. And I don't think you can have much of an ear for what you hear when you're over 20—that is, for a new kind of talk and life. The advantages and disadvantages of being a Southern writer can be endlessly debated but the fact remains that if you are, you are."

Bobbie Ann Mason, at least, among these younger writers—and there must be others—would no doubt agree with her. Asked by one interviewer what Kentucky meant to her, Mason, who no longer lives in the South, replied: "Kentucky is Home. That's where I come from and what I can identify with. In Pennsylvania or the Northeast in general, I don't identify with the culture. It doesn't have any emotional resonance for me that goes back to childhood. I don't know the language."

Southern writers know the language. But not all of them see their Southernness as an advantage, and some are uneasy about the label. What they fear—and it is a fear I can understand—is being dismissed as merely regional. Yet the South has produced its share, more than its share, of good and even great writers, and there is a kind of presumption abroad, it seems to me, that has more often than not worked in their favor.

Writing—telling stories, yarnspinning—is, quite simply, one of the things that Southerners do well, whether because of the oral tradition that folklorists are fond of citing or because of the richness of the material available to them, or possibly the motivation to excel, to be first in a section that, since the Civil War at least, had in too many things been last, or because of a combination of things, as seems likelier. Whatever the case, I would like, if I can, to rest the argument for identifying Southern writers on something more than sectional pride or chauvinism. The South, after all, does not have and never has had a corner on writing talent; the work of Southern writers is not *per se* the best writing. At its best, Southern writing transcends its regional origins. But if these writers write as they do, and very often about the things that they do, because they have grown up in the Southern milieu, the Southern culture—if there are certain approaches to the fiction that link them—this should not escape our attention. To read their stories and novels in this context is, I believe, to understand something about the nature of the literary impulse: what drives writers to write, what sources they draw upon, but also why the experience of reading them has importance for us.

To categorize these writers as Southern of course implies that there is an identifiable thing that we call the South, as I think there is: more than a geographical place, more than a state of mind, though possibly that too—a kind of La La Land (to borrow a phrase from one of Jill McCorkle's characters) with a sense of neighborhood, of shared blood, of common experience. There have been changes, true. The South of Temple Drake, of Bonnie Dee Peacock, of Rosacoke Mustian is no longer with us. Still, the South is different in specific though not always easily discernible ways from any other section. The things that once distinguished it from the Midwest or the East or West may superficially appear to be fewer, but there are important differences, and to read the twenty writers gathered here is to know it.

Most of the South's writers live in the South, though a period of residence in the North, often in New York City, is not uncommon. Those who live out of the South can frequently be found at schools where they came to teach writing classes—part of the same migration that brought their Northern counterparts to Southern campuses. Southern writers have from time to time tried to distance themselves from the South, only to discover, as Flannery O'Connor did, that "to get away from it physically for a while [was] by no means to escape it." Beverly Lowry recalls the five years she spent in New York trying to disconnect from the

South, "going for the impossible: to write as if I had no past." Others have been more successful at it, though the tidal pull seems to remain with them. Charlie Smith, who has for the last five years lived mostly in the North, says "I miss the South always, and go down there to get stirred up and refreshed, but I seem to do a lot of my best work when I'm separated from it."

The South of his boyhood continues to be a rich source for the fiction of Lewis Nordan, who has for several years lived and taught in Pittsburgh and who has called himself an expatriate, one of those Mississippians who, he says, "could not write of our sweet home, or be proud of it, until we were gone from it and certain we would not return to live." Another Mississippi writer who has lived much of his life outside the South, Richard Ford, recently came home again. But since the publication of his first novel, A Piece of My Heart, the South has not seemed to interest Ford the way it once did as a source for his work. "Maybe in time it will again," he says.

If the South has no monopoly on writing talent, neither does any single state among the states that comprise the region. But writers do appear to cluster around places where there are schools and teachers who encourage writing—schools like the University of Arkansas at Fayetteville and Hollins College in Virginia. The Durham–Chapel Hill area is another center of writing activity, and the presence of a publisher such as Algonquin Books of Chapel Hill has obviously been a factor in what at least momentarily seems to be a preponderance of North Carolina writers. No city can claim to be the South's literary capital, not even Atlanta, whose best-known writer is still, fifty years later, Margaret Mitchell.

Those looking for answers to the question of why the South has produced so many writers frequently turn to the example of Greenville, Mississippi, which boasts (quite literally) a string of writers ranging from William Alexander Percy and his cousin and adopted son Walker Percy to Shelby Foote, Ellen Douglas, journalists David Cohn and Hodding Carter, and—among the writers in this volume—Beverly Lowry. "From the time I was in elementary school," Lowry has written, "I always knew it was not only respectable to be a writer but honorable; desirable. The literary tradition was strong. Who our next writer would be was always pondered. Teachers were on the lookout. The effect of this is invaluable."

I suspect that Lowry has hit upon a truth: that in the South of the forties, fifties, sixties, teachers *were* on the lookout. Especially would this be true of towns or cities where there was already a writer or, as in Greenville, where after a time there were writers. Success of the magnitude of a Styron, an O'Connor, a Reynolds Price—even the minor successes, the writers who published one novel and were never heard from again—each stirred hopes of producing yet another writer. What had evolved, I think, was a generation, two generations—I have no doubt it is continuing—of teachers who were looking for, finding, encouraging, as they uniquely could, students who seemed promising to them. The South prided itself on its writers in part at least because teachers—those guardians of the literature and the language—had determined that to be important.

The sectional pride that I believe goes a long way toward explaining the South's abundance of writers was very much a pride of family. It was a pride so intense that it could only have come out of self-doubt, out of the desire—the necessity—to prove something. What could be proved here was that the most maligned (so the thinking went), least understood, most frequently caricatured region of the country could turn out writers who could stand next to, if indeed not above, those of any other section. If this sounds suspiciously like a kind of regional paranoia, it in fact was. There was of course, in the early years, the old fear that a writer would forget who he was and tell about the South, write about the things that nobody talked about—spill the beans, as it were—but in time that dissipated.

Much has been made of the Southern sense of place, and for the writers who came along in the fifties and afterward "sense of place" could also mean place in relation to the tradition in which they found themselves by virtue of being Southerners. How were they to remain within the tradition while at the same time trying to make their own way in the shadow of influences that were so pervasive? The very commonality of their experience—the culture, the idiom, the symbols, and so forth—was something they would have to deal with, and they would not always be successful at it. What they faced was a kind of critical consensus that everything had ended with Faulkner, or would end with Welty: they were not merely a part of something, but the tail end of it.

Now, in the middle years of the eighties, we can see that the pessimism of the early seventies was unwarranted. The writers of the South are still writing, and they appear to be writing in greater numbers than ever. It is perhaps premature to speak of a Second Renascence, but it *is* possible to say that the signs are promising. Certainly, there are some enormously talented writers among them. I should add that there are many more writers who emerged in the late seventies or eighties (and who fit my definition) than I have included. Had I attempted a complete list—and no publisher would have indulged me—this book would have expanded to three or even four volumes.

One of the things that gives the work of Southern writers its distinctive character is voice, and this is as true in the eighties as it was when Welty began publishing. What we hear in fiction with a narrator is the character *talking to* us, *telling* us, and one of the glories of Southern writing is that *how* he tells us, the rise and fall of his voice, the pauses, the arrangement of the words and phrases—all of this put down on the page to be read, but especially to be heard—is as important as the story itself. The *how* is a function of place, and place is the difference between nowhere and somewhere, as the narrator of Leigh Allison Wilson's story "Country Blues for Melissa" reminds us. Having told us that her family "lived, literally, out in the middle of nowhere," she corrects herself and says: "It's a lie. We were a family profoundly Somewhere, and we each of us clung like cornstalks to the soil and air and hills of

East Tennessee. . . . We were honest-to-God, hoedowning, shit-kicking, life-loving hillbillies, and we were smack in the middle of an overpowering somewhere." These are of course not the Southern hillbillies of old, but a modernized version: the father of the girl who is telling the story is a gentleman farmer who was once a corporate lawyer in Atlanta. But a sense of place is a sense of place. The narrator interrupts her story and says: "To all irregionalists everywhere, to all mainstreaming, trend-following, media-addicted, suburban intellectual-mystic peoples everywhere, we ask you, from the bottom of our hearts, we ask you: From whence come *your* words?"

Wilson's story is only one of several pieces in this volume that make use of a first-person narrator. In the excerpt from Louise Shivers's 1983 novel *Here to Get My Baby Out of Jail* the voice is that of twenty-year-old Roxy Walston, the wife of a young North Carolina tobacco farmer. Roxy's story of her obsession with Jack Ruffin, the redheaded drifter who comes to the farm to help with the work, is told in a simple, artless way that underplays the drama of it. It is passion talked about almost—but not quite—dispassionately. In the selection from *Machine Dreams*, the 1984 novel by Jayne Anne Phillips, the voice we hear is Mitch Hampson's, as he remembers his early years in rural West Virginia and a time when an orphaned boy could find a home in an extended family of aunts and uncles and cousins. Elsewhere in the novel we will hear from others—Mitch's wife Jean and their daughter Danner: a succession of voices that give this family chronicle its richness and its vitality.

The narrator in Padgett Powell's *Edisto* (1984) is a precocious twelve-year-old named Simons Manigault, a sort of South Carolina Holden Caulfield, who refers to his mother as "the Doctor" (she is a college teacher) or "the Duchess" (a name given her by the blacks in the juke joint the boy frequents) and to his father as "the Progenitor." Powell tells the story, or has his character tell it, in a language of purest invention. And in *The Dixie Association* (1984) there is Hog Durham, the ex-con who has been sprung from prison in McAlester, Oklahoma, to play first base for the Arkansas Reds, a ragtag team in the minors. In the pages that I have selected from Donald Hays's comic first novel, Hog tells the story of how the Reds took on the Selma Americans in Patriot Park in Selma, Alabama, before a Police Night crowd and a high school band that played "Dixie" like, he says, "they'd been bribed by yankees." Hays's novel is not by any means the only example, but certainly it is one of the best examples I know of what these new Southern writers can do with humor. There is of course more than meets the eye in Hog's story. What he and Chief Eversole, the big Indian pitcher, and the rest of the Arkansas Reds are playing against is not just another team, but the Selma, Alabama, team and the Selma police and in turn a South—that part of the South—that waves Confederate flags and mouths lies like "law and order."

Some of these other writers—Ellen Gilchrist, James Wilcox, T. R. Pearson, Lewis Nordan, and Raymond Andrews, to name but a few—can also be marvelously funny when they put their minds to it. In the Gilchrist story that I have included, "There's a Garden of Eden," we come upon the aging Alisha Terrebone, whom "scores of men, including an ex-governor and the owner of a football team, consider . . . to be the most beautiful woman in the state of Louisiana." The last we see of her she is being rowed through the rain-flooded streets of New Orleans in a canoe by a young Zen Buddhist carpenter who has just taken her to bed with him. With Gilchrist, the absurd is never quite so absurd that we cannot believe it. The same thing can be said of Wilcox. In both North Gladiola (1985) and his earlier novel, Modern Baptists (1983), he gives us the wonderfully wacky world of Tula Springs, Louisana, where, in the excerpt I have taken from North Gladiola, his heroine is about to perform for the black-tie opening of the town's first BurgerMat. Reputedly a former Miss Mississippi, though she was in fact only a two-time winner of the swimsuit competition, Mrs. Coco has immersed herself in culture and is now the leader of an unlikely string quartet in which her slob of a son George Henry plays first violin and she plays cello.

T. R. Pearson's humor lies in his nonstop narrative voice and in the outrageously improbable names he gives his characters—a send-up of the South's fondness for talk and for full names, preferably with two middle names in them. The shortest distance between two points in a Pearson novel is a detour past the cotton mill and the cemetery, and before we have reached the end of our journey we have learned a good deal more than we knew before about Braxton Porter Throckmorton III, Mrs. Coleen Ruth Hoots Newberry, Mrs. Louise Tullock Pfaff, and others who inhabit the fictional small town of Neely, North Carolina. In *A Short History of a Small Place* (1985) the narrator, young Louis Benfield, Jr., starts out by telling how the town spinster, Miss Myra Angelique Pettigrew, leaped to her death from the town water tank. But one story leads to another—and another. It is calculated digression, and it succeeds admirably while raising the question of how far—how far past his first two novels—Pearson can carry it without falling into self-parody.

Lewis Nordan, like Wilcox and Pearson, finds humor in the lives of his small-town characters, but Nordan's use of the grotesque distinguishes him from many of the South's other new writers. There are oddballs and eccentrics in the fiction of Leigh Allison Wilson and others, but none can match the gallery of freaks and cripples that we get in *Welcome to the Arrow-Catcher Fair* (1983), Nordan's first collection of stories. Nordan's characters include a paraplegic in a motorized wheelchair, a wife who keeps a mummified corpse in the broom closet, a woman with no face ("Terrible sight to see, even after the skin grafts"), and a family of midget construction workers. In one of Nordan's stories, a small-town undertaker works away on the corpse of the man lying naked on the embalming table in front of him while his aged grandmother tells one outrageous tale after another—tales that he is sure she is making up but that nevertheless compel him to listen to her. In the story I have included here, "Storyteller," a retired high school football coach keeps his listeners enthralled with the tale of how a circus elephant was put to death by hanging in Pocahontas, Arkansas. Then he releases them with a wink and a laugh and begins another. The mood changes. The storyteller has a voice for every story and every audience.

Raymond Andrews's humor is spontaneous, frequently ribald, exuberant; it is rooted deeply in the Southern black experience. The center of Andrews's fictional Muskhogean County, Georgia, is the town of Appalachee, where in his first novel, *Appalachee Red* (1978), we meet a lively group of characters that includes the big black man who gives the book its title. There is also Baby Sweet Jackson, "the Black Peach," who shares the back seat of the chauffeur-driven black Cadillac with Red when he dazzles the town with his entrance, and there is the cowboy sheriff, one-eyed Clyde "Boots" White, who wears a pair of pearl-handled Colt forty-fives and conducts vice raids on horseback at the head of a motorized posse. What we see in this novel and in Andrews's two subsequent novels is the pure joy of storytelling—the ease and authority of a writer who has stories and stories to tell and who will still be here when the sun comes up, telling them. As a black, Andrews sees things clearest of all from the black side of the picture, though with a wise understanding of the paradoxical interdependence that allows Southern blacks and Southern whites to live together.

Most of the white Southerners among the new writers of the South have black characters in their fiction, as one would expect them to, but in many cases these characters are shadow figures, like those in Padgett Powell's *Edisto*, or little more than props, as, for example, Aunt Willa Bristow, who ministers to Miss Myra Angelique Pettigrew and her pet monkey in *A Short History of a Small Place* by T. R. Pearson. Perhaps the most notable exception is the indomitable Fannie McNair in Jill McCorkle's novel *July 7th* (1984), who cooks and cleans for the Fosters, a wealthy white family, but who is largely ignored as a human being until the moment they realize she has overheard something that can destroy them. Then, to be sure she understands, Mr. Foster says: "You may as well hear it all, Fannie. You're family and anything that you ever hear in this house goes no further, do you hear?" But Fannie, who doesn't need to be told what family is—whose six-year-old grandson is "the blessing of her life"—thinks, "Family member, foot." She knows a lie when she hears one.

But for these white writers, the great civil rights revolution that swept the South in the fifties and sixties is largely absent from their fiction. It may be that this is territory on which they fear to tread, or on which they tread uncertainly; during those years of the sit-ins and the Freedom Rides the younger ones of the group would only have been children. It is more likely that their silence simply echoes the fact that the most pressing questions having to do with the rights of blacks in a white society, especially questions having to do with segregation sanctioned by law, have now been settled. Nowhere anymore, outside Klan gatherings, if indeed there, do Southerners argue that blacks (which in the South can take various forms: Negroes, nigras, niggers, coloreds) should be kept in their place, because their place is quite simply everybody's place in the post-sixties South, all of us alike, in danger of becoming what a character in Josephine Humphreys's *Dreams of Sleep* (1984) calls "Ohio warmed over." The old IMPEACH EARL WARREN signs that once dotted our highways have been replaced by others inviting us to visit Twitty City or to fly Delta or to sleep tonight in that great Southern silo in the sky, the Peachtree Plaza.

Which is not to say that there are no battles left to be fought, no hearts and minds to be changed. This, in fact, is what we see in the stories and novels of these writers, some of them: the old ways, the old habits of mind, dying. When the father in Bobbie Ann Mason's story "Drawing Names" refers to the chocolate-covered creams that he once called "nigger toes," he drops the "nigger." Likewise, Raney's mother in Clyde Edgerton's *Raney* (1985) has started saying "blacks" when her daughter's husband is around, and so has Raney, who is the narrator of the novel. "Charles," she tells the reader, "has this thing about niggers."

Raney is the story of a girl from rural North Carolina who marries a boy from urban Atlanta, but it is also the story of the modern South—two Souths, trying to accommodate, trying to learn to live with each other. Though Charles and Raney's differing attitudes toward sex are finally resolved in the feed room of Raney's father's general store, perhaps a little too tidily, there is no similar resolution of their divergent attitudes toward blacks. The problem is no longer whether she will let her young husband try all those things they presumably do in Atlanta, but whether she will invite Charles's friend from his Army days—black Johnny Dobbs—to stay overnight with them instead of taking a room at the nearby Ramada. What *has* been settled by the end of the novel, and ultimately it may be more significant than where Johnny Dobbs hangs his hat, is that he is to be their baby's godfather.

The South is sometimes of two minds about change, not merely because it wants its cake and wants to eat it, but because it cannot always be certain in its heart about its own motives. Nor can it be certain about what should be kept and what gladly discarded. But change is inescapable—it is the inevitable condition of things—and it is the thread, one of the threads, that runs through the work of these new Southern writers. "Use to," says the grandfather in Bobbie Ann Mason's story, "the menfolks would eat first, and the children separate. The womenfolks would eat last, in the kitchen."

"Times are different now, Pappy," one of his granddaughters reminds him. "We're just as good as the men." Whereupon her husband, who is getting a separation, says, "She gets that from television."

In *Dreams of Sleep* Will Reese, cloistered in his windowless, air conditioned office in a suburban Charleston medical complex, wistfully recalls his father's office, "where the hot summer air blew in through open arched windows, and men's voices rose from Broad Street below, hailing each other, yelling parts of jokes across the street." Later in the Humphreys novel he stands in front of a Victorian mansion that has been cut into twelve apartments and thinks: "Once this whole house was the home of one family. Is this how things fall apart, then? . . . Houses turn into apartments, estates into subdivisions. We can't sustain the things we used to sustain: dynasties, clans, big families; we can't even maintain their monuments."

And in Jill McCorkle's novel *July 7th* Sam Swett, the young North Carolinian who is making his way south after a stab at New York City, listens to the waitress across the counter from him and laments the loss of his Southern accent. "His mother sounds that way and he used to, a while ago; it seems that sometime or another he had made a conscious effort to change his voice so that he wouldn't sound like everyone else in the South. . . . God," he thinks, "he has no accent. He is the example of what everyone will soon sound like. Such a shame for that girl's voice to change. He would like to lock her away and protect her as a relic of passing time."

The change that we see in Mary Hood's stories in her first collection, *How Far She Went* (1984), is hardly seen as change, and it is seen almost out of the corner of the eye. Hood works by indirection. In one of the stories she describes an idyllic valley where "you could pick up one of the little early apples from the ground and eat it right then without worrying about pesticide." Her world is in fact a kind of Edenic world in which people tend the family graves in churchyard cemeteries and families gather for annual reunions where they count the loss of aunts and uncles and the addition of cousins, and where the eldest of them has the privilege of saying the blessing. But it is also a world in which there is loneliness and grief, and where something always threatens. In the title story, it is the two bikers who roar their motorcycles across the graves in a country cemetery and toss empty beer cans into the air and shoot at them—who pursue a teenage girl and her grandmother. In another of Hood's stories, one of the characters refers to the bikers who have invaded his property as "goddam weekenders." This once pleasant landscape lies just beyond the reach, but not far enough beyond the reach, of cities.

Even now, the deer have "fled across the lake with the moon on their backs," and lawns creep "from acre to acre."

Though Mary Hood's fiction is rooted in a particular place (rural Woodstock, Georgia), in many ways she seems one of the least Southern of these writers, mainly because she does not insist upon her Southernness. But neither do some of the others of these—for instance, Richard Ford, whose latest novel, *The Sportswriter* (1986), is set in New Jersey and whose recent stories have Western settings. Or Pam Durban, whose settings, whether they are Northern or Southern, seem almost incidental. What we remember most after we have read the stories in *All Set About with Fever Trees* (1985), Durban's first collection, is the characters: the angry mill worker Ruby Clinton in the story "Heat," raging over the death of her son and her whole sorry life; country singer Alice Dyer in "A Long Time Coming, A Long Time Gone," the story I have included—Alice with the big voice that "came from someplace that was forever a mystery to her." Pam Durban's extraordinary gift for description, for creating a mood and revealing character through description, is nowhere, I think, better illustrated than in this story, particularly in the all-night recording session in Knoxville. The scene outside the recording studio during the break Alice takes at 4:45 in the morning is one that I would call uniquely Southern—that is, one that would not have been written, certainly would not have been written in just the way it is, by a writer who was not a Southerner.

Beverly Lowry's Lolly Ray Lasswell, baton twirling her way to local fame in *Come Back, Lolly Ray* (1977), the first of Lowry's novels, might as easily have come from Kansas or Indiana as Mississippi, but she is this particular Lolly Ray because of the world, the culture, that produced her. There are no signs reading SOUTH. But there is the heat, the levee, we are told that Lolly Ray's mother is at home in the trailer park warming the cornbread, and there is the tacky World War II memorial where the Air Force lieutenant waits for a glimpse of the girl: on it are "the names of every white Eunolite who died in World War II." An

improbable touch, perhaps, but Lowry has established the place
and the cast of mind for us; even the name of the town, Eunola,
seems precisely the right one.

One of these writers who does insist upon his Southernness, or
at least upon the Southernness of his characters, is Charlie
Smith. In the very first sentence of his novel *Canaan* (1984) the
author tells us that "Jacey Burdette was born in Hawaii, but he
was a southerner nonetheless," meaning his father and mother
were Southerners, and their fathers and mothers, and so on back:
he is the point on the family line at which (Smith goes on to
explain) the Burdettes of Georgia and the Bonnets of Charleston
come together. The novel's theme of a family's decline is of
course a familiar one in Southern fiction. Jacey (Jackson Cole-
ridge Burdette IV), his father J.C., his grandfather, old Jack Burdette, and a rogues' gallery of uncles and cousins run through this
curiously compelling novel, but it is Jacey's mother, Elizabeth
Bonnet Burdette, who overshadows all of them. Elizabeth Burdette is in fact the Southern belle raised to the fiftieth power:
completely self-absorbed, unabashedly sexual, reckless, ungov-
ernable. There is no other character in recent fiction quite like
her. If *Canaan* suffers from excess and, at moments, the suspicion that it is at heart a sort of Deep South *Dynasty*, it also has
enormous narrative force, and there can be no mistaking Smith's
talent.

Andrew Lytle's dictum that "there is for any Southern writer of
imagination an inescapable preoccupation with his native scene
and especially with its historic predicament" raises an important
question as we look around us at the new generation of these
writers. Richard Ford feels no constraints to set his stories in the
South, and resists categorization generally. Indeed, the Ford story
that I have included takes place in sight of the Bitterroots, in
western Montana. But the fact remains that the writer who wrote
the story is a Southerner, with a Southerner's ear and a Southerner's sensibilities. The story by Madison Smartt Bell that I have
selected, "Monkey Park," is set in the South, as are several of

xxviii

Bell's other stories, but neither of his first two novels could be called Southern by any stretch of the imagination. *The Washington Square Ensemble* (1983) and *Waiting for the End of the World* (1985) both have as their setting the netherworld of New York City. The drug pushers and urban outlaws of Bell's novels seem light-years away from the three characters in his story who pay a moonstruck visit to the monkey park in Opelika, Alabama; but the fact that Bell can write with equal authority of urban crime and violence—urban madness—and that Ford can write convincingly of a New Jersey sportswriter or a good old Western boy, or would choose to, should not surprise us. Ford has lived in both New Jersey and Montana, and Bell, who grew up on a farm in Tennessee, the son of a country lawyer, lived in Brooklyn for several years after his graduation from Princeton.

Nor do any of the other writers who emerged in the late seventies or eighties appear to be preoccupied with the Southern scene, even when they make use of it. That is, their use of Southern characters and settings seems a good deal less self-conscious than Lytle's specifications suggest to us. As for the South's "historic predicament"—however we read that—well, Lytle is now two generations removed from them. History is ever in the process of moving forward, extending itself into the past day, the past hour, so that phrases like "historic predicament" ultimately lose their meaning, or become a matter of multiple choice: *Which* predicament?

The South is not quite the ghost-haunted place that it was. It is less isolated than it was, and it has lost some of its old feeling of kinship, of community. But much of what it once provided its writers it can still provide—things such as a common language and a tendency toward irony, the intuitive knowledge that things are not always or even often what they seem to be (is not the South itself an irony?)—and of course the knowledge that place matters. I have no doubt it will continue to offer a wealth of possibilities to its writers. What we see, or will yet see, in the best of them—and this must be something not too far from what Andrew Lytle has in mind—is a sense of history. Without it, the highway from Selma to Montgomery becomes just another road, another stretch of blacktop, and the greatest Southern experience, the greatest national experience, is reduced to the banality and triviality of the TV miniseries *North and South*, beside which *Gone with the Wind* seems like Shakespeare next to Neil Simon.

History, for Charlie Smith, is J. C. Burdette walking on the oak-shaded lawn of the house where Jefferson Davis came in defeat to write his story of the rise and fall of the Confederate government: "He liked . . . to imagine Davis there, imagine that bitter, phlegmatic man standing in his sandy yard staring into a distance of wave light from which he could not, not ever, expect relief."

For Jill McCorkle, too young to remember Selma or Little Rock or George Wallace standing at the schoolhouse door, history is Fannie McNair remembering herself as a young woman "going to the movies, having to sit in the balcony where it said 'colored,' using a bathroom that said 'colored.'" It is for Richard Ford, in the first of his novels, *A Piece of My Heart*, the ancient streak of violence that allows one man to kill another, and his cousins to provide him a safe hideaway from the law for forty-five years in the name of family.

Meanwhile, across the South, in places like Woodstock, Georgia, and Apex, North Carolina, and out of the South, wherever they are, they are writing. It is a concentration of talent and creative energy that can only be glimpsed—but I hope fairly represented—within the pages of this anthology.

CHARLES EAST

Baton Rouge, Louisiana

The New Writers of the South

Appalachee Red

RAYMOND ANDREWS

Appalachee Red's big new hardtop black Cadillac with its fish-tails, long cloud-tickling radio aerial, and particularly its black-uniformed black chauffeur shook the town of Appalachee and the entire surrounding area by the very roots, especially the white community, where the belief was deeply ingrained that any nig-ger, red or otherwise, with means enough to own, and gall enough to display, a car as big and as expensive as a Cadillac posed a bigger threat to their existence than . . . than . . . than Communism! This was much worse! This was out and out dis-respect for the white man himself! And to a Southern white man a disrespectful nigger was the most heinous creature stalking, or strutting, God's earth. And to Southern manhood's way of think-ing, the disrespectful nigger was at his most disrespectful when he owned something materially a white person didn't own and no white person in all of Muskhogean owned a Cadillac! Thus, the county had on its hands a disrespectful red nigger, who if he had settled for a less expensive and, especially, a smaller car like a Ford or Chevrolet (preferably used) would've been just an uppity nigger.

Following right on the heels of the Nigger Cadillac's arrival on the Appalachee scene was a strong feeling among most of the area's whites that some understanding regarding this new nigger's

true position in the town should be made clear to him by someone and that he should act accordingly . . . meaning, be a nigger or be on his way. The man's illegal gambling and liquor operations were no secret to any of these people, nor were his dealings
with the county sheriff, yet they had always figured that since
these illegalities didn't affect them personally they could shrug
them off as nothing more than "nigger stuff." But a nigger owning
a Cadillac was no longer nigger business . . . this was now white
man's business!

And what really got next to the quick of these white citizens
was that early each Sunday morning, when decent folks were on
their way to church, their children—those whose eyes weren't
being shielded by their parents' hands—had to watch that big
evil-looking black car being driven right through the heart of
town by a nigger chauffeur. And to compound their frustrations
all the more they felt helpless to do anything about such a nigger,
who because of the ever-drawn curtains on the Cadillac's back
windows none of these aroused citizens had so much as seen.
And what was proving even worse was their inability to find out
anything at all about this invisible nigger, who he was or where
he was from even after many had taken it upon themselves to
query members of the town's black community about the Cadil-
lac-owning man. But the more questions they asked about him,
the deeper the mystery surrounding the man's identity and origin
became to these people, whose sudden interest in this invisible
nigger soon had the area's entire white community—ever wary of
any nigger in white skin—regarding him as some mythical mon-
ster from another world . . . a situation which greatly aided the
subject in his apparent quest not to be interfered with by anyone
in anything he undertook in the town.

Meanwhile the area's blacks immediately took Appalachee
Red's Cadillac to their hearts and souls, as to them the car not
only represented an object too rich even for the blood and apparently the pocketbook of the county's richest, but by owning such
a vehicle Red had changed from being the villain to suddenly

2

becoming the good guy, as far as most of these blacks were concerned, by having the nuts to show up the white folks right to their faces by outdoing them at their—supposedly—own thing! True, many of these blacks often reminded one another, the car had been paid for by their money, but, yet and still, many felt it was worth donating a few dimes at craps just to stand and watch that big black Kitty cruising through the heart of town right under the noses of Mist' Charlie and Miz' Mary, her hands covering the little blue eyes of li'l Hiley Belle by her side, and with Red having all of that pretty and meaty Baby Sweet wrapped all around him there in that roomy back seat and they both holding their heads high and looking straight ahead as if not wanting to hurt their eyes on all the "po' white trash" piled neck-deep alongside the Drive just a-trying to peep through those litty-bitty curtains with everything they had!

This unfavorable reaction of the white townspeople, mostly those belonging to the middle and lower income groups, to the Nigger Cadillac eventually led them to call for an investigation into this new nigger's business affairs, a matter which brought them before the town and county governing bodies . . . all arrows inevitably and ultimately pointing to the office of Sheriff Clyde "Boots" White, just then entering his second term as the county's top law-enforcer. And into the sheriff's office marched these critics of nigger Red's conduct, announcing that he had "gotten out of his place, gone too far this time" and tried the patience of too many by having both the money and gall to possess such a big car, with a nigger chauffeur to boot, in a white man's town. The sheriff heard them all out and yet did not have to divulge a single detail regarding his and the subject's no-longer secret alliance, because before the first question could arise from these solid citizens concerning the two men's affiliation, Boots shut the county's white mouth down cold over all this Red-talk with just three little words . . . "Red's no niggah." Thus ended the Nigger Cadillac controversy.

Boots had never believed Appalachee Red to be a nigger, nor

even a white man for that matter. But the sheriff believed him to be one of those foreigners he had occasionally heard about coming to America from across the water, usually to live in the North. His reasoning was that Red was much too clever and bold to have any nigger blood in him, but yet not quite a white man because of the big man's total inability to extend any sort of warmth or comradeship to another white man, namely the sheriff. That left only the foreigner possibility . . . a possibility which Boots seemed to have developed a lasting fear of.

This awkward fear had first come to grip Boots's soul on that long-ago Thanksgiving Day back in 1945, while he stood paralyzed on his spot on the porch of the police station watching the stranger walk down the main Drive with that catlike stride of his. And for the next several days the chief of police was to undergo a haunting experience, beginning the very next night when he suddenly found himself locked out of his black gal's room. That following morning he had gone down to the hotel and gotten the black bitch fired from the job he had been kind enough to get for her in the first place. And then when he walked around to the niggers' section later that evening and ran smack into an empty Alley, and on Saturday night at that, he knew goddamn well that something had gone awful wrong in the town. The confirmation of this had come the moment he rushed into Sam's Café, wanting to know from the owner what the hell was going on upstairs . . . only to stop stone-cold dead in his tracks right there in the doorway. Sitting atop the counter staring right at him was that big cat-walking stranger. The chief of police had left the back street that night feeling spooked.

Then followed those long nights of no pussy—except at home and those rare times he had bothered to get it he enjoyed no sense whatsoever of violation or defilement and thus didn't want it. But every time he thought of his now-lost black pussy, his mind—and hard—would be brought up short by the image of that big bastard stranger sitting atop Sam's counter staring coldly out at him like

4

he, the chief of police, wasn't a white man! That man he knew had to be one of those goddamn foreigners.

Then one night about a month later, shortly before going off duty he had gotten a telephone call, someone, a man, telling him that he was needed right away at Sam's Café . . . and for him to come alone. And before he could even think to ask the reason why he was needed, the man had hung up. But he had known whom the voice on the other end had belonged to, that was why he had started shaking so in the knees, causing him not to sit but to drop down in the nearest chair. And it was knowing who had called that made him not want to go around on that back street alone, where he hadn't been since that night he had gone looking for Sam and come up with the man who'd just telephoned, whom he knew he had to go see alone, because, for whatever reason he had to be at the café right away, he knew it to be strictly a matter between him and that big bastard stranger. And that was what was scaring the shit out of him just then.

He never remembered how he reached the café, by car or foot, yet he remembered standing on the outside porch shakingly reaching out for the front doorknob and then turning it with the care of one who expected to be greeted by a giant jack-in-the-box. With both feet just inside the doorway he came to a halt, yet didn't let go of the knob he held beneath the taut pale knuckles of his right hand, as if fearful of letting go of the tangible object and losing all touch with reality in the process. Standing immobile in the middle of the room, wide body blocking from view the stove directly to his back, facing the front door, was the stranger, those cold dark eyes latching instantly onto the single eye of the policeman, which was watery from the wind outside. The stranger wasn't much more than an inch taller than the chief, but when the chief, no longer able to just stand there and hold that piercing stare, spoke from his end of the room, he felt himself talking up to the big man.

"Somebody heah call fuh me on the telephone?" The words

began in his belly as a growl but through a process of purification came off his lips as a whine.

"I did. Come in and shut the door." The authority behind the man's voice caused the lawman's hand to drop abruptly from the knob and quickly push the door closed behind him with an unintended bang, Boots flinching slightly at the surprising sound. He closed the door yet he didn't make any effort to step deeper into the room.

"I called you because, as the new owner of the café . . . and building . . . I felt you, the town's law, and I should meet one another."

"Noo ownah?" The whine had changed to a whisper.

"Yes. Three months ago my cousin . . . Sam . . . sent for me to come help him run the café here because of his health going bad. And since my coming here last month he's done nothing much but sit upstairs in his room . . . drinking . . . and thinking of his dead wife while I took care of the café, which prompted him to turn the place over to me . . . legally. And now that the building is mine, I have many plans in mind for its future. And that's why I thought you, as the chief of police, should be the first person in town to know about this change of ownership . . . because many of these plans I have in mind for the café and building will depend upon you and me doing some business together . . . some business in which both of us can earn ourselves a dollar here, a dollar there." During this entire speech, Boots had stood staring, open-mouthed and blinking-eyed, in utter disbelief at the barely moving lips of this man who called himself a cousin of the nigger Sam, yet was standing here before the chief of police, a white man, talking about their doing some business together! But for the first time since becoming a "white man," Boots felt unsure of his station while facing this here . . . "non-white man" . . . who on this night hadn't once lifted his penetrating stare off the policeman, nor shifted from his set position in front of the stove . . . nor taken his hands from the rear pockets of his khaki trousers, leaving them instead to rest back with thumbs sticking out over the sides. What, Boots felt, could even he as a white man do to anyone whose hands he couldn't see?

"Are you interested in making yourself a few extra dollars?" The man was talking again.

"How?" Surprising even himself, Boots still had his voice . . . though it had changed from a whisper to a whimper.

"That we can discuss later. But first take this down to the courthouse the first thing in the morning and see that it's handled properly." The stranger brought from his left rear pocket—Boots flinching noticeably at the man's motion—a folded sheet of white paper which, without moving from his tracks, he extended to the policeman. The man's right hand remained in his back pocket. "Then come back here the same time tomorrow night and we'll talk business."

"Whazzat?" Boots had fastened his eye on the extended piece of paper.

"Cousin Sam's will."

"Will?"

"Yes, he died late this afternoon and this is his will leaving me, his last living relative, everything he owned. And that's why right now I am interested in getting started in fixing this building up to begin making money. Money for both myself and someone who's as important, powerful . . . and respected in this town as you, the Chief of Police of all Muskhogean County."

Even years later Boots still didn't like to recall taking—at the time it had been more like being dragged—those few degrading-for-a-white-man steps up to the man who called himself the cousin of the nigger Sam, and accepting from his extended hand the folded piece of white paper. But he had been fearful of turning his back on the man and walking out of the door without the paper in his hand . . . especially so long as the big bastard stood there with his right hand still hidden from view there in his back pocket. On that night also he had flatly refused to walk up to see Sam's body but not because of any fear he had of the

7

dead . . . rather a strong fear of the living one who on that night offered to escort him up the back stairs to the room of the dead man. Nor did the lawman bother calling in the county coroner, who he knew would only have gotten mad as hell at being called away from his family on Christmas evening just to look at some dead nigger. On that next day Sam had been buried.

And on that following night, as per instructions, Boots returned to the café (after having dutifully and personally seen to it earlier that morning that Sam's will reached the county courthouse where it immediately proceeded on its way toward, and finally achieved, official documentation). Boots came off the Alley that second night still shaking in his shorts and firmly convinced that this man who called himself Red was no cousin of the nigger Sam. And this feeling was not just due to the lawman's religious belief that nowhere under God's sun did there strut a nigger with balls enough to walk into Appalachee, or any *real* American town, and take away a white man's black gal or anything else belonging to a white man. He started to get the feeling while he listened all that evening to the man's plans for the future of the building, and this planning had sent Boots away believing him to be much too shrewd and bold a person to be anybody's nigger, yet too mystic to be a "real" white man, and he appeared too four-square, from what he'd heard about Jews, to be one of them—all of which meant to the lawman that he had to be something else . . . a foreigner being the only other answer. A foreigner from up North who might've been running away from the law, or a wife, and who ended up here in Appalachee, where, by going among the town's niggers, he figured no one would ever bother looking for him. But what, Boots thought, about Sam's death . . . and the will? Well, the lawman reasoned to himself, it was too late to do anything about the first matter and as far as the will went—if Red didn't get the building then the chief of police sure as hell wouldn't stand to benefit any. Thus, the will stood. And Boots was to come away from the café on that night following Sam's burial believing Red not to be a black man but some kind of foreigner, which the lawman felt somehow was a little closer to the status of a white man than that of a Jew, nigger, or Jap. And on this basis Appalachee's Chief of Police decided to do business with Appalachee Red.

Early in 1946 Red was declared "holder of a clear and unencumbered title to" the old White House and all of its contents by the local court. No one stepped forward to contest Samuel Wallace's will, no one but the black Doctor Allen, long an unpopular figure among the area's whites and the butt of many of their doctor jokes. The day before Sam's death Dr. Allen and his wife had gone to Savannah for a week's visit with friends; when he returned, he somehow learned of the will's existence and made an attempt to see it, only to be told over at the courthouse to mind his own "witch doctor" business. The new owner began work immediately on remodeling the building, along with outlining the final plans for his and the chief policeman's "business." (This business—illegal gambling and the sale of liquor—was not considered to include the café with its considerable income, something Boots hadn't counted on in the beginning but reluctantly agreed to.) To keep their business operating long and successfully, Red proposed that the chief run for county sheriff in that year's elections; Boots was completely taken by surprise, but, again, he finally gave his consent. From the time he first joined the force the apex of Boots's dreams had been to someday become Appalachee's Chief of Police, a position he had finally achieved (through the direct intervention of his father). But the idea of being sheriff had never really appealed to him, mainly because he would not be able to wear the beautiful blue policeman's uniform if he got stuck with such a position. But after he listened to Red, it didn't take too long for him to realize the power he would hold as the sheriff of all Muskhogean County . . . even though this was suggested to him by a non-white man, a fact the lawman's mind over the years didn't exactly forget, but would always refuse to linger over for too long at a time.

For the election itself, Boots got Red's promised support. During campaign time both the outsides and insides of Appalachee's building were plastered with posters especially made for the black community of the would-be sheriff wearing a big, forced, tooth-revealing grin (so that he appeared to be straining under a severe case of constipation, many remarked upon seeing the signs) pictured below the words

VOTE CLYDE WHITE FOR SHERIFF

and above those of

WILL GIVE THE COLORED SECTION
BACK TO THE GOOD COLORED FOLKS

And in black translation this meant "Vote for Clyde White and get Boots's white ass off the Alley." There were other pictureless posters scattered about Red's of other officeseekers running on the prospective sheriff's ticket but the one of Boots was of most concern to the black community. But what had in the end lured most of those blacks who visited the polls on voting day was the sign just beneath each poster inside the café guaranteeing all those casting ballots for Boots and other candidates on his ticket the entire afternoon off from work, with pay, to do so . . . along with a free meal of their choice at Red's—signed by the management. And what wasn't mentioned on these little signs was the free half-pint of liquor that all who voted for Boots and his party, whether these voters were male or female, were to receive in addition to the free meal. But word of mouth proved sufficient to relay this latter campaign promise.

The black vote put Boots barely over the top, as he had run against a very popular incumbent, Jake Robinson, sheriff for twelve years and the only person in over thirty years to be elected to a county office, in his case three times, without the blessings of old Ezra White up at Yankee Town. But most important to most blacks was that their votes had helped get Boots off the Alley—a pre-election agreement between the lawman and Red that if

Boots won at the polls then Red would become sole overseer of the welfare of the back street.

Appalachee Red's personal gift to a flabbergasted and more than appreciative Boots for winning the election was a complete Western-style cowboy outfit, all white and silver, including a ten-gallon hat, leather gloves, boots and spurs, and two pearl-handled Colt forty-fives with star-studded holsters and bullet-lined belt . . . plus a white eyepatch. So thrilled was Boots over this gift that he immediately had Red order him a second, duplicate outfit, though this time paying for it himself. And by the time the new sheriff was inaugurated, taking the oath in this new uniform of his, he had bought himself a white horse (along with matching saddle, whip, rifle, and other unnecessary gear) whom he named "Silver Tony." Thus, once he had taken office, the new sheriff was easy to spot now even by the area's whites, having always been the most salient of souls to blacks' eyes. And now late each Sunday night after closing time Silver Tony could be seen standing outside Red's with his reins tied to a post on the café's porch. The new sheriff was often heard complaining during this time about the town not having enough hitching posts . . . not to mention water troughs.

And although they laughed at him (behind his back of course), the majority of Muskhogean blacks felt a welcome sense of relief at having Boots as county sheriff, cowboy-style or not, as it meant once again having the back street to themselves. And they knew credit for easing the pressure on most of them by ridding what they now referred to as Red Alley of "Cowboy Boots"—the new sheriff had also been renamed by the blacks—must somehow be attributed to Appalachee Red, who since taking over his dead cousin's café and building had apparently arranged to keep the law's visits back here at a minimum. That is, all except for the sheriff's late-Sunday night visits to the café, which no one ever worried over, yet which most were ever-curious about. It had soon become an accepted fact by both the area's blacks and whites

11

that Red and the new sheriff were working closely together, as shortly after Cowboy Boots took office the House of Red became the only spot in the county where a black could gamble or buy liquor without running into trouble with the Man.

Despite the surprising black vote, the person most instrumental in Cowboy Boots's becoming county sheriff had been none other than the Original Bastard of Yankee Town himself, Ezra White. Having turned eighty-one the year his youngest son won the election, old Ezra—although no longer prison warden, a position now held by his oldest son, Winfred—still ruled strongly as district political boss. Besides being political boss and Klan leader and owner of most of the land, businesses, houses, and souls in and around Yankee Town, Ezra owned a giant liquor distillery located in the dense pine area just west of the town—also his; he had spent nearly half his life refusing sawmill and pulpwood contractors permission to set up shop there. The still was not only the area's largest and oldest but most productive as well.

Ezra had always made sure that his still was the only one operating in the vicinity, but until his son took office as sheriff in early 1947, Ezra had only been interested in supplying customers in and around Yankee Town, and had not concerned himself with who supplied the rest of the area's or how. Free enterprise. But when Red came onto the Muskhogean scene, he revealed to Boots his master plan—for the two of them establishing central control over the county's vice, black vice in particular. To the lawman's astonishment this plan included a historical knowledge of—and future designs on—the White family's liquor still. So, at Red's suggestion, Boots approached his father, Ezra, with an idea for centralizing the area's liquor supply by liquidating every still in the county except the one at Yankee Town, which would become Muskhogean's sole and official illegal whiskey source. Thus it came to pass in the year of 1947 that free enterprise in the bootleg liquor business came to an end in Muskhogean County, Georgia, U.S.A. . . . and all due to a red nigger.

Cowboy Boots had been in office only a matter of hours before Red's master plan went into effect. The machinery began working that Saturday evening, following the installation of the gambling equipment above the café, when the new sheriff charged the Great Wall of Appalachee astride Silver Tony—the lawman's deputies, as was to be the procedure throughout his reign as county sheriff, trailing by car at the heels of the beast—and, with hooves thundering, swooped down upon an unsuspecting and disbelieving Dark Town, and in minutes had closed down every den of vice operating over here . . . except the local whorehouse and the church.

And for the next several months these same thundering hooves of the great white horse, Silver Tony, were heard throughout the area as the new sheriff, closely followed by his motorized posse, galloped over the whole of Muskhogean County—and in many instances just across its borders—apprehending every black involved in the making, distributing, selling, buying, or possession of any liquor not traceable to the House of Appalachee Red and even forcing everyone he caught with such liquor on them (or in them) to tell whom they bought it from. Also arrested were those caught operating or involved in any way in gambling, including those who were caught with dice or playing cards in their possession. Instrumental in helping to smoke out these lawbreakers was Red's "spy," Big Apple, financed and backed by The House of Red to roam the far reaches of the black community listening for and bringing back to Red in person any information or suspicion regarding the whereabouts of floating crap or skin games, the location of liquor stills or liquor-sellers in the county, and the names of all the people involved in such operations—whereupon Red would relay these findings of his trusted spy to the sheriff, who in turn would just as quickly leap astride Silver Tony and carry out official raids on these illegal establishments. And within a year after the sheriff's sweeping program of law and order began, he had swept all of the county's black lawlessness and disorderliness into one great heap atop Appalachee Red's café, where now all of those blacks who wanted to gamble and buy liquor could do so without having to keep one eye peeled back over their shoulder for the Man. "Justice is merely incidental to law and order" is what the Man said.

Yes, they poured up the back steps with their nickels, dimes, quarters, halves, and dollars, because now it was the only game in town, including the pool game as well. Earnest Moore's old two-table poolroom a few doors up from Red's was shut down shortly following the opening of the casino. The owner's license was revoked "indefinitely" because, according to the law, of Earnest's having contributed to some cause called "juvenile delinquicy." It seems the police had walked into the poolroom one day and caught a couple of high-school kids in the act of betting (a nickel apiece, some said) on a game. And after having earlier lost most of his teenage crowd to Red's and now with his poolroom shut down, Earnest soon closed his store altogether and began concentrating on driving the county's lone black taxi and later opening up an auto repair shop over in the tranquility of Light Town.

At strategic points throughout the county Ezra soon had set up distributing centers with appointed distributors for his liquor, which in short order had the big still up at Yankee Town operating around the clock and causing many to begin referring to the liquid product both as moonshine and "sunshine." Red, of course, became the sole outlet for the county's black liquor market—the only way he would have it—while for Muskhogean's much larger white community there were now several outlets within the county. And for those freelance bootleggers, whether black or white, in the county who did not believe that, since family White distillery had been constructed with the money of the people of Muskhogean, it was therefore operated by the people of Muskhogean and for the people of Muskhogean, whether these people were black or white, such heretics soon found themselves being trampled beneath the thundering hooves of Silver Tony.

For Red's soon-flourishing gambling trade though, the unwritten license for this operation had not been issued as freely by the district political boss as had the one for selling liquor—consumers of the latter were believed by the county's righteous not to be able to do more than get drunk and end up in jail after busting a head or two, or getting theirs busted, and wind up not making church on Sunday. But gambling to these same believers entailed much more, involving the nucleus of America's morality . . . money. And Red's was to be the only gambling casino permitted in the county by Boss Ezra, simply because it took in only black money, which Red split with father and son White. When the town and county white leaders first became aware of Red's casino, a mild grumbling was heard from many of them. This had nothing to do with the illegality or the immorality of the operation (they all knew that niggers had no morals); it was just that they themselves weren't getting any of this "nigger money." But the Whites and Red knew that if another finger got into the pie, then there would be more fingers than apple slices. That was when Red came up with the suggestion that he agree to relinquish the casino on Monday nights (normally a dead night) to these grumbling county leaders so they could gamble among themselves and thus feel a part of the scene and, perhaps, stop grumbling. The Whites agreed to the idea; Boots presented it to the local leaders, who at first appeared leery of such an outright proposal, but finally consented to give it a try, though only after receiving a promise that the café itself would be closed on these nights. Being who they were, they didn't particularly cotton to the idea of sharing a building with niggers while they were involved in such intimate doings as gambling, even if the niggers were downstairs. Red agreed to close the café and have everyone off the premises, except himself and Baby Sweet, by sundown on each Monday since none of these respectables wanted to be seen entering a nigger establishment during daylight hours. Thus, during the winter months the respectables were at Appalachee Red's from six until midnight and those times of the year when the sun hung high until late, they came around nine and usually stayed way past twelve. And true to the nature of man these Southern gentlemen wholeheartedly accepted the idea of their using the casino once a week—still not sharing in the "nigger money," but instead chancing their own dollars. Yet the mere thought that their social status permitted them to gamble in an illegally operated gambling casino without fear of their souls' being contaminated by such illegality proved enough to end their grumbling about the operation. But perhaps the most ironic thing about this Monday night setup—"White Night," as it soon became known among the local blacks—was that these men (a clique whose number was to remain fixed at fifteen), rather than being crap or pool shooters, or even slot-arm jerkers—gambling games provided by the controversial casino—were players of poker, a game which it was possible to play in practically any locale or setting. Yet they preferred to play their poker in the casino around three tables brought up beforehand from the café, each seating five plus a dealer. Players relinquished five percent (on seven cards) and three percent (on five cards) of their winnings to the house dealers—Cowboy Boots, the new chief of police, and his second in command. Yet, these men felt satisfied that they, too, were now a part of the illicit "action."

Monkey Park

MADISON SMARTT BELL

At five o'clock in the afternoon the light comes in yellow across the brown curling paint at the edge of the window sill and makes the stained white walls of the kitchen glow golden, makes the tired enamel at the bottom of the sink look like old ivory. Carolee's just back from her job, she's a waitress in a lunch place this month, and she's in a pretty good mood. She finishes off the dishes from breakfast, and the hot water is pleasant over her hands, the last clot of suds moves toward the drain and Carolee flicks it away with a worn-out sponge that's shaped like an apple. She watches the afternoon light on the wall and it makes her feel warm and electric, like she wants something to happen.

Then something does happen. Carolee hears this awful noise, like a cross between a chain saw and a jackhammer, it's getting closer and closer and finally it comes around the corner of the house and stops under the kitchen windows. Carolee looks out through the vines that are crawling along the window panes and sees that the noise belongs to a big old wreck of a car, long and grey with blood-red flecks on it, like an enormous sickly shark. The car coughs and groans and chokes and dies, and the driver gets out and bangs the door and it's Perry. Perry walks around the tail-fins of the car and starts up the cracked concrete walk to the back door, and Carolee can even hear his feet rustling over

17

the tough little weeds that grow up between the cracks, which means that Perry is definitely here.

Oh hell, Carolee thinks, but she can't not be glad to see Perry, so she dries her hands on the dish towel and dabs at the water spots on her jeans. Then she flips her hair back away from her eyes and goes around to the back door to let Perry in.

"So what are you doing back in town," Carolee says.

"Shrimpers in Bayou le Battrie," Perry says.

"Oh," Carolee says. "But this isn't Bayou le Battrie, you know."

"I know," Perry says. "I quit."

"Well come in the kitchen and drink some beer," Carolee says. So they go in the kitchen and Carolee gets out a bottle of Strohs and pours it into two glasses. They sit down beside the table in there, which has an enamel top with black speckles in it, and they don't say anything. Carolee lights a Lucky Strike and pushes the pack over to Perry and they smoke and watch the smoke whirling and spinning across the wide shafts of orange light in the kitchen. After a few minutes or so Carolee gets up and takes another beer from the fridge and pours it into the two glasses. Then she stands there with her fingers touching the table.

There's a little green tattoo smudged on the back of Perry's dirty pale hand, though she can't quite tell what it is. It looks like it could be initials or something, but it seems that Perry has tried to get rid of it, so it really isn't readable at all. Well, Perry doesn't look like someone that ought to have a tattoo. He doesn't even look much like someone that ought to work on a shrimp boat. He's little and light and not very strong-looking, though he has a nice enough face and all that. He's got messy black hair and dark eyes and the sun never tans him or even burns him somehow, he just stays pale and grubby all the time. All of a sudden Carolee is afraid that Perry is going to say, "Aren't you glad to see me?" so she wills him not to say this, and he doesn't.

Instead Perry gets down on the floor and lies on his side, with his knees drawn up to his belt buckle and his hands cocked in front of him like the paws of a begging dog.

"I have now metamorphosed into a shrimp," Perry announces. "I've looked into too many nets. I've seen too many little grey squiggles. I'm done for. I am a shrimp. I have a pointy nose and little feelers and no bones. I eat tiny garbage all over the big wide sea."

"Oh God," says Carolee. "Shut up and get off the floor."

Perry gets up and wiggles his fingers in front of his face.

"I will now clasp you in my shrimply embrace," he says. He makes a dive at Carolee but she dodges out of the way, and Perry turns around in the corner of the kitchen and puts his hands back in his pockets. That's when Carolee notices the green bruise healing around his left eye-socket. It almost looks like make-up, only there's a line of an old cut there too, and Carolee wonders if he really did quit the boat or if somebody just pitched him headfirst onto the docks one day.

"Well, I do smell like a shrimp, anyway," Perry says. "You can admit that."

"You smell like a lot of shrimp," Carolee says. Then she stalks over to Perry and gives him a quick hard hug, pushes him away and goes back to the windows, but the light is fading now, so she turns back around and half sits on the sill. Perry has enough sense not to be grinning.

"I have money," Perry says. "I have shrimp in the car. Shrimp for supper. Eh?"

"Alright," Carolee says then. "Go upstairs and take a shower."

"Maybe I should bring the shrimp in," Perry says.

"I'll get the shrimp," Carolee says. "Go on and get in the shower. I'll bring you up a towel in a minute."

There's a window in the bathroom tucked up under the eaves and Perry can look out over the tarpapered kitchen roof and see Carolee going out to the car, walking with quick reedy movements.

Perry watches her peering into the ruined interior, finding the cooler and swinging it up over her narrow chest. She steps out from the car and closes the door with a brisk backward kick. The cooler is heavy, Perry knows, but Carolee stands there for a minute holding it, looking up at the window under the roof. Perry can't see her face too well at this distance, but he knows perfectly well what it looks like, freckles splayed over the urgent bird-like features, the sandy hair that keeps drifting over her eyes. Carolee shifts her glance and marches into the house, and Perry dunks his head back under the shower stream. He hears the back door slam closed behind Carolee, over the running water, and he lets water run in and out of his ears, thinking how her eyes look when they catch the sudden light beams in the kitchen, translucent, glowing, oceanic green.

Then Perry picks up a piece of soap from the tray in the shower and squeezes it until he's got enough lather to wash his hair with and when he's done that he rubs the soap lump all over himself, 'til all the fish slime is gone. Carolee cracks the bathroom door and hangs a red towel over the key that sits in the lock of it.

"Jesus, Perry," she says. "There's water all over the floor. There's a shower curtain on the shower, you know."

"I wanted to look out the window," says Perry. "I'll clean it all up when I get out."

"You better," Carolee says. Then she bangs the door shut, hard enough to rattle the key in the lock, but the towel keeps on hanging there.

Carolee even goes out and finds Perry's old duffle bag in the trunk of the car, so when Perry has finished his shower and dried up the floor he finds clean clothes waiting for him outside the bathroom. So Perry puts these clean clothes on and goes downstairs, rubbing his hair around with the dripping red towel. He goes into the kitchen where Carolee is. Perry's eyes are red and stinging from the soap that got in them and the evening air feels cool on his wrists and the back of his neck.

"Is Alphonse around?" Perry says.

"He's not in the house," says Carolee. "He's in town, alright, if that's what you mean."

"Oh," says Perry, and he drops the wet towel over the back of a chair. "I saw Art in Bayou le Battrie. He told me that Alphonse was thinking about a two-month job in Brazil."

"He decided not to take that job," Carolee says. "He's still working for Rock City." Alphonse is a solid blond cheerful man with a degree in Building and Construction. He inspects constructions while they are being built. That is his profession. Sunset is over and the light in the kitchen is now a subaqueous grey.

"I don't see how you can be married to someone named Alphonse," Perry says.

"You don't have to see it," Carolee says. "It isn't your problem." Perry lights another one of Carolee's Lucky's and doesn't think of anything else to say. But cigarettes do taste good after showers. Carolee rolls up the dish towel and pops it toward Perry's limp collar.

"Besides, it's not his fault he's named Alphonse," she says. "His family is French from New Orleans."

"I don't believe that for a minute," Perry says. "I think his family is crazy is all." Carolee wraps the dish towel around her wrist and turns to look out the window.

"It's getting dark in here," she says.

"Alright," Perry says. "How do we do the shrimp?"

"Boil them?"

"Fry them?"

"Too much trouble."

"Do them in butter, no bread."

"Still have to clean them."

"I'll do it," Perry says. He goes out to the car and stands beside it, finishing the nub of the cigarette. The light snaps on at the kitchen windows, and Perry drops the butt and grinds it carefully into the dry red dirt. It's getting very dark now and the light is blue and up above the scrubby pine tops Perry can see the eve-

21

ning star. He reaches into the glove compartment through the open car window and gets out a red plastic shrimp peeler and carries it back to the house.

"Maybe you better not start yet," Carolee says. "Alphonse might be back to supper, only I don't know when."

"That's alright," Perry says, shrugging. "I'll just clean them now and put them in the fridge." Carolee goes to help him but Perry waves her away.

"Make sauce or something," he says. "There's only one peeler anyway." So Carolee sits at the table and watches him cleaning the shrimp with his deft bony hands, pushing the peeler from neck to tail, flicking the shells onto a newspaper and the shrimp into a bowl. Then the telephone rings in the living room and Carolee goes in there and picks it up. There's no light on in there and only a little dimness seeping in at the windows by now.

Carolee comes back in the kitchen.

"Alphonse is working late," she says. "Alphonse is having dinner with a business acquaintance. He wants us to meet him at the Wheel at ten."

"Fine," says Perry, slinging shrimp around. "I'm hungry right now, anyway."

"He wants to talk to you," Carolee says. "He's still on the phone." The peeler clicks into the sink and Perry walks out of the kitchen and picks up the telephone, which is sitting on one of those little round tables with a pole lamp sticking up through the middle. Perry puts the receiver to his ear and starts switching the light on and off. Carolee notices he forgot to wash his hands, so he's leaving shrimp goo all over the telephone and hanging sand veins on the pull chain of the lamp.

"Hey there good buddy," Alphonse says. "Good to hear you, good to hear you're back in town. Yeah, Carolee tells me you're back in town, so how're you doing, old buddy?"

"The same," Perry says. He pulls at the light chain. Alphonse's voice feels like it is right there in the room and slapping Perry on the back.

22

"Hey, sure, I know what you mean, hey. Nothing too much changes, does it? Naw, nothing too much changes. Hey, but I hope you'll be hanging around some this time, no trouble to us to put you up, got plenty of room and all. So hang around a few days, old buddy, maybe we'll take off and go fishing."

"Thanks, Alphonse," Perry says. "Thanks for the invite. I don't quite know how long I'll be around, though. I don't exactly know what's going to happen."

"Well that's fine, old buddy, that's just fine," Alphonse says. "I know just exactly what you mean. But anyway, I'll see you tonight, you're coming on up to the Wheel tonight, with Carolee, aren't you, right?"

"I'll be there," Perry says. "Take it easy, Alphonse. Until ten."

Perry hangs up the telephone and goes back to the kitchen, and Carolee goes in the living room and starts cleaning off the phone and the light stand. She cleans them very carefully so there won't be any fish smell and by the time she gets through the shrimp are already getting pink and rosy in the skillet that Perry has put them in, with onion and butter and a trace of garlic, and the shrimp smell very good indeed.

"We don't need any sauce anyway," Perry says. "These are just right how they are." So they both sit down at the table with salt and pepper and shrimp and beer, and Carolee feels good because eating something this good makes her feel purely happy. Then the shrimp have all been eaten and Carolee gets up and opens another bottle of beer. But Perry covers his glass with his hand.

"No more right now," he says. He looks up at the clock on the wall and it's still only seven.

"I got a little number out in the car," Perry says. "You want to do a little number, maybe? Carolee?"

So then they do the little number, standing out by the car in the vague starlight, and then they go in the house and drink a lot of water to ward off the cotton-mouth. They go in the living room and sit on the sofa and Carolee plays Billie Holiday and then

Hank Williams, and then Billie Holiday again. The songs are pained and lonely, but Carolee feels fine and free and floating, and there is no light in the room except for the tip of one of Carolee's cigarettes that Perry is smoking, and Carolee's elbow is touching Perry's elbow, and Perry's knee is touching Carolee's knee, and Carolee jumps off the sofa and runs up the stairs to her bedroom. Then she comes back to the bannister and calls down the stairs.

"Come on up here, Perry," she says. "I got a real stage make-up kit now, I'll make you a face."

Then Perry climbs up to Carolee's bedroom and she makes him put out the cigarette, and she lights a candle and sets it up in a saucer on the floor. Then she puts the make-up box on the floor near the candle and works on Perry for a while with the things in the box, and she criticizes him whenever he twitches. Perry wants to look at himself when she's done, but Carolee says no. She scoots the candle over to the bottom of the full length mirror on the closet door and crouches there, working on her own face for a long time, while Perry sits in the corner feeling foolish and sticky. Then Carolee reaches behind her and takes Perry by the wrist and pulls him over so their faces are together over the candle and they're looking at themselves in the mirror.

Perry's face is simple and harsh, his skin is whiter than ever now, and he's got black lips and black slashes over his eyes and that's all, it makes him look like a mime or a ghost. Carolee's face is more subtle and dangerous, she's lengthened her nose and raised her cheekbones and added some colors here and there. She looks as deathly as Perry does, also beautiful and fierce and disdainful.

"That's scary," Perry says, and he starts when he sees the lips of his mask moving. "You look scary, Carolee."

"Do you like it?" Carolee says.

"I don't know if I like it," Perry says. "Oh, you did a good job, alright." In the mirror Perry sees Carolee turn her head and look at him hard over the candle, so he has to turn and look at her too.

"Don't look like that," Perry says. Carolee keeps looking.
"It's ten already," Perry says.

So then they get up and go in the bathroom and Carolee finds some cold cream to take the faces off with, and they wash the faces off with this, standing side by side over the sink. When that's done they go down and outside to the car, and Perry arranges some of his clothes over the seat so that the springs won't stick into Carolee. Perry turns the key and nothing happens at all so he gets out and digs around under the hood and the car starts like a bomb going off. Perry presses a button on the steering column and the car begins to crawl backwards down the gravel drive to the street. Then he presses another button and the car begins to move forward. It still sounds like a bomb going off.

"Like the car?" Perry yells to Carolee. "It's got a push button transmission, the latest thing in cars."

"I guess so," Carolee says. "It makes a hell of a lot of noise."

"That's a special option on this car," Perry says. "It saves having to make conversation."

So they don't make any conversation until Perry has parked the car outside the Wheel, which is something like a cross between a nice little neighborhood bar and a roadhouse. It gets its name from a big old wooden wagon wheel that hangs over the door, and Alphonse is standing to the left of this wheel when Perry and Carolee arrive. Alphonse has a seersucker jacket stretched across his big shoulders, with a lot of pens in the top pocket, and he keeps looking this way and that, until Carolee calls to him. Then he walks over to meet them, gives Carolee a peck on the cheek, and squeezes Perry's hand so hard that Perry makes a face. So they all go into the Wheel.

They sit down in a row at the bar and Perry buys everybody a mixed drink, only Carolee just takes a beer. Perry and Alphonse are sitting together and Alphonse tells Perry all his new jokes, and Carolee doesn't listen too closely to this, because Alphonse's new jokes are not new to Carolee. She looks around the Wheel and thinks that it's changed quite a bit since she was a teenager, when all there was to the Wheel was three-legged chairs on a sawdust floor with beer and pool and the odd knife fight. Now there's varnished pine panels all over the walls, and the chairs and bar-stools were designed by someone, and there's a big leather cushion along the edge of the bar, which keeps your elbows from getting sore. But the rednecks are still there with their girls and big cars, even if they do have on long hair and satin shirts now, and they still start fights all over the pool tables, even though they have nicer cues to bash each other with these days.

So Carolee sits there and thinks all these things, and she listens to the jukebox with one ear and hears Alphonse talking and Perry laughing with the other. Pretty soon Perry buys another round of drinks and Perry and Alphonse start to play an electronic game that they have in the Wheel now. The bartender brings a little box over to Perry and Alphonse, and Perry and Alphonse push buttons on this box, and all sorts of stuff begins to go on on a big lighted screen over the bar: a picture of a man with a gun shoots little lights at pictures of geese, and points are scored from this somehow. Alphonse beats the hell out of Perry at this game, be-cause Perry has never been any good at games of this kind, and after Alphonse has beaten him a few times Perry asks Alphonse to go and shoot pool.

Alphonse beats Perry at pool too, but not so badly, and by now Alphonse is drunk enough to start telling his jokes all over again, and Perry keeps laughing at the jokes and buying more drinks. Perry is acting like everybody's rich uncle, he keeps buying all the drinks and won't let Alphonse buy even one round, and Perry even keeps giving Carolee handfuls of quarters to go play the jukebox with. So Carolee plays things on the jukebox and she sits at the bar and drinks her beers, and Perry and Alphonse come stand beside her stool and talk to her between shots on the pool table. Everyone's having a wonderful time, and Carolee herself is feeling no pain, until Perry comes over and recites one of Alphonse's jokes to her, in such a way that the joke does not seem funny at all.

But Perry has to go make a shot right away, so Carolee doesn't have time to react because Alphonse comes over instead, and Carolee sees that Alphonse is now so drunk that he needs a big piece of the bar to hold himself up with, though he still seems to be winning the pool games. Then Carolee looks over at Perry and notices that he doesn't seem to be drunk at all, though he's been drinking as much as anybody and probably more. Well, Perry has always been like that, he drinks himself drunk and then he drinks himself sober again, only tonight there seems to be something deliberate and scientific about the way he is doing it, and Carolee might wonder what he is cooking, only it seems to be too much trouble, so she gets another beer and forgets about it. Then it's the last call, and then they turn up the house lights and unplug the jukebox and start sweeping the floor, and then the only people left in the Wheel are Perry and Alphonse and Carolee.

Perry looks dead sober under the bright lights that are on now, and he takes the cue from Alphonse, who is weaving just a tiny bit, and then Perry runs the table even though this game just started, and then he slams the cue back in the rack. Alphonse's eyes bug out a little at this, and Carolee herself feels suddenly sober, but that turns out not to be entirely true when she gets up onto her feet. Then they are all standing out on the curb, and the taillights of the last jacked-up car are drifting down the highway away from the Wheel, and Alphonse and Perry are on either side of Carolee with their arms linked through her elbows.

"Let's go do something," Perry says. "I feel like doing something."

"It's late," Carolee says. "There's no place open now."

"We can go to the monkey park," Perry says, "Let's go to the monkey park."

The monkey park is in Opelika, which is the next little town down the road, so they all get in the front of the big grey car, with

Carolee in the middle. Alphonse has a brand new Volvo he'd be happy to drive, but Alphonse doesn't know the way and Perry wants to drive himself, so now Alphonse is shifting around on the ragged seat trying to find a spot with no springs sticking out.

"This is some car you got, old buddy," Alphonse says. "You going to customize it? Hey?"

"I like it how it is," Perry says. Then he starts the motor and it drowns out everything.

But when they get on the highway the car goes into some kind of cruising gear and shuts up considerably, and then even when Perry slows it down to go along the quiet little streets of Opelika it still doesn't seem to be making very much noise. Carolee looks out down the streets and thinks of the people asleep in the little white houses on either side, and the car floats along so softly that she doesn't really notice when it slips off the road and stops.

Then Perry gets out and clicks his door shut and Carolee and Alphonse get out on the other side and stretch their stiffening legs. The stars are out and fairly bright but it's still too dark to see faces. There's a little rise up from the roadside and when they get to the top of this they are looking down a long gentle slope, the edge of a deep basin full of trees. At the bottom of the basin, in a clearing there, is a thing that looks like a very big bird bath.

So Perry starts running down the slope toward the bird bath, and Carolee and Alphonse follow him down slowly, Alphonse stumbling just a little. When they get down there it is plain that the thing is not a bird bath at all, though Carolee knows this already, in any case. It's a green metal saucer that sits on a green metal post, and in between there is a ring of ball bearings, so that when Perry gives the saucer a little light push it starts spinning and keeps going for more than a minute.

"I love this thing," Perry says softly. "I think about it all the time when I'm on the boat."

Then Perry stops the coasting saucer with his hand and climbs into it. He sits there with his feet braced on the rim.

"Give me a push," he says, and Carolee takes hold of the rim of the saucer and runs around and around with it 'til she feels dizzy herself, and then she steps away from it, stands still and breathes hard. Perry freezes in the saucer and stares straight out, and Carolee and Alphonse are braided into the whirling trees so thoroughly that Perry can't pick them out at all, and Perry can't pick anything else out either because everything has blended and flattened itself into one continuous streaming ribbon of vision. Then Perry rolls over onto his back and closes his eyes and tucks up his legs like an embryo. He can feel all the liquor he drank shrinking away until it disappears altogether and only Perry is left there alone with a cold clear mind, solid and calm and perfectly stationary, while the whole rest of the world shrieks by all around him. When Perry opens his eyes again he is looking up into the waning moon that has just risen, and the white light burns a big circle at the top of Perry's sky, and Perry watches the circle until it fragments itself into twelve moons and then six moons and then only two or three, so Perry sits up again, and now he can see a few Alphonses and Carolees flashing by. The saucer stops coasting and Perry gets out.

Then Carolee comes over and gets into the saucer. Perry runs with it until it's spinning fast and then he dodges out to the side. When he turns back around he can't see Carolee because she's lying down flat in the dish, and she stays down for a long time. When the saucer begins to slow down some Carolee sits up and moves toward the edge. Carolee's eyes are open wide and full of the light of the moon, but to Perry she looks like she's in a trance, so deep he thinks she may never come out of it. The dish holds its speed for quite a long time, and Perry begins to wonder if Carolee may not stay there forever, whirling and dreaming and rotating across his line of sight as evenly as his own pulse. But Carolee stretches her foot to the ground and stops it. She gets out of the dish and stands there beside it looking down at her feet.

"Well, Alphonse," Perry says.

"I don't know," Alphonse says.

"You're going to love it, old buddy," Perry says.

"Go on, Alphonse," Carolee says.

Alphonse climbs heavily into the saucer.

"What do I do?" he says.

"It doesn't much matter," Carolee says. "Just keep some of your weight on the center."

So Alphonse gets himself settled in, and Perry and Carolee push him together, until the saucer is going so fast that Carolee can't keep up with it. "That's enough," Carolee says, stepping away, but Perry doesn't hear her, or anyway he doesn't stop. The saucer is going so fast now that Carolee can't see Alphonse at all, and she wonders if he has been whirled away into nothingness, and after a while she can hardly see Perry any more either. But finally Perry breaks apart from the saucer and runs away from it in a long crooked line, stopping himself on a tree about halfway up the slope. Perry stands there and leans on the tree, while the saucer hisses and whirls on its bearings. It's a long time before the saucer seems to slow down at all, and Perry straightens up and stands near the tree as still and silent as if he were a tree himself. Then the breeze starts to blow the treetops together, and the branches sound almost like distant applause, and there is enough moonlight for Carolee and Perry to see each other's faces, across the top of the hurtling saucer.

Eventually the saucer does slow down and stop, and something begins to move around inside of it, and this something is Alphonse. Alphonse gets out and starts walking around, only he can't seem to find anybody, he can't even seem to bump into a tree. He wanders around in big sloppy circles, with his hands pressed over the top of his face. Then Perry goes over to him and takes him by the arm, whispers in his ear and leads him up the slope into the shadows. Carolee hears all sorts of strange noises coming from there, and she hears Perry's voice as steady and soothing as the night breeze, and after a while Perry comes back by himself.

"Alphonse is sleeping," Perry says, walking toward Carolee. "Alphonse is taking a nap for a while."

"Is he okay?" Carolee says.

"He's just fine," Perry says, still coming on. "He just felt like going to sleep for a while." Perry doesn't stop coming and Carolee can't think of any more questions, so she turns around and starts walking the same way Perry is, walking rather quickly in order to keep ahead of Perry. Then it occurs to her that they are going toward the monkey cage, so then she has something to say.

"Let's go and look at the monkeys," Carolee says, and Perry doesn't say anything at all.

Then Carolee is standing in front of the monkey cage, which is no bigger than an elevator in an office building, and Carolee thinks that the monkeys would probably look pretty shabby in daylight, but by night they seem mysterious and alluring. There's five or six or seven of them, all about the size of five-year-old children, but they're slender and graceful and their movements around the cage seem polished and decorous. The monkeys have fan-shaped puffs of hair around their eyes, and they have long plumed tails. A couple of monkeys come to the front of the cage and gaze at Carolee with what seems to be wisdom and compassion, and a couple more climb up to the top and hang by their feet, to see what Carolee looks like upside down.

Then all the monkeys chitter together and turn their backs and the two at the top drop to the bottom and start combing and stroking each other's fur. Two monkeys come back to the front and reach out through the wires of the cage, and one monkey points a long black finger at Perry.

So then Carolee notices that Perry has caught up with her and in fact he's been there for quite some time, with one hand gripping her on the waist and the other one stroking her hair over and over. Carolee notices, now, but she doesn't do anything about it just yet, she just stands there stiffly with both hands holding on to the rail that someone has put up around the cage to keep her from being able to reach her fingers in where the monkeys could bite them. Perry nuzzles her neck and starts whispering into one of her ears, and Carolee doesn't listen to the things that he says, she listens to the monkeys clucking instead, but the monkeys are beginning to look very misty and far away.

"Just stop it," Carolee says. "You might as well just stop it."

"But why—"

"Stop it."

"But I—"

"Stop."

Then Perry stops and even moves a little away from Carolee, only dropping his hand over hers on the rail. The monkeys chitter and clutch at each other and climb up and down all over the cage.

"Where do you think they come from?" Perry says.

"I think they've always been here," Carolee says.

"You think they like it in Opelika?" Perry says.

"I don't think they care," Carolee says.

By the time the next silence is over Carolee can see chinks of daylight in the night sky. She looks at the monkeys and they do look worse in the strengthening daylight. The monkeys are all combing and stroking each other again.

"You know why they do that way?" Carolee says. "They're just picking salt off of each other's skins."

"You didn't have to say that," Perry says.

"Yes I did," Carolee says. But she lets her hand turn itself over and take hold of Perry's.

"Alright, you did then," Perry says. "I have to drive down to New Orleans this morning, because Art says he'll get me a job on a rig." Carolee says nothing to that.

"I'll send you all some postcards," Perry says. "Probably I'll even be back sometime." Carolee doesn't say anything to that either, but she also doesn't let go of Perry's hand, so they just stand there and look into the monkey cage, and they don't say anything to each other at all until the sun tips its rim over the edge of the basin and they hear Alphonse calling to them through the trees.

A Long Time Coming,
A Long Time Gone

PAM DURBAN

Alice held the eight-by-ten glossy photograph and looked into her own laughing face, at her flashing eyes and the hair tumbling in dark loose ways, at the fringed white buckskin shirt unbuttoned down to *here*. She took it all in. "Lord have mercy," she groaned to herself, smiling, "Will you please look at that?" It had happened in a moment, a flash had gone off, and the photographer had caught her, not as she was now, but as she would be, blossomed out into this joyful creature who laughed as though she'd just caught sight of the face of a loved one who's been a long time away. She picked up a skinny turquoise pen with a peacock feather coming out of the end and signed the corner of the photo. "Love ya," she signed in a hand as sleek and foxy-looking as the woman in the picture, "Alice Dyer." The 'r' trailed off into a musical note set with a star where the note should be.

Alice had moved back home last July after she had had enough of John Wallace Siddon, her second husband, and the running around they'd done on each other. They went through people so fast you'd have thought they were racing each other to find the ace in a deck of playing cards. Now, here it was, spring again, and outside the window of Alice's room, as usual on any day in late

33

March in Memphis, Tennessee, her mother was walking around in the throes of her annual spring labor—preparing the flower beds for planting. She moved slowly, like an old animal walking a familiar path. She wore a pair of men's black high-top tennis shoes, black nylon socks, and a gray housedress with a hand-kerchief stuck under the belt. She was walking in the flower bed that surrounded the sundial, shaking some kind of white powder from a sack made out of an old net curtain and watching where it fell. If she missed a spot, she backed up and gave the bag an extra shake. Honestly, sometimes Alice wondered if her mother weren't rowing with just one oar in the water these days. "Hey," Alice yelled out the window. "What's that you're slinging?"

"Bone meal," her mother said without looking up. "Sweetens the soil."

That woman, Alice thought. You'd think she'd get tired of doing the same thing year after year. But never a spring went by that her mother didn't plant zinnias and marigolds and nastur-tiums right back in the same beds where others of their kind had lived and died the year before. Even the spring Alice was twelve, the spring her father died, did his wife stop her planting? No, she did not. He hadn't been two days in the ground when she was back out there with her string and markers and packages of seeds, down on her hands and knees in the dirt again like nothing had happened. Never a spring went by that Alice didn't get restless all over again, watching her mother drop seeds into the earth. Or watching her sit out there of an evening as the season went on, with her hands folded in her lap and her face blank, as if she were listening for the first green shoots to pop up from under the dirt. Well, Alice had her own season. It started like spring—with a restless stirring inside tight husks and casings—but it wasn't spring, it was like two seasons—*always* and *never*—trying to hap-pen at once. It began with a seed, a kind of hunger, and ended with a dream such as a seed might dream that never left the earth, as it lay in the ground and dreamed of its flower.

She pushed through the back door, letting it slam behind her, and stood blinking in the strong sunshine. The ground was lightly steaming where her mother had turned a new bed. "Mama," she called. "Now I want you to tell me why you go to such trouble when you'll just turn around and do the exact same thing next year?"

Her mother was back down on her knees again by this time, sifting it through her fingers as if, Alice thought, there could be a single clod or pebble left after all this time. Without raising her head she said, "Well, sure it's trouble, but, Lord, if you get to pick your trouble, I'll pick this." And she returned to her sifting.

Alice lingered until the strong smell of turned earth began to crowd so close to her she had to rush back inside and slam the window, get out the guitar, sit on the edge of the bed and play and play and play, every song she'd ever written until she felt like herself again and not like anybody's hungry child. This season, there was a special reason to practice and get ready—she was going to play a big folk festival in Knoxville, Tennessee. But even if she hadn't been, she would have gone on singing because singing was about the only thing she really wanted to do. She couldn't type worth a damn, never could stand waitress work, or clerking in a store, couldn't seem to stay married. But ever since she could remember she had had this voice and when she sang, Lord, when she sang, it felt like some answer was about to come to her to a question that she could never quite put into words, though all her life she had been asking it. When she sang she felt something coming that would change her and make her whole, something she'd been waiting for for so long she could almost taste it. And she felt that if she just kept singing and keeping watch, one day this thing would come to her and it would be full, it would be rich, it would satisfy the hunger and fill up the empty places and make her know why she was alive on this green earth.

The festival was held in a valley watched over by the blue presence of the Great Smoky Mountains. It was twilight when she went on stage. The audience knew her well from other times and

35

places—a tall winter tree of a woman, dressed all in white: buck-skin skirt and shirt with fringe on the hem and sleeves—and they knew where she would take them—down into the roots of that tree and up the long, bare branches stretched out against the sky. Finally, she stood like a statue—head bowed and her arm resting on top of the guitar—waiting for the cue to begin her last song. When the spotlight changed to blue, Alice came to life. She whomped down on the guitar, threw back her head, stomped the stage and started in on the song about freedom that she always saved for last because it ended things on just the right note. When she came to the chorus her voice broke free and soared off toward the mountains. *"Free as the rain that falls on the water,"* she sang. *"Free as the lonesome sky. Free as a child without any mother. Free as the years flying by."*

In the audience, people closed their eyes and swayed against one another, while her voice took them places, and showed them things. It was a big voice, bigger than she was, and it came from someplace that was forever a mystery to her and the shadow of that place lay across it. Some people thought about a river, an old slow wide brown winding river, flowing in shade and then in sun. One person saw the shadow of a hawk cross a field of ripe wheat and disappear into a stand of pines. Another heard the whistle on a long train gone around the bend and out of sight. *"Free as the rain that falls on the water,"* Alice had made her way around to the chorus again. *"Free as the lonesome sky,"* she sang. *"Free as a child without any mother. Free as the years flying by."*

When the song was over and she opened her eyes, she saw the audience rising in one long wave that began in front of the stage and rolled all the way to the back of the amphitheater. They were standing up for her, and they were clapping and clapping. She blew them kisses and she felt calm and dreamy as though a soothing hand had been laid on her head. And then somebody struck a match, held it up. Then another, another, and soon the whole place was dancing with tiny flames. "Thank you," she said, "God bless you, thank you." She slipped down the steps and around back of the stage, through the hands that reached out to pat her, while the applause started again out front and went on in one continuous roar. And she stood there hugging herself, eyes shining with the light of those matches that had been held up to her as though they were lighting the way somewhere.

That's when a man—his name was Malcom, he said, but she thought of him as Good-Natured because of his sweet round face with the little features perched on it, like the face of the man in the moon—appeared out of the backstage crowd and took her hand. He was so serious and he stuttered so much she had to laugh as he told her who he represented—Mountain Laurel Records—and what and why and who—herself—and would she consider doing a record with them. Right here, right in Knoxville, soon? In April? "We've had our eye on you for a few years now," he said. "We're a small label, but we like to think we're a progressive label."

"You don't have to sell me, darling heart," she said, "I'm ready." She stood there after he was gone, holding the card he'd given her, watching dusk turn the mountains purple and thinking *it's coming now, it's almost here.*

Two weeks later, there she was, going through the door of the recording studio on Good-Natured's arm. The night was hers, that's what he'd said, bought and paid for so that she could make her record. He'd lived up to his name and had brought her a Mason jar, a half-pint of clear whiskey made somewhere back in the hills, tied up with a bright red ribbon. It was a gift you'd give to a star. And really, she guessed she was just about a star. Here she was in a recording studio, not a big fancy one, and not in Nashville or anything, but a studio just the same, with that tangle of cords and wires all over everywhere, the crushed coffee cups and music stands standing every which way, like everybody there had more important things to do than clean up after themselves, and a big control booth lit up like Christmas. Here she was, wearing her new red high-heeled boots, and the wide denim skirt cinched tight with a belt of Navajo silver, the white buckskin shirt with a bandanna tied at the neck and her hair brushed and brushed to the sleek gloss of a bay horse's mane. Here she was, sizing up the competition, the racks of albums out in the foyer beside the drink machine. A lot of gospel groups recorded in this studio, and their album covers showed sweet-faced women in long skirts and men with long clean jaws and sideburns, all gathered round the old rugged cross. She winked, poked Good-Natured in his soft stomach. "I'd like to make me a gospel album one of these days," she said. "Think I could pass for saved?"

"Well," he said, "I wouldn't know about all that."

She gave the whole bunch of albums a shove. Devotion always made her thirsty. She tossed her hair back and tore the red ribbon off the jar of whiskey, unscrewed the cap and took a nice long pull. It spread all the way through her, waking every slumbering appetite. She took another sip, another. And then the musicians were coming through the door and she was there to greet them and offer them her whiskey. "Travis Ferrell," Good-Natured said, "lead guitar." Alice curtsied and offered him a drink. She liked his bedroom eyes, his thick blond hair, the way that turquoise and silver bracelet nestled in the hair on his forearm. "Toy Lovett, he plays bass." He was dark as a foreigner. He liked her whiskey. "Bobby Sunday, he's your drummer." He looks it, Alice thought, fat and sloppy and with his shirttail hanging out. When he handed the jar back, she wiped its lip with her bandanna. "Cat Adams," Good-Natured beamed. "Best rhythm-guitar player in Knoxville," he said. "And twice Tennessee State fiddle champion." He had his hand on the shoulder of this little scrawny woman with black hair that stood up from her head like chicken feathers and about six earrings stuck through one earlobe. She was wearing a T-shirt that looked like a man's old undershirt, and black corduroy pants, and she walked right on in there like she owned the world, like she didn't care that she was little or skinny and she didn't need anything from anybody to fill her up or change her, like she had everything she needed right there in the guitar case and the fiddle case she carried in either hand. "I would shake hands," she said, "but my hands are full."

"That's all right," Alice said. "Don't feel like you have to." She took three quick sips of the whiskey. It burned all the way down and caught her up in its wild energy and spun her around. It was like celebrating with yourself about everything good that hadn't happened to you yet. Thirst made you do things like that, hunger did too, and Jesus had blessed them both. While they set up their equipment and tuned, she sipped and hummed and walked around and sharp spears of thought fired through her head like stars shooting down through the summer sky. She went out to the drink machine and got herself a Coke. She poured whiskey into it and stirred it with her finger, watching the ice dissolve. She ignored the worried looks Good-Natured kept shooting her. She knew the whiskey was for later, but when she was thirsty time might as well not exist and the world might as well be water because she was going to drink her fill.

She settled the earphones onto her head and hooked her heels over the rungs of the stool. The earphones were too tight, they pinched her head and made her ears feel hot and a sighing sound came through them that was like the sound of a radio station that's gone off the air. She was beginning to feel confined, hemmed in. That was not a good sign. They were all staring at her like sheep at a pasture fence, waiting for her to begin. She hadn't bargained for this. She didn't know exactly how she'd imagined, no, dreamed it would be, but it was something like a combination of the way she'd felt when all those people held up their matches and times when her father had come home and brought her something from where he'd been. Once, it had been a wooden apple with "Blowing Rock, North Carolina" written on the side, in gold. You opened it up, and there was another, smaller apple, then another, then another, smaller and smaller, until you opened the last one, which was tiny as a pea, and inside there was a real apple seed. She guessed she had hoped it might be like that.

"All right," she said, holding up a hand for quiet. "From the top," she said, ready to launch herself into the song that begged Jesus to take the pain of love from her life. It began with an announcement played on the fiddle by Cat Adams with such energy that it made the gooseflesh rise along Alice's arms. A woman of many talents, Alice thought, as she clasped her hands around one knee and began to sway. Then the bass slipped in and it was time—dum ah dee DUM DUM: *"Lord, to you I am crying,"* Alice sang (dum DUM dum). Her voice made her nervous, coming back at her that way through the headset, but she recovered and went on. *"Here on your sweet earth below"* (dum ah dee DUM dum), *"Where you gave us sweet love for one another"* (dum DUM dum), *"But then Lord la la la la la la-la-la.* Get the idea? All right bridge, O.K. now chorus, *So call your love back home to hea-vun"* (dum dum), *"We don't know how to use it here below. Where . . ."* (DUM DUM DUM).

She snatched the earphones off and held them tight. "Wrong," she said. "Wrong, wrong. It's supposed to go softly there, pianissimo, right?"

"Alice," it was Good-Natured's voice, coming from the control booth. "Please don't yell into the microphone that way, Ronnie'd like to keep his eardrums." Ronnie was the engineer. She guessed he deserved to hold onto his eardrums.

"Sorry," she said, taking another sip of the whiskey. "I just get so impatient and excited. I'm just like a damn little kid on Christmas morning."

The lead-guitar player ran quietly through a scale. "Maybe if we had charts," he said.

"Oh, charts," Alice said, "I don't work with charts, love, I work with the feel of the whole song. I'm looking for that spark, see, I'm looking for that elusive something called chemistry." Good old whiskey, she thought, it made her strong as a searchlight's beam, looking here, there, cutting through the night with a diamond-bright light, signaling Here I am to anyone who might be watching.

40

"This is costing somebody a whole lot of money," a woman's voice said. "Do you want to spend it getting soused?"

Alice whirled on her stool and discovered, with a shock that magnetized all the sharp unruly feelings whirling around in her head and drew them toward a red hot center, that she loathed the woman behind that voice—Cat Adams with her fiddle and guitar, and the way she played, as though there was a note, one note, that might keep the world from blowing to pieces, and every time she picked up an instrument she had to find it again and play it. And it was her note too, you knew that by listening to her, nobody gave it to her, so nobody could take it away. Alice pointed her finger. Her nails were painted red to match her boots. "Ms. Adams," Alice said, "you want to keep your job?"

"It's your dime, Ms. Dyer," Cat said. "You spend it like you want to." She wiped the neck of the fiddle with a cloth that she took from her case and then she laid that fiddle in the case and put the cloth down over it as gently as if she were putting a baby down for its nap.

"You're wrong there," Alice said. "It's somebody else's dime, but brother I sure know how to spend it. Isn't that right?" She aimed her voice toward the control booth. She held out both legs and studied the toes of her boots. They were expensive Tony Lama boots, custom-made at the factory in El Paso, Texas. They had taps on the heels; each had a star on the toe. She'd bought them to wear dancing with somebody she hadn't met. They were so shiny that when the light shone on them she caught a glimpse of her face, a white shape with stars where the eyes should be, in their polished surface.

"Alice." It was Good-Natured again, standing up with his arms folded, looking stern as a judge. "Alice, could we please get serious here." He held up his wristwatch.

She sipped the whiskey, nodded, straightened out her skirt. I am serious, she said to herself. You don't know how serious I am.

"All right," she said. "Key of A again. For real this time." She closed her eyes and imagined that she was a magnifying glass

41

gathering the rays of the sun and aiming them down onto her song. Sometimes that worked. Cat Adams saved the world with her fiddle one more time and Alice began asking Jesus to take the love that he had given back out of the world because people didn't know how to use it. It was good this time at first. The old excitement came back like it did every time she sang. Something was coming, everything in her leaned forward to meet it, like you would for the first glimpse of somebody getting off a train. She felt a smile waiting to bust out on her lips any minute. Then she began to listen to what she was singing and she felt herself falter. Something was coming, all right. It moved over the horizon and into sight. It was Jesus again, empty-handed as ever.

See, Jesus had let her down and he shouldn't have done that. She'd waited for him for a long time and then after she'd left Wallace, she'd found him and for a while everything was peaches and sweet heavy cream. But the thing that had finished it between her and Jesus had happened late one evening not long after she'd come back home, while she was swinging in the swing on the side porch at her mother's, reading scripture from the pocket-sized New Testament the Gideons had come around handing out door to door. This book had an alphabetical index of readings to turn to if you needed help with life's problems. "Adultery" came first (why is it that help always comes too late?), then "Adversity" and so on down through "Tribulation" and "Worldliness." In the section recommended under "Tribulation" she had come to the part about seeking first the kingdom of God and how everything else would be added unto you. That's good, she thought, and you know, it's true. Seeking was something she knew about for sure. Then she'd turned to the second reading listed under "Tribulation" and it was the one about how the kingdom of heaven is within you and when she read that, she slapped the book shut so quick she thought she might be able to forget that she'd seen it. She'd sent that book flying as far as she could throw it out across the yard. But what was written there had already taken root in her and nothing could tear it loose again.

42

Her palms had felt clammy then and her heart was knocking and pounding like a crazy something in a cage. She'd dragged her feet until the swing barely moved and she heard the creak of the porch swing and the rasping of the cicadas, she heard the bugs pinging against the porch light over her head, she smelled the river and felt its heat swarming all over everywhere. She felt the lonesomeness of every place that Jesus had vacated. Because if the kingdom of heaven and Jesus were all within, then he wasn't coming from anywhere and he wasn't going anywhere, he was just there all the time, died and risen both and it was up to you to know him both ways and from the inside out if you wanted to live in his kingdom. And so she guessed she wouldn't, thank you.

So she sang with a heavy heart, not about who Jesus was, or what love was, but about what they *weren't*. They did that song half a dozen times, a dozen. They went away from it and did a few more songs and then they came back and tried Jesus again, but her heart wasn't in it. Her heart was sitting right there like a good dog that's been told not to move until somebody comes back to claim it. Then Ronnie wound the tape back through the last few versions of the song and started it rolling forward again. The moment of truth, she thought, and she sat up straight to wait for it. All right then, let's have the moment of truth. Everything you did had one. Trouble was, it was never the right kind of truth, you could count on that. It brought no comfort and it didn't fill you up, not in any way. Her voice flowed out of the speakers and filled the studio. It was the sound of a person with a heavy heart trying her best to sound lighthearted. She tried for a joke. "Hold it," she said weakly, "Ronnie, honey, turn me off."

The tape rolled on and her voice went round and round inside her head as though it might go on forever, telling the same old story. If somebody wanted to drive me crazy, she thought, all they'd have to do is to lock me up in a room with the sound of my own voice to tell me what's what. She sat quietly then, listening, with a smile on her face and her hands gone to ice. "Lord God," she said to herself, "that's me." And she felt something coming again, only it wasn't Jesus this time, it was the emptiness and the stony stillness such as could have been felt in Jesus' tomb with the stone still over the entrance and no dawn coming. Then, mercifully, the song was done.

"No," she said. "That's all wrong. Not a thing right about it."

"Maybe one there that's worth saving," Ronnie the engineer said. "But that's about it." He flipped a bunch of switches up in the control booth. He was a small, quick, dark man with his hair pulled back in a thin ponytail. He jumped around up there like a monkey or something.

She had a brainstorm. "Ronnie," she said, "why don't we put some echo on that one? We could mix down the bass and throw on some echo and I bet it'd sound a whole lot better."

"Honey," he said, "I'm afraid a little echo isn't going to solve the problem here." His face was smiling at her, except for his eyes, which were sad. "Nothing to do but try it again."

"You know, there's not but one thing I can think of that's fun to do more than once," Alice said. At least she'd gotten the players laughing. Even old Cat Adams threw back her head and laughed. Alice slapped her knee and sipped the whiskey. Laughter was always good. It brought back a sense of perspective. She watched them over the rim of the jar, then held it up to the light. Half empty, she thought. Then she corrected herself, angrily. No, it's still half full. She pressed her lips together tightly for a moment and brushed furiously at her skirt.

"Sweetheart," Ronnie said. He stood up in the control booth and leaned into the microphone so he could see her and talk to her at the same time. He started counting on his fingers. "Loretta Lynn, Tammy Wynette, Crystal Gayle, Dolly Parton. I have worked with those ladies and every single one of them's willing to do a song as long as it takes to get it right," he said. "You're no better than them now are you?"

Her face felt like a big tin moon with a bright light fixed on it from someplace far away. Everybody was watching, waiting. "Well, darling," she said, "I guess I'm just in a class by myself."

"Shit," Cat Adams said. "Why don't we act professional about this instead of wasting time talking about echo and all that nonsense?" She was staring directly at Alice with those intense green eyes. The others studied their instruments, the ceiling, the floor.

Then Good-Natured was at her side, only he wasn't living up to his name anymore. His face was tight and flushed. "Let's get serious here, Alice," he said. He held his wristwatch up for her to see. 4:45.10, 4:45.11, 4:45.12. It was a kind that blinked the time, seconds and all, and beeped at you every hour. She felt relieved. When a man spoke to her sternly that way she felt as though a burden had been lifted off her shoulders. "O.K.," she said, in her smallest voice to let him know that she knew what was what. "Malcom," she said. "I need a few minutes here to pull myself together and then I promise I'll do what I came here to do." She crossed her heart. "Promise," she said, "I'll be right back. Now don't go away."

"Alice," he said. Her name sounded like a warning.

"Promise," she said, and slipped out through the door—safe. The sky was wide as an ocean you couldn't see across, restless with clouds and with the black shapes of mountains thrown up against the stars. It was the coldest time of night, the hour just before dawn, when all the warmth has escaped the earth and the sun has not yet risen to give it back. She began to walk and shake her head to clear it. Good old night, she thought. Good old walking. Good old whiskey and good old quiet stars, so far and so many it would take a person longer than two lifetimes to wish on every one. She tipped her head back and let the sky bathe her face, hands in the pockets of her skirt, swirling it around her legs. The stars on the toes of her red boots flashed as she walked. Now and then the moon flashed off the silver disks of her belt and made the white buckskin of her shirt shine, the wind went up under her hair and she moved along like a ship under full sail.

The longer she walked, the better she felt. She walked along the edge of the lot that paralleled the highway, then she turned and started back toward the mountain that rose straight up out of the earth just behind the studio. The air was colder there, as though even at night the mountain cast a shadow. Over in the east the sky was starting to lighten, which made the mountain look even darker. The closer she got, the blacker and higher it seemed, until it towered above her, blocking the sky. It looked like someplace God might have gone—colder than the earth, high, and darker than the sky, with the stars hovering above, offering light. But if God was up there, he was keeping real quiet and not letting on that he was any different from darkness itself.

She shook her head. You sure have some funny thoughts late at night. She walked out until she came to the highway again. Even at this hour a few cars came winding down the road between the mountains at the end of the valley, heading south, their headlights sparkling against the dark. Even at this hour. Good song title. Hum a few bars and I'll give it a go. She waved to a van with Alabama plates. It flashed its high-beams and went on down the road. She waved at an old Chevrolet bearing Tennessee plates. It slowed and stopped beside the guardrail and the man driving leaned across the seat and looked up at her. He was older than she and he had an open country face, brown and lined and soft-looking as a leather pouch turned inside out. In the back seat were three large burlap sacks with pictures of horses on Purina labels. The front seat of his car was clean, and a small whisk broom hung from the cigarette-lighter knob. A tray rested on the hump in the floor. It held a cup of steaming coffee and a sausage biscuit, with a bite taken out of it, on a McDonald's napkin. The radio was turned down low and an early-morning radio voice read the market futures for soybeans and corn.

She leaned over and caught a whiff of the inside of the car. It smelled of coffee and sweet feed and sausage biscuit. She had the queerest feeling in her body, as though all her senses and even her skin had roused up at the sight and smell of that car and that man. The feeling rose in her till she felt it coloring her cheeks and warming her scalp. It was a feeling of joy such as you'd feel when somebody you loved and who'd been away for a long time

46

had at last come home. And it was as though while he'd been gone he'd had something of hers with him and now he'd brought it back. But what was it? Where was it? A map lay on the seat, a wallet, a little sprig of forsythia. When he saw her looking at the wallet, he moved it closer to him. Alice stepped back from the guardrail.

"Need any help do you, lady?" he asked.

She shook her head. "No," she said. "I guess not. I was just out walking, thinking some things through, you know. I was just waving to people, that's all. But thank you, though," she said. "You've helped me a lot."

"All right then," he said. He eased the transmission lever back into D and coasted back onto the asphalt and down.

Alice practically flew across the parking lot, she twirled and danced. Why, that man had given her hope again. Just a stranger, and here he'd come riding out of the night that way, reminding her of what she was about. The door banged back, startling them all. The guitar player had been sitting on the floor with his knees drawn up and his head resting on his arms. Cat Adams was stretched out on the floor with a book propped on her chest. Good-Natured sipped coffee out of a styrofoam cup and walked around. The clock on the wall said five A.M. She had only been gone for fifteen minutes. She clapped her hands and they looked at her, bleary and sour. The faces of the men were stubbled with new beards. God they were a ragged crew. She saw the coffee stains on the carpet, the old tired green color of the walls, the rips in the amplifier coverings, and Cat Adams's old scarred guitar with the wood around the pick guard gouged out. Why was it that everything in this world was bound to disappoint?

They climbed to their feet and she climbed back onto her stool and picked up the earphones and the jar of whiskey. "Now," she said, her eyes shining just the way they had shone when all those people lit their candles for her. "I'm going to tell you what I discovered on my little walk outside." She took a sip out of the jar. Up in the control booth, Good-Natured rubbed his forehead so hard that when he stopped his skin stayed red, as though he had a rash. She tucked her skirt around her legs. "Well," she said, "I discovered two things—the mountain and the road. Listen to me now. Those two things. We can climb that mountain, which means we can do that same old song over and over again until we wear ourselves out, or, now hear me out, we can trust to the road and what's coming down it. And who knows what we might find there?"

"So what's it going to be then?" Cat Adams said. She had the fiddle tucked up under her chin, plucking the strings and twisting the tuners.

"Well what do you think?"

"Eureka," the drummer said. He hitched up his pants and climbed in behind the drums. She tried to catch Cat's eye. Surely another woman would have to understand about wanting something so badly you didn't care what you did to get it, or who saw you. But that woman kept tuning her fiddle.

"We're going to do a number called 'Free as the Rain,'" Alice said. "Key of G. We'll run it through a few times so you know it and then we'll do it for real. It's easy, just your standard changes, G to C and then on the chorus it's D, G, A and so on. Got it?" she said. "Then here we go." She closed her eyes and swayed on her stool. She let them go through the opening chords five or six times, until the feeling rose in her again—something's coming, Alice, it's almost here. Then Alice began to sing. Cat Adams was smiling, eyes closed, sawing away on her fiddle. Then she let the guitar player have his say, and they were into the chorus. The bass was going like a heart beating time along its rough zig-zag way.

"*Free as the rain that falls on the water,*" she sang.
"*Free as the lonesome sky.*
"*Free as a child without any mother.*
"*Free as the years flying by.*"
She heard her voice coming back at her through the head-phones. It was taking her down, like a seed toward the earth. She

48

was going that way again. And she sang about that falling. Then she saw the country down below where she was going. It was a wide and stony place with one dark tree, a honey locust still locked in winter, standing up tall and throwing its shadow, so she sang about that tree and the shadow it cast. And when she reached the bottom, she looked all around her and she sang about the stone, she sang about the cold moon that shone there, in a voice that was clear and wide and dark as emptiness itself. Now listen, everybody, her voice said, I am going to tell you about a place I know. She sang about that place in a voice that rang off stone.

"*Free as the rain that falls on the water*," she sang.
"*Free as the lonesome sky.*
"*Free as a child without any mother.*
"*Free as the years flying by.*"

She had had her say, She took off the earphones and laid them down in her lap and listened while the music came out of the headset, tinny and distant, like a radio playing two houses away. The others kept going, heading for home. They had made a circle and they were playing together. They spoke and answered with their instruments until the separate strands of what they were playing joined and became one song. Even the fat drummer whisking the snare with his brush knew the way. She felt a tenderness opening inside her, a kind of patience, towards whatever struggled to be born. It opened in her like a single wide flower. Then, with a flourish on the fiddle, they were done. They grinned at each other and the bass player bowed her way. She saluted them with her jar.

The only person not smiling was Good-Natured. "Alice," he said. He spoke as gently as he could, but she knew the news was bad. You just developed an ear for things, like the sound of certain footsteps or certain cars. Ronnie flipped switches up in the control booth. She slung her purse over her shoulder and picked up the jar of whiskey. There was a shallow film of liquid left in the bottom and she drained it down before she answered. She watched while it coasted toward her down the side of the jar so slowly she thought it might evaporate before it got there. It spread in her mouth like oily heat. She dropped the empty jar into the wastebasket on top of the red ribbon. "Umm?" she said.

"Well, that was a take," he said. "But, Alice, we don't have any more time here, honey. You used it all up."

"What'd I do with it?" she joked. Nobody laughed. She pushed through the restroom door. In the mirror she saw that the lipstick had worn off her mouth and her hair looked limp and stringy. Her face had settled around its bones the way it did when she was tired. She looked at the woman in the mirror, the one who had sung about the emptiness and felt a kind of mercy come to her after the emptiness was done. She had the strongest desire to leave her face bare that way, not to touch it, to go out of there wearing that face, and all that it had seen, as her own, and to let other people worry what they thought about it. That might be a place to start. But the longer she stared the more she began to believe that if she looked into this other woman's eyes long enough, that woman would begin to speak, and when she did, she would tell Alice things she did not want to hear. She reached around in her tooled handbag until she found a manila envelope where she'd stashed a few of the publicity photos, just in case. She eased them out of the envelope and looked into her laughing face. There you are, she said.

She assembled her makeup supplies—foundation, blush, powder, lipstick, eyeliner and shadow—on the washbasin and started in on herself. Cat Adams came in and stood looking at her with her narrow pointed face and those intense green eyes, just like a cat crouched under a bush watching a bird. "Look here," she said, "Malcom tells me there may be enough there to do a forty-five. 'Course, they don't usually do forty-fives, but in this case," she shrugged, and mimicked Malcom's voice, " 'a definite maybe.' " Alice held the mascara wand poised in front of her eyelashes. She smiled at Cat. "Thanks, babe," she said. "But I'm an all-or-nothing person." She put the finishing touches on her face, and brushed her hair until it crackled and stood out around her head. She put on her bright-red lipstick and blotted her lips, tossed some cologne on her wrists and up under her hair.

"Now then, I feel better," she said, heading for the door. Then she stopped. "Something I've been wanting to ask you," she said. "Who gave you that name anyway? Who calls you that?"

"My husband."

"Oh." That's what she'd been afraid of. She looked at Cat and felt dizzy all of a sudden, as though she had become aware of some steady kind of motion, rolling like a tide, carrying everything and everyone toward something plain and true and terrible as a name that exactly fit. "Excuse me," she said. "I need some fresh air."

Ronnie locked the door behind them. The lock made a satisfying solid sound as it caught. At least that's done, it said. At least that's over. It was dawn. There was a leftover moon hanging on in the pale sky as though it didn't have the sense to set. They were all standing outside like a bunch of refugees, Alice thought, tossed off their ship. All except Alice. She felt the dawn on her face and she breathed deep. She felt that tenderness again, welling up inside her, toward all creatures and their weariness. She felt that she was going to be like this for a very long time. "Listen," she said. "You all look tired. You wait here, I'll go get the van." Good-Natured tossed her the keys.

She stepped quickly through the pale morning, listening to the birds, the traffic on the highway, watching the chimneys begin to pour smoke. A flock of redwing blackbirds descended onto a clump of cattails standing in a roadside ditch. They hung there swaying and calling to one another, in their clear melodious voices, ruffling their feathers and flashing the bright scarlet bars on their wings. Suddenly she was furious at them, sitting there like that, preening. There wasn't but so much beauty to go around in the world and it wasn't fair for birds to get so much of it. She ran at them yelling "Shoo, get out of here, birds," and watched them take off in a great confusion of wings until they were lost against the rising sun.

From somewhere up the valley, a rooster crowed. It was all right. She unlocked the van and paused with her hand on the key. In the shopping center across the highway, a Bunny Bread truck and a Sealtest milk truck were backed up to the front door of the Winn-Dixie. She heard men's voices, racks clanging, and saw the drivers wheeling hand trucks stacked with cases of bread and milk. She closed her eyes and breathed deep, breathed deeper. Quietly now, Alice, softly now. She could have sworn she caught a whiff of fresh bread drifting over the lot, invisible and yet full of comfort too, the smell of home and morning coming round. The mountains were still purple in the growing light, purple and silent and waiting for the light to strike them.

By the time Good-Natured dropped her off at the motel the pink and pearl-gray of dawn had vanished. Spring trees on the mountains stood up like pale green smoke and the sky was so pale it looked almost white. "Well, thanks for a lovely evening," she joked. His eyes, when he finally looked at her, were the pale, joyless white of that sky.

"I'm sorry you won't think about the forty-five," he said. "I'll come take you to the airport at three. Please be ready."

"You can count on me," she said. "I'm the best at being ready of anybody you've ever seen. I am the champion of the world at being ready."

She closed her door and leaned against it, and for an instant the objects in the room left their places and seemed to float inches above the surfaces where they had rested, as though she'd surprised them in the act of running away. She closed her eyes and pinched the bridge of her nose and when she looked again everything had settled back down. She whipped the curtains shut against the brightening morning.

She undressed quickly, brushed her teeth, slapped cream on her face, and crawled between the sheets. She liked motels;

motels were the best places in the world. Motels were like resting-places between two points: where you'd been and where you were going. And they had two double beds to choose from. You could pick either one and lie there on the crisp, almost cold sheets with the luxury of two pillows under your head and the sheet folded over the satin border of the blanket and your hands folded over the top of the sheet, thinking about things until you drifted off to sleep.

She looked at the photograph of her father that traveled with her everywhere and now sat on top of the TV. He was dark as an Indian, and his white shirt glowed. He had his foot up on the running board of his truck, and the truck was piled high with peaches. Up close, you could see leaves on some of the stems. Apples, turnips, peaches, pecans. He had hauled vegetables and fruit all over the Southeast and into Texas and he'd never worked for a soul other than himself until his dying day. He would go away, come back, go away again. She used to believe that he went away on his trips and backed his truck in somewhere and peaches and apples, turnips, pecans, onions, peanuts, and sweet honeydew melons tumbled into it right out of the sky. Then one time he stayed gone, and he was dead off the side of a mountain up in North Carolina, hauling a load of apples.

Sometimes, though, in times such as these, she felt as if he were about to turn up again, his truck loaded down with can-taloupes from the low country of Carolina or pecans from the valley of the Rio Grande. He used to drive his truck right up into the yard and under the tulip poplar tree, and he'd call to her. "Come on out here, little sister," he'd call. "Climb up there and pick you out the best one you can find to keep for yourself." He didn't say pick out just *any* one, he said the best one. She figured that all her life she'd tried to do just that.

Oh, she knew he wasn't coming back, not *really*. She wasn't crazy (though sometimes she wished she was). She could just feel it in the air, and she would catch herself perking up whenever a truck went by, or a train late at night, blowing its whistle, or a barge on the river near home, sounding its horn. It seemed like those horns and whistles and wheels were saying something to her. Sometimes it seemed that the whole round world was speaking. Alice, it called, something's coming, Alice. It hooted and it moaned. A change is bound to come. Get ready.

Raney

CLYDE EDGERTON

Now. The honeymoon. I do not have the nerve to explain everything that happened on the first night there in the Holiday Inn.
We had talked about it some before—or Charles had talked about
it. And we had, you know, necked the same as any engaged couple. And I had told Charles way back, of course, that I wanted my
marriage consumed *after* I was married. Not before. Because if it
was consumed before, then I would have to carry the thought of
that throughout my entire life and it's hard to undo that which
has already been done.

I've read books. I've had talks with my mama. And I've read
the Bible. You'd think that would prepare a woman for her wedding night.

It didn't. First of all, Charles had rib-eye steaks rolled into our
room on this metal table with drawers which could keep the
steaks warm. And there in the middle of the table was a dozen red
roses. All that was nice.

But in this silver bucket with ice and a white towel was, of all
things, a bottle of champagne.

It was a predicament for me, because on the one hand it was
all so wonderful, and Charles had planned it all out like the
man is supposed to do—I mean, my dream was being fulfilled.
Charles was getting things right. But on the other hand, there in
the middle of the table rearing its ugly head, as they say, was a

bottle of champagne. I've seen enough bottles of champagne after the World Series on TV (when the ballplayers make fools out of themselves and cuss over the airways) to know one when I see it.

Well, I'm not a prude. Getting drunk at your wedding is one thing, but I can understand a little private celebrating, maybe—as a symbol of something wonderful happening. Something symbolic. So I didn't say anything about the champagne. It's very hard to find fault on your wedding night with a dozen red roses staring you full in the face—even though a still, small voice was warning me.

Charles poured me a glass and I said to myself, Why not just a sip, like medicine, and I tried a sip, but that's all. It tasted like Alka-Seltzer with honey in it. I politely refused anymore. And didn't think Charles would drink over a glass. (I figured you couldn't buy it except in the bottle, and that's why he got it that way.)

We finished eating and Charles pushed the table, with the dishes, out into the hall. I said excuse me, went into the bathroom, put on my negligee and got ready, you know, and came back out to find Charles standing there in his Fruit of the Loom, drinking champagne out of a plastic cup. It was a terrible scene to remember.

I was planning to do what Mama explained to me: get in the bed and let Charles carry out his duties. And I was thinking that's what Charles would be planning to do. But. He had a different idea which I do not have the nerve to explain. It turned into an argument which finally turned into a sort of Chinese wrestling match with my nerves tore all to pieces. Charles kept saying nothing was in the Bible about what married people could or couldn't do. I finally cried, and Charles said he was sorry. It was awful. I cried again the next morning and Charles said he was sorry again. This may be something I can forgive but I don't think I'll ever forget it. Not for a long time.

On the second day, we didn't say much at breakfast, or after. We went to the beach for a while, ate hot dogs for lunch, and then came back to change clothes. Charles asked the manager about us playing music in the motel lounge that night. (We took our instruments in case we got a chance to play.) When he found out we'd do it free the manager said fine.

So on the second night, rather than going to this country music show like we'd planned, we met the manager in the lounge. Charles wore bluejeans and I wore my blue-checkered blouse, jeans, and cowgirl hat. The manager came in and lit all the candles in these orange candle vases. There were only three or four people there. The only thing I didn't like about it was that they served beer. But the bartender went out of his way to be nice.

We decided to play half an hour and see if we could draw an audience. We started with several banjo pieces and then I sang "This World Is Not My Home" and "I'll Fly Away." I like the way those two songs fit together. It gives me something to talk about when I introduce them. Charles is good about letting me talk about the songs. I have played with people who hog it all.

A crowd gathered, and sure enough they liked the music and clapped and somebody requested "Your Cheating Heart" and Charles tried it. He's been learning it for the last month or so. He forgets words pretty easy. Nobody noticed but he sang the same verse twice. He looked at me and I managed to wink in spite of the fact I was still in turmoil from the night before.

We had told the manager we couldn't play past nine-thirty that night. We told him it was our honeymoon and all. The truth is we only know about two hours worth of songs. But I did want to get back up to our bed and start our marriage in the proper manner. It's something I had been thinking about since I was sixteen or seventeen years old and the night before had *not* worked out at all like I thought it would. It had made me a bundle of nerves and I had discovered something in Charles I didn't know existed— something corroded, and him drinking a whole bottle of champagne brought it out. He still hasn't taken serious my principles about drinking. That first night was a awful experience which I can't bring myself to talk about, but I must say things went better on the second night. I was able to explain to Charles how I was supposed to come out of the bathroom in my negligee, go get in the bed, get under the cover, and then he was supposed to go to the bathroom, come out, come get under the cover, and accomplish what was supposed to be accomplished. It all worked the way it was supposed to, and was wonderful, I must say.

Next morning when I came out of the shower, before we went down for breakfast, Charles was talking on the phone to his other main friend besides Buddy Shellar: Johnny Dobbs, who lives in New Orleans. They were all three in the army together.

"She has a great voice," he was saying. "Raney, get your guitar. Wait a minute, Johnny."

Charles put the phone receiver on the bed, got out his banjo, hit a couple of licks and said to me, "Do 'This World Is Not My Home.' Wait a minute, let me introduce you to Johnny." So he did, over the phone, and Johnny sounded real nice.

"Charles," I whispered, "do you know how much this is costing?"

"I'll pay for it," he said. "I've been telling Johnny about your voice."

So I sang "This World Is Not My Home," and Charles asked Johnny if he could hear it clear over the phone and he said he could and then Charles wanted me to do my chicken song—the one I wrote. Charles thinks it's the funniest thing he's ever heard. It *is* a good song, and since Charles was paying. . . . It goes like this:

> The town council chairman came by late last May.
> Said we're sorry, Mr. Oakley, 'bout what we must say.
> But the airport's expanding, we mean you no harm.
> The new north-south runway's gonna point toward your farm.
>
> My chickens ain't laying; my cow has gone dry,
> 'Cause the airplanes keep flying to the sweet by and by,

To the lights of the city, to the Hawaiian shore,
While I rock on my front porch and tend to get poor.

I talked to the governor, and told him my desire:
Could you please make them airplanes fly a little bit higher.
"My chickens ain't laying," I tried to explain.
But my words were going north on a south-bound train.

My chickens ain't laying; my cow has gone dry,
'Cause the airplanes keep flying to the sweet by and by,
To the lights of the city, to the Hawaiian shore,
While I rock on my front porch and tend to get poor.

I talked to a doctor; he gave me a pill.
I talked to a lawyer; you should have seen the bill.
I talked to a librarian; he grinned and winked his eye.
And he gave me a little book called, "Chickens Can Fly."
(Charles says the book is by B. F. Skinner)

I read the little book. Taught my chickens to fly,
To aim at the intakes as the jet planes flew by.
My chickens are gone now, but the answer is found:
My kamakazi chickens closed the new runway down.
My kamakazi chickens closed the new runway down.

When I finished, Charles said Johnny really liked it. They talked another fifteen minutes before Charles finally hung up.

I hugged Charles and said something about the night before. Charles said we ought to *talk* about our "sexual relationship" sometime, and I said okay, but Lord knows I won't be able to *talk* about it. It's something you're supposed to do in a natural manner, not *talk* about. That's why you don't find it talked about in church and school—or at least you shouldn't: it's not supposed to be talked about. It's something which is supposed to stay in the privacy of your own bedroom.

Next morning when we left, the manager was at the desk and he gave us an envelope with a twenty dollar bill in it. Said it was some of the best entertainment they ever had and would we please come back and that he once worked in a hotel in Reno, and he'd heard some better, but he'd sure heard a lot worse.

II

Charles is in the bedroom covered up in the bed. There are eleven broken monogrammed glasses here on the kitchen floor and every window in the house is locked from the inside.

This all started last Saturday afternoon when I called Mama as usual. I try to call her every day. We've always been close and I say those television commercials about calling somebody— reaching out and touching—make sense. Belinda Osborne drives to see her mother every day—forty miles round trip—which I'm not about to do. That is too close. Three times a week is often enough. (Belinda's mother *is* sick a lot though.)

I'd like to be living closer to home and I know Mama and Daddy were disappointed that we didn't move into the Wilkins house, and I would have, but Charles insisted we live here in Listre because it's close to the college. I finally said okay when he promised he would still go to church with me at home in Bethel.

But: he's been going to church less and less, and we've only been married six weeks. He'll take me to Sunday School and drop me off, still wearing his pajamas under his clothes. He's done it twice. Deacon Brooks said since Charles was Methodist he must think he's too good for Free Will Baptists. He pretended he was kidding, but I could tell he was serious.

Well, as I said, I called Mama last Saturday afternoon and she told me that she had come by with Aunt Naomi and Aunt Flossie to see us that morning but we were gone. They came on in to use the phone to call Annie Godwin so it wouldn't be long distance. (We don't lock the door normally.) Aunt Naomi went to the kitchen to get a glass of water and accidentally broke one of the monogrammed glasses Cousin Emma gave us for a wedding present. Mama told me all this on the phone. I didn't think twice about it. I figured I'd just pick up another glass next time I'm at the mall. I know where they come from.

Sunday, the very next day, we're eating dinner at home in Bethel with Mama, Daddy, Uncle Nate; Mary Faye, and Norris.

Mama fixes at least two meats, five or six vegetables, two kinds of cornbread, biscuits, chow-chow, pickles, pies, and sometimes a cake.

Mama says, "Where did you tell me you all were yesterday morning?" She was getting the cornbread off the stove. She's always the last one to sit down.

"At the mall," I said.

"I like where you moved the couch to," says Mama. "It looks better. We waited for you all fifteen or twenty minutes. I'm sorry Naomi broke that glass," she said.

I hadn't mentioned it to Charles. No reason to. He says—and he was serious: "Why were you all in our house?"

I was mortified in my heart.

"We were just using the phone," says Mama. There was a long silence. It built up and then kept going.

"Pass the turnips, Mary Faye," I said. "I couldn't figure out what was wrong in there so I moved things around until it looked better and sure enough it was the couch. The couch was wrong."

My mama ain't nosy. No more than any decent woman would be about her own flesh and blood.

Listen. I don't have nothing to hide. And Lord knows, Charles don't, except maybe some of his opinions.

We finished eating and set in the den and talked for a while and the subject didn't come up again. Charles always gets fidgety within thirty minutes of when we finish eating. He has no appreciation for just setting and talking. And I don't mean going on and on about politics or something like that; I mean just talking—talking about normal things. So since he gets fidgety, we usually cut our Sunday visits short. "Well, I guess we better get on back," I say, while Charles sits over there looking like he's bored to death. I know Mama notices.

Before we're out of the driveway, Charles says, "Raney, I think you ought to tell your mama and Aunt Naomi and Aunt Flossie to stay out of our house unless somebody's home."

To stay out of *my* own house.

He couldn't even wait until we were out of the driveway. And all the car windows rolled down.

When we got on down the road, out of hearing distance, I said, "Charles, you don't love Mama and never did."

He pulls the car over beside the PEACHES FOR SALE sign across from Parker's pond. And stares at me.

The whole thing has tore me up. "Charles," I said, and I had to start crying, "you don't have to hide your life from Mama and them. Or me. You didn't have to get all upset today. You could understand if you wanted to. You didn't have to get upset when I opened that oil bill addressed to you, either. There ain't going to be nothing in there but a oil bill, for heaven's sake. Why anyone would want to hide a oil bill I cannot understand."

He starts hollering at me. The first time in my life anybody has set in a car and hollered at me. His blood vessels stood all out. I couldn't control myself. It was awful. If you've ever been hollered at, while you are crying, by the one person you love best in the world, you know what I mean. This was a part of Charles I had never seen.

Here's what happened yesterday. We went to Penny's Grill for lunch. (I refuse to cook three meals a day, I don't care what Mama says.) When we got back, there was Mama's green Ford—parked in front of the house.

"Is that your mother's Ford?" says Charles.

"Where?"

"There."

"Oh, in front of the house? I think it might be." That long silence from the dinner table last Sunday came back, and I hoped Mama was out in the back yard picking up apples because I knew I couldn't stand another scene within a week. I couldn't think of a thing to say. I didn't want to fuss at Charles right before he talked to Mama, and I certainly wouldn't dare fuss at Mama.

Charles got out of the car not saying a word and started for the house. I was about three feet behind, trying to keep up. The front door was wide open.

Charles stopped just inside the door. I looked over his shoulder and there was Mama coming through the arched hall doorway. She stopped. She was dressed for shopping.

"Well, where in the world have you all been?" she says.

"We been to eat," I said.

"Eating out?"

"Mrs. Bell," says Charles, "please do not come in this house if we're not here."

I could not believe what I was hearing. It was like a dream.

Mama says, "Charles son, I was only leaving my own daughter a note saying to meet me at the mall at two o'clock, at the fountain. The front door was open. You should lock the front door if you want to keep people out."

"Mrs. Bell, a person is entitled to his own privacy. I'm entitled to my own privacy. This is my—our—house. I—"

"This is my own daughter's house, son. My mama was never refused entrance to my house. She was always welcome. Every day of her life."

I was afraid Mama was going to cry. I opened my mouth but nothing came out.

"Mrs. Bell," says Charles, "it seems as though you think everything *you* think is right, is right for everybody."

"Charles," I said, "that's what everybody thinks—in a sense. That's even what *you* think."

Charles turned half around so he could see me. He looked at me, then at Mama.

Mama says, "Son, I'll be happy to buy you a new monogrammed glass if that's what you're so upset about. Naomi didn't mean to break that glass. I'm going over to the mall right now. And I know where they come from."

Charles walks past me and out the front door, stops, turns around and says, "I didn't want any of those damned monogrammed glasses in the first place and I did the best I could to make that clear, plus that's not the subject." (I gave him a monogrammed blue blazer for his birthday and he cut the initials off before he'd wear it.)

So now Mama's at the mall with her feelings hurt. Charles is in the bedroom with a blanket over his head, and I'm sitting here amongst eleven broken monogrammed glasses, and every door and window locked from the inside.

Evidently Charles throws things when he's very mad. I never expected violence from Charles Shepherd. Thank God we don't have a child to see such behavior.

We didn't speak all afternoon, or at supper—I fixed hot dogs, split, with cheese and bacon stuck in—or after. I went to bed at about ten o'clock, while Charles sat in the living room reading some book. I felt terrible about Mama's feelings being hurt like I know they were; I hadn't known whether to call her or not; I couldn't with Charles there; and I couldn't imagine what had got into Charles.

I went to bed and was trying to go to sleep, with my mind full of upsetting images, when I heard this *voice* coming out of the heating vent at the head of the bed on my side. I sat up. I thought at first it was somebody under the house. I let my head lean down over the side of the bed close to the vent. It was *Charles*—talking on the phone in the kitchen.

Now if we'd been on speaking terms I would have told him I could hear him, but we weren't speaking. And besides, I won't about to get out of bed for no reason at eleven P.M. And so I didn't have no choice but to listen, whether I wanted to or not.

Charles was talking to his Johnny friend. I could hear just about everything he said. If we had been speaking, I wouldn't have hesitated to tell him how the sound came through the vent. But we weren't speaking, as I said. He was talking about—you guessed it: Mama.

". . . She just broke in, in essence . . . just walked through the door when nobody was home. . . . It's weird, Johnny. . . . What am I supposed to do?"

Now why didn't he ask *me* what he was supposed to do? He didn't marry Johnny Dobbs.

I agree that some things need to be left private—but the *living room?* The living room is where everybody comes into the house. That's one of the last places to keep private on earth. I just can't connect up Charles's idea about privacy to the living room.

He went on about Mama for awhile and then said something about everybody saying "nigger," and that when Johnny came to see us for him not to drive in after dark—which I didn't understand until it dawned on me that maybe Johnny Dobbs was a, you know, black. He didn't sound like it when I talked to him over the phone at Myrtle Beach. Charles and his other army buddy, Buddy Shellar, at the wedding kept talking about "Johnny this" and "Johnny that" but I never thought about Johnny being anything other than a regular white person. They were all three in the army, which of course everybody knows has been segregated since 1948, according to Charles, so I guess it's possible they roomed together, or at least ate together.

He didn't sound, you know, black.

I'll ask Charles about it when we're on speaking terms and I tell him about how the sound comes through the vent; but if he *is* a nigger, he can't stay here. It won't work. The Ramada, maybe, but not here.

Sweethearts

RICHARD FORD

I was standing in the kitchen while Arlene was in the living room saying goodbye to her ex-husband, Danny. I had already been out to the store for groceries and come back and made coffee, and was standing drinking it and staring out the window while the two of them said whatever they had to say. It was a quarter to six in the morning.

This was not going to be a good day in Danny's life, that was clear, because he was headed to jail. He had written several bad checks, and before he could be sentenced for that he had robbed a convenience store with a pistol—completely gone off his mind. And everything had gone to hell, as you might expect. Arlene had put up the money for his bail, and there was some expensive talk about an appeal. But there wasn't any use to that. He was guilty. It would cost money and then he would go to jail anyway.

Arlene had said she would drive him to the sheriff's department this morning if I would fix him breakfast, so he could surrender on a full stomach. And that had seemed all right. Early in the morning Danny had brought his motorcycle around to the backyard and tied up his dog to the handlebars. I had watched him from the window. He hugged the dog and kissed it on the head and whispered something in its ear, then came inside. The dog was a black Lab, and it sat beside the motorcycle now and stared with blank interest across the river at the buildings of town, where the sky was beginning to turn pinkish, and the day was opening up. It was going to be our dog for a while now, I guessed.

Arlene and I had been together almost a year. She had divorced Danny long before and had gone back to school and gotten real estate training and bought the house we lived in, then quit that and taught high school a year, and finally quit that and just went to work in a bar in town, which is where I came upon her. She and Danny had been childhood sweethearts and run crazy for fifteen years. But when I came into the picture, things with Danny were settled, more or less. No one had hard feelings left, and when he came around I didn't have any trouble with him. We had things we talked about—our pasts, our past troubles. It was not the worst you could hope for.

From the living room I heard Danny say, "So how am I going to keep up my self-respect. Answer me that. That's my big problem."

"You have to get centered," Arlene said in an upbeat voice. "Be within yourself if you can."

"I feel like I'm catching a cold right now," Danny said. "On the day I enter prison I catch cold."

"Take Contac," Arlene said. "I've got some somewhere." I heard a chair scrape. She was going to get it for him.

"I already took that," Danny said. "I had some at home."

"You'll feel better then," Arlene said. "They'll have Contac in prison."

"I put all my faith in women," Danny said softly. "I see now that was wrong."

"I couldn't say," Arlene said. And then no one spoke.

I looked out the window at Danny's dog. It was still staring across the river at town as if it knew about something there.

The door to the back bedroom opened then, and my daughter Cheryl came out wearing her little white nightgown with red valentines on it. BE MINE was on all the valentines. She was still asleep, though she was up. Danny's voice had waked her up.

"Did you feed my fish?" she said and stared at me. She was barefoot and holding a doll, and looked pretty as a doll herself.

"You were asleep already," I said.

She shook her head and looked at the open living-room door. "Who's that?" she said.

"Danny's here," I said. "He's talking to Arlene."

Cheryl came over to the window where I was and looked out at Danny's dog. She liked Danny, but she liked his dog better. "There's Buck," she said. Buck was the dog's name. A tube of sausage was lying on the sink top and I wanted to cook it, for Danny to eat, and then have him get out. I wanted Cheryl to go to school, and for the day to flatten out and hold fewer people in it. Just Arlene and me would be enough.

"You know, Danny, sweetheart," Arlene said now in the other room, "in our own lifetime we'll see the last of the people who were born in the nineteenth century. They'll all be gone soon. Every one of them."

"We should've stayed together, I think," Danny whispered. I was not supposed to hear that, I knew. "I wouldn't be going to prison if we'd loved each other."

"I wanted to get divorced, though," Arlene said.

"That was a stupid idea."

"Not for me it wasn't," Arlene said. I heard her stand up.

"It's water over the bridge now, I guess, isn't it?" I heard Danny's hands hit his knees three times in a row.

"Let's watch TV," Cheryl said to me and went and turned on the little set on the kitchen table. There was a man talking on a news show.

"Not loud," I said. "Keep it soft."

"Let's let Buck in," she said. "Buck's lonely."

"Leave Buck outside," I said.

Cheryl looked at me without any interest. She left her doll on top of the TV. "Poor Buck," she said. "Buck's crying. Do you hear him?"

"No," I said. "I can't hear him."

Danny ate his eggs and stared out the window as if he was having a hard time concentrating on what he was doing. Danny is a handsome small man with thick black hair and pale eyes. He is likable, and it is easy to see why women would like him. This morning he was dressed in jeans and a red T-shirt and boots. He looked like somebody on his way to jail.

He stared out the back window for a long time and then he sniffed and nodded. "You have to face that empty moment, Russ." He cut his eyes at me. "How often have you done that?"

"Russ's done that, Dan," Arlene said. "We've all done that now. We're adults."

"Well that's where I am right now," Danny said. "I'm at the empty moment here. I've lost everything."

"You're among friends, though, sweetheart." Arlene smiled. She was smoking a cigarette.

"I'm calling you up. Guess who I am," Cheryl said to Danny. She had her eyes squeezed tight and her nose and mouth pinched up together. She was moving her head back and forth.

"Who are you?" Danny said and smiled.

"I'm the bumblebee."

"Can't you fly?" Arlene said.

"No. My wings are much too short and I'm too fat." Cheryl opened her eyes at us suddenly.

"Well you're in big trouble then," Arlene said.

"A turkey can go forty-five miles an hour," Cheryl said and looked shocked.

"Go change your clothes," I said.

"Go ahead now, sweetheart," Arlene said and smiled at her. "I'll come help you."

Cheryl squinted at Danny, then went back to her room. When she opened her door I could see her aquarium in the dark against the wall, a pale green light with pink rocks and tiny dots of fish.

Danny ran his hands back through his hair then and stared up at the ceiling. "Well here's the awful criminal now, ready for jail," he said. And he looked at us and he looked wild suddenly, as wild and desperate as I have ever seen a man look. And it was not for no reason, I knew that.

"That's off the wall," Arlene said. "That's just completely boring. I'd never be married to a man who was a fucking criminal." She looked at me, but Danny looked at me too.

"Somebody ought to come take her away," Danny said. "You know that, Russell? Just put her in a truck and take her away. She always has such a wonderful fucking outlook. You wonder how she got in this fix here." He looked around the little kitchen, which was shabby and white. At one time Arlene's house had been a jewelry store, and there was a black security camera above the kitchen door, though it wasn't connected now.

"Just try to be nice, Danny," Arlene said.

"I just oughta slap you," Danny said. I could see his jaw muscles tighten, and I thought he might slap her then. In the bedroom I saw Cheryl standing naked in the dark, sprinkling food in her aquarium. The light made her skin look the color of water.

"Try to calm down, Dan," I said and stayed put in my chair. "We're all your friends."

"I don't know why people came out here," Danny said. "The West is fucked up. It's ruined. I wish somebody would take me away from here."

"Somebody's going to, I guess," Arlene said, and I knew she was mad at him and I didn't blame her, though I wished she hadn't said that.

Danny's blue eyes got small, and he smiled at her in a hateful way. I could see Cheryl looking in at us. She had not heard this kind of talk yet. Jail talk. Mean talk. The kind you don't forget. "Do you think I'm jealous of you two?" Danny said. "Is that it?"

"I don't know what you are," Arlene said.

"Well I'm not. I'm not jealous of you two. I don't want a kid. I don't want a house. I don't want anything you got. I'd rather go to Deer Lodge." His eyes flashed out at us.

"That's lucky, then," Arlene said. She stubbed out her cigarette

70

on her plate, blew smoke, then stood up to go help Cheryl. "Here I am now, hon," she said and closed the bedroom door.

Danny sat at the kitchen table for a while then and did not say anything. I knew he was mad but that he was not mad at me; probably, in fact, he couldn't even think why I was the one here with him now—some man he hardly knew, who slept with a woman he had loved all his life and at that moment thought he still loved, but who—among his other troubles—didn't love him anymore. I knew he wanted to say that and a hundred things more then. But words can seem weak. And I felt sorry for him, and wanted to be as sympathetic as I could be.

"I don't like to tell people I'm divorced, Russell," Danny said very clearly and blinked his eyes. "Does that make any sense to you?" He looked at me as if he thought I was going to lie to him, which I wasn't.

"That makes plenty of sense," I said.

"You've been married, haven't you? You have your daughter."

"That's right," I said.

"You're divorced, aren't you?"

"Yes," I said.

Danny looked up at the security camera above the kitchen door, and with his finger and thumb made a gun that he pointed at the camera, and made a soft popping with his lips, then he looked at me and smiled. It seemed to make him calmer. It was a strange thing.

"Before my mother died, okay?," Danny said, "I used to call her on the phone. And it took her a long time to get out of bed. And I used to wait and wait and wait while it rang. And sometimes I knew she just wouldn't answer it, because she couldn't get up. Right? And it would ring forever because it was me, and I was willing to wait. Sometimes I'd just let it ring, and so would she, and I wouldn't know what the fuck was going on. Maybe she was dead, right?" He shook his head.

"I'll bet she knew it was you," I said. "I bet it made her feel better."

71

"You think?" Danny said.

"It's possible. It seems possible," I said.

"What would you do though," Danny said. He bit his lower lip and thought about the subject. "When would you let it stop ringing? Would you let it go twenty-five or fifty? I wanted her to have time to decide. But I didn't want to drive her crazy. Okay?"

"Twenty-five seems right," I said.

Danny nodded. "That's interesting. I guess we all do things different. I always did fifty."

"That's fine."

"Fifty's way too many, I think."

"It's what you think *now*," I said. "But then was different."

"There's a familiar story," Danny said.

"It's everybody's story," I said. "The then-and-now story."

"We're just short of paradise, aren't we, Russell?"

"Yes we are," I said.

Danny smiled at me then in a sweet way, a way to let anyone know he wasn't a bad man, no matter what he'd robbed.

"What would you do if you were me," Danny said. "If you were on your way to Deer Lodge for a year?"

I said, "I'd think about when I was going to get out, and what kind of day that was going to be, and that it wasn't very far in the future."

"I'm just afraid it'll be too noisy to sleep in there," he said and looked concerned about that.

"It'll be all right," I said. "A year can go by quick."

"Not if you never sleep," he said. "That worries me."

"You'll sleep," I said. "You'll sleep fine."

And Danny looked at me then, across the kitchen table, like a man who knows half of something and who is supposed to know everything, who sees exactly what trouble he's in and is scared to death by it.

"I feel like a dead man, you know?" And tears suddenly came into his pale eyes. "I'm really sorry," he said. "I know you're mad at me. I'm sorry." He put his head in his hands then and cried.

And I thought: What else could he do? He couldn't avoid this now. It was all right.

"It's okay, bud," I said.

"I'm happy for you and Arlene, Russ," Danny said, his face still in tears. "You have my word on that. I just wish she and I had stayed together, and I wasn't such an asshole. You know what I mean?"

"I know exactly," I said. I did not move to touch him, though maybe I should have. But Danny was not my brother, and for a moment I wished I wasn't tied to all this. I was sorry I had to see any of it, sorry that each of us would have to remember it.

On the drive to town Danny was in better spirits. He and Cheryl sat in the back, and Arlene in the front. I drove. Cheryl held Danny's hand and giggled, and Danny let her put on his black silk Cam Ranh Bay jacket that he had won playing cards, and Cheryl said that she had been a soldier in some war.

The morning had started out sunny, but now it had begun to be foggy, though there was sun high up and you could see the blue Bitterroots to the south. The river was cool and in a mist, and from the bridge you could not see the pulp yard or the motels a half mile away.

"Let's just drive, Russ," Danny said from the back seat. "Head to Idaho. We'll all become Mormons and act right."

"That'd be good, wouldn't it?" Arlene turned and smiled at him. She was not mad now. It was her nicest trait not to stay mad at anybody long.

"Good day," Cheryl said.

"Who's that talking?" Danny asked.

"I'm Paul Harvey," Cheryl said.

"He always says that, doesn't he?" Arlene said.

"Good day," Cheryl said again.

"That's all Cheryl's going to say all day now, Daddy," Arlene said to me.

73

"You've got a honeybunch back here," Danny said and tickled Cheryl's ribs. "She's her daddy's girl all the way."

"Good day," Cheryl said again and giggled.

"Children pick up your life, don't they Russ," Danny said. "I can tell that."

"Yes, they do," I said. "They can."

"I'm not so sure about that one back there, though," Arlene said. She was dressed in a red cowboy shirt and jeans, and she looked tired to me. But I knew she didn't want Danny to go to jail by himself.

"I am. I'm sure of it," Danny said and then didn't say anything else.

We were on a wide avenue where it was foggy, and there were shopping centers and drive-ins and car lots. A few cars had their headlights on, and Arlene stared out the window at the fog. "You know what I used to want to be?" she said.

"What?" I said, when no one else said anything.

Arlene stared a moment out the window and touched the corner of her mouth with her fingernail and smoothed something away. "A Tri-Delt," she said and smiled. "I didn't really know what they were, but I wanted to be one. I was already married to him, then, of course. And they wouldn't take married girls in."

"That's a joke," Danny said, and Cheryl laughed.

"No. It's not a joke," Arlene said. "It's just something you don't understand and that I missed out on in life." She took my hand on the seat, and kept looking out the window. And it was as if Danny weren't there then, as if he had already gone to jail.

"What I miss is seafood," Danny said in an ironic way. "Maybe they'll have it in prison. You think they will?"

"I hope so, if you miss it," Arlene said.

"I bet they will," I said. "I bet they have fish of some kind in there."

"Fish and seafood aren't the same," Danny said.

We turned onto the street where the jail was. It was an older part of town, and there were some old white two-story residences that had been turned into lawyers' offices and bail bondsmen's rooms. Some bars were farther on, and the bus station. At the end of the street was the courthouse. I slowed so we wouldn't get there too fast.

"You're going to jail right now," Cheryl said to Danny.

"Isn't that something?" Danny said. I watched him up in the rearview. He looked down at Cheryl and shook his head as if it amazed him.

"I'm going to school soon as that's over," Cheryl said.

"Why don't I just go to school with you?" Danny said. "I think I'd rather do that."

"No sir," Cheryl said.

"Oh Cheryl, please don't make me go to jail. I'm innocent," Danny said. "I don't want to go."

"Too bad," Cheryl said and crossed her arms.

"Be nice," Arlene said. Though I knew Cheryl thought she was being nice. She liked Danny.

"She's teasing, Mama. Aren't we, Cheryl baby? We understand each other."

"I'm not her mama," Arlene said.

"That's right, I forgot," Danny said. And he widened his eyes at her. "What's your hurry, Russ?" Danny said, and I saw I had almost come to a stop in the street. The jail was a half block ahead of us. It was a tall modern building built on the back of the old stone courthouse. Two people were standing in the little front yard looking up at a window. A station wagon was parked on the street in front. The fog had begun to burn away now.

"I didn't want to rush you," I said.

"Cheryl's already dying for me to go in there, aren't you baby?"

"No, she's not. She doesn't know anything about that," Arlene said.

"You go to hell," Danny said. And he grabbed Arlene's shoulder with his hand and squeezed it back hard. "This is not your business, it's not your business at all. Look Russ," Danny said, and he reached in the black plastic bag he was taking with him and pulled a pistol out of it and threw it over onto the front seat between Arlene and me. "I thought I might kill Arlene, but I changed my mind." He grinned at me, and I could tell he was crazy and afraid and at the end of all he could do to help himself anymore.

"Jesus Christ," Arlene said. "Jesus, Jesus Christ."

"Take it, goddamn it. It's for you," Danny said, with a crazy look. "It's what you wanted. Boom," Danny said. "Boom-boom-boom."

"I'll take it," I said and pulled the gun under my leg. I wanted to get it out of sight.

"What is it?" Cheryl said. "Lemme see." She pushed up to see.

"It's nothing, honey," I said. "Just something of Danny's."

"Is it a gun?" Cheryl said.

"No, sweetheart," I said, "it's not." And I pushed the gun down on the floor under my foot. I did not know if it was loaded, and I hoped it wasn't. I wanted Danny out of the car then. I have had my troubles, but I am not a person who likes violence or guns. I pulled over to the curb in front of the jail, behind the gray station wagon. "You better make a move now," I said to Danny. I looked at Arlene but she was staring straight ahead. I know she wanted Danny gone now, too.

"I didn't plan this. This just happened," Danny said. "Okay? You understand that? Nothing's planned."

"Get out," Arlene said and did not turn to look at him.

"Give Danny back his jacket," I said to Cheryl.

"Forget it, it's yours," Danny said. And he grabbed his plastic string bag.

"She doesn't want it," Arlene said.

"Yes I do," Cheryl said. "I want it."

"Okay," I said. "That's nice, sweetheart."

Danny sat in the seat and did not move then. None of us moved in the car. I could see out the window into the little jail yard. Two Indians were sitting in plastic chairs outside the double doors. A man in a gray uniform stepped out the door and said something to them, and one got up and went inside. There was a large, red-faced woman standing on the grass now, staring at our car. The fog was almost gone.

I got out and walked around the car to Danny's door and opened it. It was cool out, and I could smell the sour pulp-mill smell being held in the fog, and I could hear a car laying rubber on another street.

"Bye-bye Danny," Cheryl said in the car. She reached over and kissed him.

"Bye-bye," Danny said. "Bye-bye."

The man in the gray uniform had come down off the steps and stopped halfway to the car, watching us. He was waiting for Danny, I was sure of that.

Danny got out and stood up on the curb. He looked around and shivered from the chill in the air. He looked cold, and I felt bad for him. But I would be glad when he was gone and I could live a normal life again.

"What do we do now?" Danny said. He saw the man in the gray uniform, but would not look at him. Cheryl was saying something to Arlene in the car, but Arlene didn't say anything. "Maybe I oughta run for it," Danny said, and I could see his pale eyes were jumping as if he was eager for something now, eager for things to happen to him. Suddenly he grabbed both my arms and pushed me back against the door and pushed his face right up to my face. "Fight me," he whispered and smiled a wild smile. "Knock the shit out of me. See what they do." I pushed against him, and for a moment he held me there, and I held him, and it was as if we were dancing without moving. And I smelled his breath and felt his cold, thin arms and his body struggling against me, and I knew what he wanted was for me not to let him go, and for all this to be a dream he would forget about.

"What're you doing?" Arlene said, and she turned around and glared at us. She was mad, and she wanted Danny to be in jail

77

now. "Are you kissing each other?" she said. "Is that what you're doing? Kissing goodbye?"

"We're kissing each other, that's right," Danny said. "That's what we're doing. I always wanted to kiss Russell. We're queers." He looked at her then, and I know he wanted to say something more to her, to tell her that he hated her or that he loved her or wanted to kill her or that he was sorry. But he couldn't come to the words for that. And I felt him go rigid and shiver, and I didn't know what he would do. Though I knew that in the end he would give in to things and go along without a struggle. He was not a man to struggle against odds. That was his character, and it is the character of many people.

"Isn't this the height of something, Russell?" Danny said, and I knew he was going to be calm now. He let go my arms and shook his head. "You and me out here like trash fighting over a woman."

And there was nothing I could say then that would save him or make life better for him at that bad moment or change the way he saw things. And I went and got back in the car while Danny turned himself in to the uniformed man who was waiting.

I drove Cheryl to school then, and when I came back outside Arlene had risen to a better mood and suggested that we take a drive. She didn't start work until noon, and I had the whole day to wait until Cheryl came home. "We should open up some emotional distance," she said. And that seemed right to me.

We drove up onto the interstate and went toward Spokane, where I had lived once and Arlene had, too, though we didn't know each other then—the old days, before marriage and children and divorce, before we met the lives we would eventually lead, and that we would be happy with or not.

We drove along the Clark Fork for a while, above the fog that stayed with the river, until the river turned north and there seemed less reason to be driving anywhere. For a time I thought we should just drive to Spokane and put up in a motel. But that, even I knew, was not a good idea. And when we had driven on far enough for each of us to think about things besides Danny, Arlene said, "Let's throw that gun away, Russ." I had forgotten all about it, and I moved it on the floor with my foot to where I could see it—the gun Danny had used, I guess, to commit crimes and steal people's money for some crazy reason. "Let's throw it in the river," Arlene said. And I turned the car around.

We drove back to where the river turned down even with the highway again, and went off on a dirt-and-gravel road for a mile. I stopped under some pine trees and picked up the gun and looked at it to see if it was loaded and found it wasn't. Then Arlene took it by the barrel and flung it out the window without even leaving the car, spun it not very far from the bank, but into deep water where it hit with no splash and was gone in an instant. "Maybe that'll change his luck," I said. And I felt better about Danny for having the gun out of the car, as if he was safer now, in less danger of ruining his life and other people's, too.

When we had sat there for a minute or two, Arlene said, "Did he ever cry? When you two were sitting in the kitchen? I wondered about that."

"No," I said. "He was scared. But I don't blame him for that."

"What did he say?" And she looked as if the subject interested her now, whereas before it hadn't.

"He didn't say too much. He said he loved you, which I knew anyway."

Arlene looked out the side window at the river. There were still traces of fog that had not burned off in the sun. Maybe it was 8:00 in the morning. You could hear the interstate back behind us, trucks going east at high speed.

"I'm not real unhappy that Danny's out of the picture now. I have to say that," Arlene said. "I should be more, I guess, sympathetic. It's hard to love pain if you're me, though."

"It's not really my business," I said. And I truly did not think it was or ever would be. It was not where my life was leading me, I hoped.

"Maybe if I'm drunk enough someday I'll tell you about how we got apart," Arlene said. She opened the glove box and got out a package of cigarettes and closed the latch with her foot. "Nothing should surprise anyone, though, when the sun goes down. I'll just say that. It's all melodrama." She thumped the pack against the heel of her hand and put her feet up on the dash. And I thought about poor Danny then, being frisked and handcuffed out in the yard of the jail and being led away to become a prisoner, like a piece of useless machinery. I didn't think anyone could blame him for anything he ever thought or said or became after that. He could die in jail and we would still be outside and free. "Would you tell me something if I asked you?" Arlene said, opening her package of cigarettes. "Your word's worth something, isn't it?"

"To me it is," I said.

She looked over at me and smiled because that was a question she had asked me before, and an answer I had said. She reached her hand across the car seat and squeezed my hand, then looked down the gravel road to where the Clark Fork went north and the receding fog had changed the colors of the trees and made them greener and the moving water a darker shade of blue-black.

"What do you think when you get in bed with me every night? I don't know why I want to know that. I just do," Arlene said. "It seems important to me."

And in truth I did not have to think about that at all, because I knew the answer, and had thought about it already, had wondered, in fact, if it was in my mind because of the time in my life it was, or because a former husband was involved, or because I had a daughter to raise alone, and no one else I could be absolutely sure of.

"I just think," I said, "here's another day that's gone. A day I've had with you. And now it's over."

"There's some loss in that, isn't there?" Arlene nodded at me and smiled.

"I guess so," I said.

"It's not so all-bad though, is it? There can be a next day."

"That's true," I said.

"We don't know where any of this is going, do we?" she said, and she squeezed my hand tight again.

"No," I said. And I knew that was not a bad thing at all, not for anyone, in any life.

"You're not going to leave me for some other woman, now, are you? You're still my sweetheart. I'm not crazy am I?"

"I never thought that," I said.

"It's your hole card, you know," Arlene said. "You can't leave twice. Danny proved that." She smiled at me again.

And I knew she was right about that, though I did not want to hear about Danny anymore for a while. He and I were not alike. Arlene and I had nothing to do with him. Though I knew, then, how you became a criminal in the world and lost it all. Somehow and for no apparent reason, your decisions got tipped over and you lost your hold. And one day you woke up and you found yourself in the very situation you said you would never ever be in, and you did not know what was most important to you anymore. And after *that* it was all over. And I did not want that to happen to me, did not, in fact, think it ever would. I knew what love was about. It was about not giving trouble or inviting it. It was about not leaving a woman for the thought of another one. It was about never being in that place you said you'd never be in. And it was not about being alone. Never that. Never that.

There's a Garden of Eden

ELLEN GILCHRIST

Scores of men, including an ex-governor and the owner of a football team, consider Alisha Terrebone to be the most beautiful
woman in the state of Louisiana. If she is unhappy what hope is
there for ordinary mortals? Yet here is Alisha, cold and bored and
lonely, smoking in bed.

Not an ordinary bed either. This bed is eight feet wide and
covered with a spread made from Alisha's old fur coats. There are
dozens of little pillows piled against the headboard, and the
sheets are the color of shells and wild plums and ivory.

Everything else in the room is brown, brown velvet, brown
satin, brown leather, brown silk, deep polished woods.

Alisha sleeps alone in the wonderful bed. She has a husband,
but he isn't any fun anymore. He went morose on Alisha. Now
he has a bed of his own in another part of town.

Alisha has had three husbands. First she married a poor engineer and that didn't work out. Then she married a judge and
that didn't work out. Then she married a rich lawyer and that
didn't work out.

Now she stays in bed most of the day, reading and drinking
coffee, listening to music, cutting pictures out of old magazines,
dreaming, arguing with herself.

This morning it is raining, the third straight day of the steady dramatic rains that come in the spring to New Orleans.

"It's on the T.V. a flood is coming," the maid says, bringing in Alisha's breakfast tray. Alisha and the maid adore each other. No matter how many husbands Alisha has she always keeps the same old maid.

"They always say a flood is coming," Alisha says. "It gives them something to talk about on television all day."

"I hope you're right," the maid says. "Anyway, your mother's been calling and calling. And the carpenter's here. He wants to start on the kitchen cabinets."

"Oh," Alisha says, "which carpenter?"

"The new one," the maid says, looking down at her shoes. "The young one." Blue-collar workers, she says to herself. Now it's going to be blue-collar workers.

"All right," Alisha says. "Tell him I'll talk to him as soon as I get dressed. Fix him some coffee."

Alisha gets out of bed, runs a comb through her hair, pulls on a pair of brown velvet pants, and ties a loose white shirt around her waist. I've got to get a haircut, she says, tying back her thick black curls with a pink ribbon. I've really got to do something about this hair.

The carpenter's name is Michael. He used to be a Presbyterian. Now he is a Zen Buddhist carpenter. When he uses wood he remembers the tree. Every day he says to himself: *I am part of the universe. I have a right to be here.*

This is something he learned when he was younger, when he was tripping with his wild friends. Michael is through with tripping now. He wants to go straight and have a car that runs. He wants his parents to call him up and write him letters and lend him money. His parents are busy pediatricians. They kicked him out for tripping. They don't have time for silly shit about the universe.

83

Alisha found Michael in a classified ad. "Household repairs done by an honest, dedicated craftsman. Call after four."

Alisha called the number and he came right over. As soon as she opened the door she knew something funny was going on. What kind of a carpenter shows up in a handmade white peasant shirt carrying a recorder.

"Can I put this somewhere while you show me what needs fixing," he said, looking at her out of dark blue eyes.

"What is it?" she said, taking it from him, laying it on a sofa.

"It's a musical instrument," he said. "I play with a group on Thursday nights. I was on my way there."

She led him around the house showing him things that were broken, watching his hands as he touched her possessions, watching his shoulders and his long legs and his soft hair and his dark blue eyes.

"This is a nice house," he said, when he had finished his inspection. "It has nice vibrations. I feel good here."

"It's very quiet," she said.

"I know," he said. "It's like a cave."

"You're right," she said. "It is like a cave. I never would have thought of that."

"Do you live here alone?" he said, holding his recorder in his arms. The last rays of the afternoon sun were filtering in through the leaded glass doors in the hallway casting rainbows all over the side of his face. Alisha was watching the blue part of the rainbow slide along the hollows of his cheeks.

"Most of the time," she said. "I have a husband, but he's almost never here anymore."

"It feels like only one person lives here," he said. "Everything seems to belong to you."

"It's very astute of you to see that," she began in a serious voice, then broke into a giggle. "To tell the truth, that's why my husband left. He said only Kierkegaard would believe I loved him. He said the longer he stayed in this house the smaller he became.

He said he had gotten to be about the size of an old golf ball in the corner."

"Why did he let you do that to him?" Michael said.

"He did it to himself," she said. "I don't take responsibility for other people's lives. I don't believe in being a scapegoat. That's a thing Jews are historically pretty good at, you know, so I'm always watching out for it in myself. Women are pretty good at it too, for that matter."

"You're a pretty smart lady."

"No, I'm not," she said. "I'm just trying to make it through the days like everybody else."

"I should be leaving," he said. "I'm having a hard time leaving this house."

"Come back, then," she said. "As soon as you have time. I'm looking forward to getting things fixed up around the place."

Now he was back, leaning on a counter in her spotless kitchen, cradling a cup of coffee, listening intently to something the maid was telling him.

"Have you been sick?" Michael asked, looking up from his coffee.

"Not really," she said. "I just stay in bed a lot."

"Do you want me to start on these cabinets?" he said. "I could come back another day."

"Oh, no," she said. "Today is fine. It was nice of you to come out in this weather."

"It says on the television two pumping stations are out," the maid said. "It says it's going to flood and your mother's been calling and calling."

"Maybe you should go home then," Alisha said. "Just in case."

"I think I will," the maid said. "They might let the schools out early and I'm taking care of my grandchild this week."

"Go on then," Alisha said. "I can manage here."

"What about the cabinets?" the maid said. "I was going to put in shelf paper when he finished."

"It doesn't matter," Alisha said. "I'll do it. Look out there. The sky is black as it can be. You better call a cab."

Michael finished his coffee, rinsed out the cup in the sink, set it neatly upside down to dry and began to work on the hardware of the cabinet doors, aligning them so they stayed closed when they were shut.

"They go out of tune," he said, "like a piano. I wonder who installed these to begin with. He must have been an impatient man. See how he drove these screws in. I should take the hardware off and start all over."

"Will that take a long time?" she said.

"Well," he laughed, "you'd probably have to refinish the cabinets if I did that."

"Then do it," she said. "Go on. Fix them right while you're here."

"I'll see," he said. "Perhaps I will change the worst ones, like the ones over the stove."

He went back to work. Outside torrents of rain beat against the windows and the sky was black as evening. Alisha moved around the kitchen straightening things inside the cabinets. She had not looked inside these cabinets in ages. She had forgotten all the interesting and beautiful things she owned. There were shelves of fine Limoges china and silver serving pieces wrapped carelessly in cellophane bags from the dry cleaners. There were copper pans and casserole dishes. There were stainless-steel mixing bowls and porcelain soufflé dishes and shelves and shelves of every sort of wineglass from the time when she gave dinner parties. There was one cabinet full of cookbooks and recipe folders and flower vases and candles and candleholders.

She took down a cookbook called *The Joy of Cooking*. Her first mother-in-law had given it to her. On the flyleaf was an inscription, "Much love for good cooking and a few fancy dishes." Underneath the inscription the maid had written TAKE FROM THE LEFT, SERVE FROM THE RIGHT, in large letters.

Alisha laughed out loud.

"What's so funny," the carpenter said.

"I found a book I used to use when I gave dinner parties," she said. "I wasn't very good at dinner parties. I was too ambitious. I used to make things with *curry*. And the maid and I used to get drunk while we were waiting for the guests to arrive. We never could remember which side to serve the vegetables from. No matter how many dinner parties we had we never could remember."

"Why did you get drunk?" Michael said. "Were you unhappy?"

"No," she said. "I don't think so. To tell the truth I think I was hungry. I used to take diet pills so I wouldn't eat any of the good things I was always cooking. I would be so hungry by nighttime I would get drunk if I only had a glass of wine."

"Why did you do all that?" he said, wondering if she always said anything that came into her head.

"I did it so I would look like Audrey Hepburn," she said. "At that time most of the women in the United States wanted to look like Audrey Hepburn."

"Really?" he said.

"Well, all of my friends did at least. I spent most of my waking hours trying not to eat anything. It was a lot of trouble, being hungry all the time."

"It sounds terrible," Michael said. "Do you still do it?"

"No," she said. "I quit giving a damn about Audrey Hepburn. Then I quit taking diet pills, and then I quit drinking, and then I quit giving dinner parties. Then I quit doing anything I didn't like to do."

"What do you like to do?" he asked.

"I don't know," she said. "I haven't found out yet."

"Your phone is ringing," he said. "Aren't you going to answer it?"

"No," she said. "I don't like to talk on the telephone."

"The maid said your mother had been trying to call you."

"I know. That's probably her on the phone now."

"You aren't going to answer it?"

"No. Because I already know what she's going to say. She's going to tell me a flood is coming. Don't pay any attention to the phone. It'll stop in a minute."

He put down his tools and turned around to face her. "There's a whole lot going on in this room right now," he said. "Are you aware of that?" He looked very serious, wiping his hands across his sleeves.

"How old are you?" Alisha said.

"What difference does that make?" he said and crossed the room and put his arms around her. She felt very nice in his arms, soft and brave and sad, like an old actress.

"Oh, my," she said. "I was afraid this was going to happen." Then they laid down their weapons and walked awkwardly down the hall to the bedroom, walking slowly as though they were going to do something embarrassing and awkward and absurd.

At the door to the bedroom he picked her up and carried her to the bed, hoping that was the romantic thing to do. Then he saw it. "What in the name of God is this?" he said, meaning the fur bedspread.

"Something my mother gave me," she lied. "Isn't it the tackiest thing you've ever seen in your life."

"Your body is very beautiful," she said when he had taken off his clothes and was standing before her, shy and human. "You *look* like a grown man. That's a relief."

"Do you always say whatever comes into your head?" he said.

"Oh, yes," she said. "I think everyone knows what everyone else is thinking all the time anyway. Do you mind? Do you think I talk too much?"

"Oh, no," he said. "I like it. It keeps surprising me."

"Do you like my body," she said, for now she had taken off her clothes and had struck a pose, sitting cross-legged on the bed.

"Of course I do," he said. "I've been wanting to touch your tits ever since the first moment I saw you. The whole time we were walking around your house I was wanting to touch your tits."

"Oh, my," she said. "Not my tits again. For years I believed men liked me for my mind. Imagine that! I read hundreds of books so they would like me better. All the time they were only wanting to touch my tits. Think of that!"

"Now you're talking too much," he said.

Then Alisha closed her eyes and pretended she was an Indian princess lying in a tent deep in a forest, dressed in a long white deerskin robe, waiting for Jeff Chandler to come and claim her for his bride. Outside the wind and rain beat down upon the forest.

Then Michael closed his eyes and pretended he was a millionaire going to bed with a beautiful, sad old actress.

The phone woke them with its ringing. Alisha was startled for a moment. Then she settled back down, remembering where she was. Michael's legs were smooth and warm beside her. She was safe.

"You really ought to answer that," he said. "This is quite a storm we're having."

She picked up his shirt up off the floor, put it on for a bathrobe, and went into the other room to talk.

"That was my mother," she reported. "She's crying. She's almost got her companion crying. I think they're both crying. He's this real sensitive young man we found in the drama department at Tulane. They watch T.V. together. He's learning to be an actor watching T.V."

"Why is she crying?" Michael said, sitting up in bed, pulling the plum-colored sheets around his waist.

"She's crying because the basement of her house is flooding. It always does that in heavy rains. She lives on Jefferson Avenue, around the corner. Anyway, she can't find one of her cats and she thinks he's getting wet."

"Her cats?"

"She has six or seven cats. At least six cats. Anyway, she thinks the water is going to keep on rising and drown her cats."

"You'd better go and see about her then. We'd better go and help her."

"Help her? How can we help her? It's a flash flood on Jefferson Avenue. It'll go away as soon as the pumping stations start working. I told her to sell that goddamn house the last time this happened."

"It's flooding your mother's house and you don't want to go and help her?"

"It's only flooding the basement."

"How old is she?"

"My mother. She's seventy-eight. She has a companion. Besides, she does anything she wants to do. Last year she went to *China*. She's perfectly all right."

"Then why is she crying?"

"Because she thinks her silly goddamn cats are getting wet."

"Then we'll have to go and help her."

"How can we. It's *flooded* all the way down Jefferson Avenue."

"Does that canoe in the garage work?"

"I think so. No one's ever used it. Stanley ordered it last year when he got interested in the Sierra Club. But no one's ever *used* it."

"Then we'll go in that. Every time I see a flood on television and people going to get other people in boats I want to be one of them. This is my chance. We can take the canoe in my truck to where the water starts. Go on. Call your mother back and tell her we're coming to save her. Tell her we'll be right there. And, Alisha."

"Yes."

"Tell her to stop crying. After all, she is your mother."

"This is a great canoe," he said, maneuvering it down from the floored platform of the garage. "Your husband never uses it?"

"He never uses anything," she said. "He just likes to have things. To tell the truth he's almost never here."

"Then why are you married?" he asked.

"That's a good question," Alisha said. "But I don't know the answer to it."

"Well, look, let's go on over there. I can't wait to put this in the water. I'm afraid the water will go down before we get there."

"It's really nice of you to do this," Alisha said, standing close to him, smelling the warm smell of his clothes, taking everything that she could get while she could get it.

"Everybody loves to be a hero," Michael said, putting his arms around her again, running his hands up and down her strange soft body.

"Say I'm not your mother," she said.

"You're not my mother," he said. "Besides, it doesn't matter. We're probably only dreaming."

They drove down Freret Street with the city spread out before them, clean and shining after the rain. The sun was lighting up the red tile roofs of the houses, and Tulane students were on the porches with glasses in their hands, starting their flood parties.

The inside of Michael's truck was very cosy. He used it for a business office. File folders stuffed with bills and invoices were piled in one corner, and an accounting book was on the dashboard.

"Will I make love to you again?" Alisha said, for she was too old to play hard to get.

"Whenever you want to," he said. "As soon as we finish saving your mother."

They could see the flood now. They took the canoe out of the back of the truck and carried it to where the water began at the foot of Skippy Nevelson's front yard. Alisha sat in the bow and Michael waded out pushing her until it was deep enough for him to climb in.

"I don't believe I'm doing this," she said. "You're the craziest man I ever met in my life."

"Which way is the house," he said.

"It's the second house off Willow," Alisha said. "I guess we'll just go down Jefferson and take a right at Willow."

They floated along with Michael paddling. The water was three feet deep, thick and brown and slow-moving. An envelope floated by, then an orange barrette, then a purple Frisbee.

Alisha was feeling wonderful. If Skippy Nevelson was leaning out of her front window with her eyes the size of plates, if the WDSU Minicam crew was filming her for the evening news, if the levee broke and carried them all out to sea, what was that to Alisha, who had been delivered of an angel.

"What will happen next?" she asked, pushing her luck.

"Whatever we want to happen," he said, lifting the paddle and throwing the muddy water up into the air.

"Oh, my," she said to no one in particular. "This was the year I was going to stop dying my hair."

Now they were only a block away from their destination. Alisha kept her face to the front wishing she had a hat so Michael couldn't see her wrinkles. I have to remember this a long time, she told herself. I have to watch everything and hear everything and smell everything and remember everything. This may have to last me a long, long time.

Then Alisha did a stupid thing. She wrote a little script for herself. This is the very last time I will ever love anyone she told herself. I will love this boy until he leaves me. And then I will never love another human being.

And he will leave me, because no man has ever left me in my whole life and sooner or later it has to be my turn. After a while he will stop loving me and nothing will bring him back, not all the money or love or passion in the world will hold him. So he will leave me and go into the future and I will stay here and remember love. *And that is what I get for devoting my life to love instead of wisdom.*

So Alisha sat in the bow and wrote a script for herself and then she went to work to make it all come true.

"There it is," she said, spotting the house. "The one with the green awnings. See the balconies on the top. When I was a child I always dreamed of walking out there and waving to people, but the windows were always locked so I wouldn't fall to my death on Willow Street."

"That's terrible," he said. "You had a fancy place like that and you couldn't even walk out on the balconies."

"I couldn't do anything," she said. "They were too afraid I'd get hurt. That's how wealthy Jews used to raise their children. They didn't let me ride a bicycle or roller skate or swim or anything."

"You don't know how to *swim!*" he said.

"No," she said. "Isn't that dreadful?"

"Then what are you doing in this boat?"

"Hoping it won't turn over," she said, smiling a wonderful mysterious French smile, holding on lightly to the gunwales while he rowed her to her mother's doorstep.

The Dixie Association

DONALD HAYS

It was Police Night at Patriot Park in Selma, Alabama. The first 2,500 people in the stadium were given a little American flag on a stick; a bumper sticker that said: Help God Save His Country/Support Your Local Police; a black Styrofoam nightstick; and a paperback book called *The Handy Dandy Evolution Refuter.* Cops and their families, straight-A students, disabled veterans, boy scouts, and Vacation Bible School students got in free. The stadium had spaces for about 10,000 fans, but after all those seats and the aisles between them had been filled, another couple of thousand folks were herded out to some temporary bleachers that had been set up just beyond the outfield walls.

The show was supposed to commence at seven-thirty, but it must've been closer to eight by the time they got the fans seated and the cops scrubbed down and juiced up. But sitting between Lefty and Pansy in the visitors' dugout, I enjoyed myself. Ever since Pinzon had come back and helped pry Ratoplan's fingers off my neck, things had been easy and good between Pansy and me. I hadn't told her about the bank robbery, but I had told her that Mantis had been threatening me with another McAlester vacation and that that at least partly accounted for the foul moods I'd been subjecting her to. We'd spent the last couple of nights in

Little Rock laying together in her room and, among other things, listening to the rain hit the roof. And we'd spent a good part of this day touring Selma with Lefty, walking, like King and his folks had done an age ago, from Brown's Chapel to the Edmund Pettus Bridge, where the cops had turned them back. The name of the road we followed had been changed from Sylvan Street to Martin Luther King Drive, but there was still a stiff view of suffering on either side of it. A block south of where Martin Luther King intersected with Jefferson Davis Avenue was a housing project, bleak and battered. We stood outside a chain-link fence a few minutes and watched black kids shoot goals.

When we'd entered Patriot Park, Pansy had managed to talk one of the Selmans into giving her samples of the free paraphernalia. Then while I was in the clubhouse getting into my uniform, she'd stuck the bumper sticker onto my bat. Now Bullet Bob was parading in front of us with the toy nightstick protruding up out of his fly. Pinzon was at the far end of the dugout with my bumperstickered bat in one hand and the little flag in the other. He sang a tune he'd composed for the occasion.

My name is Teddy Roosevelt.
  I am a bully man.
I have shot Injuns in the West
  And spics in Greaserland.

Now I am the president
  Of this Almighty land.
God, I know, is on my side.
  His stick is in my hand.

When he finished the song, he stretched himself belly-down against the dugout steps, put the bat to his shoulder like a rifle, said, "Don't let them take you alive," and commenced taking play shots at the crowd.

Lefty had gotten *The Handy Dandy Evolution Refuter* from Pansy, and now and then I heard him laughing over parts of it.

"Educating yourself?" I asked him.

"In the beginning was the word and the word was wrong," he said.

Then we heard sirens and looked across the diamond and saw a gate swing open in the fence down the right-field line and in came the Dallas County Honorary Posse, riding at a gallop, three abreast, in uniforms of Confederate gray, a pistol in each holster, a rifle brandished high in each right hand. There must've been 150 of the stupid fuckers. They circled the field twice, getting further and further out of formation, and then rode out the hole they'd come in. Going out the gate, each rider fired his rifle into the air. And the delighted crowd roared.

"The South will, by God, rise again," I said.

"Several times a day," Lefty agreed.

When all the posse had cleared off, two groundkeepers, dressed for the night in old police uniforms, trotted out of the Selma dugout and set up a microphone on top of home plate. Then they left and the sirens commenced again. This time a cop car, red and blue lights flashing on top, flags flapping from the fenders, led the procession through the gate. It was followed by three motorcycles and four more misery wagons. When the lead car passed our dugout, I saw that Bull Cox himself, wearing his sheriff's costume, was at the wheel. They circled the field just once, slowly. A high school band, sitting in the section of seats directly behind home plate, played "Dixie." They sounded like they'd been bribed by yankees.

Bull parked beside the pitcher's mound and strutted to the mike. The other cop cars took the infield positions, first, second, short, and third, and faced homeward. The three motorcycles positioned themselves in the outfield, one in left, one in center, one in right. Each of the drivers—helmeted, legs spread, arms folded across chest—stood just to the left of his vehicle. Bull stood at the mike and watched his men get into position. Then he turned, waved his Stetson at the crowd, and whooped and hol-

lered a couple of times. They waved their little flags and whooped
right back at him. The band kept trying to get "Dixie" right and
had finally got within hailing distance when Bull shoved his hat
back on his head and held out a palm for silence.

"You got to hand it to ole Bull," Bullet Bob said. "You can't
beat him for putting on a show."

"Wait till I get him in Little Rock again," Lefty said.

"Shit, it'll be over by then," Bullet Bob said. "That's the last
series of the year."

"The pennant race may be over," Lefty said, and then paused.
"One way or another. But I'll give them a show that'll make this
look like a wake."

"Man, there's no way you can top this, Genghis Mohammed,
Jr. said. "They gonna end it by hanging a nigger boy from the
rafters."

Pinzon favored us with another ditty:

> Niggers from a rafter.
> Meskins from a tree.
> Let's bring back the poll tax
> And set this country free.

Bull thanked the crowd for showing up and making the night a
success. "It does my heart good to know that I live amongst folks
that still honor two of the things that made this country what it is
today—law and order and baseball." Here he stopped and tried to
make his voice take on the weight of thought. "And if we didn't
have law and order we couldn't have baseball. In some of the big
cities, folks are afraid to leave their homes and go to the ballpark.
They're afraid they might get mugged on the way to the game or
come back home to find out that a burglar has busted into their
house. It's not a fit way to live, and, thank God, we've managed
to keep it from coming to that down here."

Bull rambled on for a while about hard work and safe streets
and Sunday school. Then he told the crowd that it was time to

present the annual Law Enforcement Officer of the Year Award, which this year was going to a rookie deputy—born, raised, educated, and born again right there in Selma—named Junior Boggs. Junior was president of the Bearcat Boosters, coach of the midget league Amvet Warriors, and a member of the Sulphur Springs Freewill Baptist Church. His wife was the former Joy Lynn Biggerstaff. They had two fine children, Billy Bob and Bitsy. One Saturday back in February, Junior had rescued the local TV weathergirl, Lornetta Gooch, daughter of Harley and Viola Gooch from over by Marion Junction, from a man who'd escaped from a Florida insane asylum and was holding Lornetta hostage, demanding the TV station give him an hour of prime time so that he could present his plan for achieving world peace. Well now, ole Junior wasn't having none of that. He sneaked in the back way, somehow managed to slip up behind the lunatic, sunk a .38 slug in the back of his head, and saved the evening for "Love Boat" and "Fantasy Island."

Pinzon said, "Ah, to be in Selma, now that Junior's there."

"Lornetta Gooch herself will present the award," Bull announced.

Lornetta sprung up out of the American dugout and sashayed to the microphone. She had her feet in patent leather spike heels, her face under several layers of Max Factor, her frosted hair in a $75 frizz, and her body in a white one-piece bathing suit with a banner slantwise across her chest that said "KALA TV 5." The fans moaned and whistled and waved their flags.

"Damned if that ain't a prime piece," Bullet Bob said.

"Fucking her would be an act of patriotism," I said.

When Lornetta got to Bull she went up on tiptoes and gave him a sweet little kiss on the cheek. Bull grinned like a stump freak in an amputee ward. Then he leaned down to the microphone and said, "Lordee, I do hope Beulah ain't here."

The crowd laughed. Lornetta giggled and worked up a blush. "Well, Lornetta," Bull said, "we're getting off to a late start and these folks're apt to miss the ten-o'clock edition of 'Eyewitness

98

News.' So I wonder if you wouldn't be good enough to go ahead and tell us what the weather's going to be up to?"

"Fair to partly cloudy," she said, just as cute as a button on Peggy Lou's Easter dress. "Highs in the low nineties. Lows in the high seventies. Ten percent chance of afternoon or evening thundershowers."

She smiled. Bull smiled. I suppose the crowd smiled. Bullet Bob said, "I bet ole Bull's getting him some of that."

"Lucky girl," Genghis Mohammed, Jr., said.

Bull walked back to his car and dragged out a trophy that was about the size of a healthy midget. On a pedestal a bronzed cop stood in full regalia, chest out, legs spread, hands on hips. He carried it to Lornetta and was going to give it to her, but she shook her head and stepped to the microphone.

"A family of four could set up housekeeping inside that trophy," Lefty said.

"It'd be hot in there this time of year," I said.

"Ladies and gentlemen," Lornetta began, in a serious speech-class voice, "it's a great honor for me to be here tonight for Police Night. And it's a special thrill to be able to present this award to Deputy Junior Boggs. I owe my life to his bravery." She extended her left arm toward the Selma dugout. "Junior . . ."

Junior looked to be about five years and forty pounds beyond the high school football field. Bands of fat had formed around him but hadn't had time yet to do much serious falling. Swollen with ignorant pride, he long-stepped his way across the infield. When he reached Bull and Lornetta, he stopped, turned, and looked back at the dugout, out of which a choir appeared, wrapped in robes the color of old blood. They lined up, joined hands, and, to the accompaniment of the ball park organ, sang "Let the Lower Lights Be Burning." I joined in on the chorus.

> Let the lower lights be burning!
> Send a gleam across the wave!
> Some poor fainting, struggling seaman
> You may rescue, you may save.

"Why, Hog," Pansy kidded, "you have the voice of an angel."

"I sung bass, Hon, in the Slammer Tabernacle."

The choir doused the lower lights, and Lornetta returned to the mike. "For outstanding service to your community, for courage far beyond the call of duty, Deputy Sheriff Junior Boggs, I do hereby present you this award as Law Enforcement Officer of the Year."

Trophy extended, Bull stepped toward Junior, but Lornetta slipped between the two lawmen, wrapped her arms around Junior's neck, and kissed him flush on the mouth. "Junior," she said, letting him go, "thank you so very much for saving my life. I'll be grateful to you forever."

Junior laid his right hand on the butt of his holstered pistol, wiped his eyes with his left, and said, "Why, you're quite welcome, Miss Lornetta."

Then he accepted the trophy from Bull. I don't think he much wanted to make a speech, but Bull and Lornetta pushed him forward. The trophy was so big that he had to hold it off to one side to keep it from blocking him away from the microphone.

"Some of y'all that know me know I ain't never been much on public speaking. But I would like to take this chance to say how proud I am to accept this award. I never expected ever to get such a honor. I just go along doing what I been trained to do and what I know way down deep in my heart is right." He stopped, swallowed a time or two, looked at the trophy, and then switched it from one side to the other. "I'd just like to thank Sheriff Cox for being so good to me, and my momma and daddy—Mr. and Mrs. Burl R. Boggs, Star Route 1. Most of y'all know them—for raising me up the way they done." He started to let it go at that, then thought of something else. "And I'd like to put in a good word too for Coach Buster Spoon. When I's in high school Coach Spoon always taught us that if you wanted to amount to anything you had to put out 110 percent effort 110 percent of the time. I just really do hope I can go through life that away." He raised the trophy a little and took another look at it. "I·thank each and ever' one of y'all for this very much. I won't never forget it."

Lornetta hooked her hand around Junior's free elbow and turned him toward the choir, which roared into "Stand Up, Stand Up for Jesus."

Bull stretched both arms, palms up, out in front of him, and the crowd stood and began singing with the choir. Everywhere the little American flags, held tight in fevered hands, jumped jubilantly back and forth, up and down through the bristling air.

I don't know whether Eversole had been sitting quietly all along at his end of the bench or had just then been drawn out of the clubhouse by the sound of the rising tumult. I just remember that suddenly there he was, the huge dark man, standing, just off to my right, on the first dugout step. His long, thick arms hung down at his sides, a glove on one hand, a ball in the other. I leaned a little to my left to get a clear look at his face. I didn't see anger in it, but I sensed that it was there, that Eversole had simply covered it with several coats of determination. And not a grim determination either. There was almost a satisfied look to the face. I thought it was the face of a man who, after a long search, had finally found the perfect enemy and was now ready to go out and do them in.

The choir began the final verse. Lornetta, as formally as she could, led Junior toward them. I wish I could have seen their faces. I imagined the light of heroism glowing through the faint pink of Junior's man-child cheeks. I imagined Lornetta, Miss America for the moment, smiling all over herself while tears streamed down her face, dredging rivulets through the makeup. Southern man, stout and strong, southern woman, meek and mild, lost in similar delusions.

It was farce, all right, but for just a minute there I felt a rush of sympathy, an urge toward brotherhood. Folks get by however they can. They do work they don't like to feed their kids. Year by year, the work grinds them down. The kids grow up to be strangers. Husbands and wives cling together out of habit and fear and sometimes love. Or they break apart because one or the other or both suddenly feel for somebody else the stirring of passion, almost forgotten, always confusing. And when and if they ever stand back and take a hard look at it all, none of it seems to make any sense. So they need patriotism and they need religion. They need ceremony, then, even if the ceremony is a farce, so that they can fool themselves into believing in something. And, hell, anyway, their ceremony was no bigger a farce than anybody else's.

Oh, they were enemies to me, but not in the pure way they were to Eversole. Sitting there on that dugout bench, I fancied I had some understanding of them. And I knew that a part of me would always be kindred to them. But I knew too that another part of me—I think it's the best part, I know it's the strongest—would have to fight them for every breath. Because their ceremonies, and everybody else's, have made it a world of cops and robbers. And I'm one of the robbers.

How Far She Went

MARY HOOD

They had quarreled all morning, squalled all summer about the incidentals: how tight the girl's cut-off jeans were, the "Every Inch a Woman" T-shirt, her choice of music and how loud she played it, her practiced inattention, her sullen look. Her granny wrung out the last boiled dishcloth, pinched it to the line, giving the basin a sling and a slap, the water flying out in a scalding arc onto the Queen Anne's lace by the path, never mind if it bloomed, that didn't make it worth anything except to chiggers, but the girl would cut it by the everlasting armload and cherish it in the old churn, going to that much trouble for a weed but not bending once—unbegged—to pick the nearest bean; she was sulking now. Bored. Displaced.

"And what do you think happens to a chigger if nobody ever walks by his weed?" her granny asked, heading for the house with that sidelong uneager unanswered glance, hoping for what? The surprise gift of a smile? Nothing. The woman shook her head and said it. "Nothing." The door slammed behind her. Let it.

"I hate it here!" the girl yelled then. She picked up a stick and broke it and threw the pieces—one from each hand—at the laundry drying in the noon. Missed. Missed.

Then she turned on her bare, haughty heel and set off high-shouldered into the heat, quick but not far, not far enough—no road was *that* long—only as far as she dared. At the gate, a rusty

103

chain swinging between two lichened posts, she stopped, then backed up the raw drive to make a run at the barrier, lofting, clearing it clean, her long hair wild in the sun. Triumphant, she looked back at the house where she caught at the dark window her granny's face in its perpetual eclipse of disappointment, old at fifty. She stepped back, but the girl saw her.

"You don't know me!" the girl shouted, chin high, and ran till her ribs ached.

As she rested in the rattling shade of the willows, the little dog found her. He could be counted on. He barked all the way, and squealed when she pulled the burr from his ear. They started back to the house for lunch. By then the mailman had long come and gone in the old ruts, leaving the one letter folded now to fit the woman's apron pocket.

If bad news darkened her granny's face, the girl ignored it. Didn't talk at all, another of her distancings, her defiances. So it was as they ate that the woman summarized, "Your daddy wants you to cash in the plane ticket and buy you something. School clothes. For here."

Pale, the girl stared, defenseless only an instant before blurting out, "You're lying."

The woman had to stretch across the table to leave her handprint on that blank cheek. She said, not caring if it stung or not, "He's been planning it since he sent you here."

"I could turn this whole house over, dump it! Leave you slobbering over that stinking jealous dog in the dust!" The girl trembled with the vision, with the strength it gave her. It made her laugh. "Scatter the Holy Bible like confetti and ravel the crochet into miles of stupid string! I could! I will! I won't stay here!" But she didn't move, not until her tears rose to meet her color, and then to escape the shame of minding so much she fled. Just headed away, blind. It didn't matter, this time, how far she went.

The woman set her thoughts against fretting over their bickering, just went on unalarmed with chores, clearing off after the uneaten meal, bringing in the laundry, scattering corn for the chickens, ladling manure tea onto the porch flowers. She listened though. She always had been a listener. It gave her a cocked look. She forgot why she had gone into the girl's empty room, that ungirlish, tenuous lodging place with its bleak order, its ready suitcases never unpacked, the narrow bed, the contested radio on the windowsill. The woman drew the cracked shade down between the radio and the August sun. There wasn't anything else to do.

It was after six when she tied on her rough oxfords and walked down the drive and dropped the gate chain and headed back to the creosoted shed where she kept her tools. She took a hoe for snakes, a rake, shears to trim the grass where it grew, and seed in her pocket to scatter where it never had grown at all. She put the tools and her gloves and the bucket in the trunk of the old Chevy, its prime and rust like an Appaloosa's spots through the chalky white finish. She left the trunk open and the tool handles sticking out. She wasn't going far.

The heat of the day had broken, but the air was thick, sultry, weighted with honeysuckle in second bloom and the Nu-Grape scent of kudzu. The maple and poplar leaves turned over, quaking, silver. There wouldn't be any rain. She told the dog to stay, but he knew a trick. He stowed away when she turned her back, leaped right into the trunk with the tools, then gave himself away with exultant barks. Hearing him, her court jester, she stopped the car and welcomed him into the front seat beside her. Then they went on. Not a mile from her gate she turned onto the blue gravel of the cemetery lane, hauled the gearshift into reverse to whoa them, and got out to take the idle walk down to her buried hopes, bending all along to rout out a handful of weeds from between the markers of old acquaintance. She stood there and read, slow. The dog whined at her hem; she picked him up and rested her chin on his head, then he wriggled and whined to run free, contrary and restless as a child.

The crows called strong and bold MOM! MOM! A trick of the ear to hear it like that. She knew it was the crows, but still she looked around. No one called her that now. She was done with that. And what was it worth anyway? It all came to this: solitary weeding. The sinful fumble of flesh, the fear, the listening for a return that never came, the shamed waiting, the unanswered prayers, the perjury on the certificate—hadn't she lain there weary of the whole lie and it only beginning? and a voice telling her, "Here's your baby, here's your girl," and the swaddled package meaning no more to her than an extra anything, something store-bought, something she could take back for a refund.

"Tie her to the fence and give her a bale of hay," she had murmured, drugged, and they teased her, excused her for such a welcoming, blaming the anesthesia, but it went deeper than that; *she* knew, and the *baby* knew: there was no love in the begetting. That was the secret, unforgivable, that not another good thing could ever make up for, where all the bad had come from, like a visitation, a punishment. She knew that was why Sylvie had been wild, had gone to earth so early, and before dying had made this child in sudden wedlock, a child who would be just like her, would carry the hurting on into another generation. A matter of time. No use raising her hand. But she *had* raised her hand. Still wore on its palm the memory of the sting of the collision with the girl's cheek; had she broken her jaw? Her heart? Of course not. She said it aloud: "Takes more than that."

She went to work then, doing what she could with her old tools. She pecked the clay on Sylvie's grave, new-looking, un-healed after years. She tried again, scattering seeds from her pocket, every last possible one of them. Off in the west she could hear the pulpwood cutters sawing through another acre across the lake. Nearer, there was the racket of motorcycles laboring cross-country, insect-like, distracting.

She took her bucket to the well and hung it on the pump. She had half filled it when the bikers roared up, right down the blue gravel, straight at her. She let the bucket overflow, staring. On

106

the back of one of the machines was the girl. Sylvie's girl! Her bare arms wrapped around the shirtless man riding between her thighs. They were first. The second biker rode alone. She studied their strangers' faces as they circled her. They were the enemy, all of them. Laughing. The girl was laughing too, laughing like her mama did. Out in the middle of nowhere the girl had found these two men, some moth-musk about her drawing them (too soon!) to what? She shouted it: "What in God's—" They roared off without answering her, and the bucket of water tipped over, spilling its stain blood-dark on the red dust.

The dog went wild barking, leaping after them, snapping at the tires, and there was no calling him down. The bikers made a wide circuit of the churchyard, then roared straight across the graves, leaping the ditch and landing upright on the road again, heading off toward the reservoir.

Furious, she ran to her car, past the barking dog, this time leaving him behind, driving after them, horn blowing nonstop, to get back what was not theirs. She drove after them knowing what they did not know, that all the roads beyond that point dead-ended. She surprised them, swinging the Impala across their path, cutting them off; let them hit it! They stopped. She got out, breathing hard, and said, when she could, "She's underage." Just that. And put out her claiming hand with an authority that made the girl's arms drop from the man's insolent waist and her legs tremble.

"I was just riding," the girl said, not looking up.

Behind them the sun was heading on toward down. The long shadows of the pines drifted back and forth in the same breeze that puffed the distant sails on the lake. Dead limbs creaked and clashed overhead like the antlers of locked and furious beasts.

"Sheeeut," the lone rider said. "I told you." He braced with his muddy boot and leaned out from his machine to spit. The man the girl had been riding with had the invading sort of eyes the woman had spent her lifetime bolting doors against. She met him now, face to face.

"Right there, missy," her granny said, pointing behind her to the car.

The girl slid off the motorcycle and stood halfway between her choices. She started slightly at the poosh! as he popped another top and chugged the beer in one uptilting of his head. His eyes never left the woman's. When he was through, he tossed the can high, flipping it end over end. Before it hit the ground he had his pistol out and, firing once, winged it into the lake.

"Freaking lucky shot," the other one grudged.

"I don't need luck," he said. He sighted down the barrel of the gun at the woman's head. "POW!" he yelled, and when she recoiled, he laughed. He swung around to the girl; he kept aiming the gun, here, there, high, low, all around. "Y'all settle it," he said, with a shrug.

The girl had to understand him then, had to know him, had to know better. But still she hesitated. He kept looking at her, then away.

"She's fifteen," her granny said. "You can go to jail."

"You can go to hell," he said.

"Probably will," her granny told him. "I'll save you a seat by the fire." She took the girl by the arm and drew her to the car; she backed up, swung around, and headed out the road toward the churchyard for her tools and dog. The whole way the girl said nothing, just hunched against the far door, staring hard-eyed out at the pines going past.

The woman finished watering the seed in, and collected her tools. As she worked, she muttered, "It's your own kin buried here, you might have the decency to glance this way one time . . ." The girl was finger-tweezing her eyebrows in the side mirror. She didn't look around as the dog and the woman got in. Her granny shifted hard, sending the tools clattering in the trunk.

When they came to the main road, there were the men. Watching for them. Waiting for them. They kicked their machines into life and followed, close, bumping them, slapping the old fenders, yelling. The girl gave a wild glance around at the one by her door and said, "Gran'ma?" and as he drew his pistol, "Gran'ma!" just as the gun nosed into the open window. She frantically cranked the glass up between her and the weapon, and her granny, seeing, spat, "Fool!" She never had been one to pray for peace or rain. She stamped the accelerator right to the floor.

The motorcycles caught up. Now she braked, hard, and swerved off the road into an alley between the pines, not even wide enough for the school bus, just a fire scrape that came out a quarter mile from her own house, if she could get that far. She slewed on the pine straw, then righted, tearing along the dark tunnel through the woods. She had for the time being bested them; they were left behind. She was winning. Then she hit the wallow where the tadpoles were already five weeks old. The Chevy plowed in and stalled. When she got it cranked again, they were stuck. The tires spattered mud three feet up the near trunks as she tried to spin them out, to rock them out. Useless. "Get out and run!" she cried, but the trees were too close on the passenger side. The girl couldn't open her door. She wasted precious time having to crawl out under the steering wheel. The woman waited but the dog ran on.

They struggled through the dusky woods, their pace slowed by the thick straw and vines. Overhead, in the last light, the martins were reeling free and sure after their prey.

"Why? Why?" the girl gasped, as they lunged down the old deer trail. Behind them they could hear shots, and glass breaking as the men came to the bogged car. The woman kept on running, swatting their way clear through the shoulder-high weeds. They could see the Greer cottage, and made for it. But it was ivied-over, padlocked, the woodpile dry-rotting under its tarp, the electric meterbox empty on the pole. No help there.

The dog, excited, trotted on, yelping, his lips white-flecked. He scented the lake and headed that way, urging them on with thirsty yips. On the clay shore, treeless, deserted, at the utter limit of land, they stood defenseless, listening to the men coming on, between them and home. The woman pressed her hands to her mouth, stifling her cough. She was exhausted. She couldn't think.

"We can get under!" the girl cried suddenly, and pointed toward the Greers' dock, gap-planked, its walkway grounded on the mud. They splashed out to it, wading in, the woman grabbing up the telltale, tattletale dog in her arms. They waded out to the far end and ducked under. There was room between the foam floats for them to crouch neck-deep.

The dog wouldn't hush, even then; never had yet, and there wasn't time to teach him. When the woman realized that, she did what she had to do. She grabbed him whimpering; held him; held him under till the struggle ceased and the bubbles rose silver from his fur. They crouched there then, the two of them, submerged to the shoulders, feet unsteady on the slimed lake bed. They listened. The sky went from rose to ocher to violet in the cracks over their heads. The motorcycles had stopped now. In the silence there was the glissando of locusts, the dry crunch of boots on the flinty beach, their low man-talk drifting as they prowled back and forth. One of them struck a match.

"—they in these woods we could burn 'em out."

The wind carried their voices away into the pines. Some few words eddied back.

"—lippy old smartass do a little work on her knees besides praying—"

Laughter. It echoed off the deserted house. They were getting closer.

One of them strode directly out to the dock, walked on the planks over their heads. They could look up and see his boot soles. He was the one with the gun. He slapped a mosquito on his bare back and cursed. The carp, roused by the troubling of the waters, came nosing around the dock, guzzling and snorting. The girl and her granny held still, so still. The man fired his pistol into the shadows, and a wounded fish thrashed, dying. The man knelt and reached for it, chuffing out his beery breath. He belched. He pawed the lake for the dead fish, cursing as it floated

110

out of reach. He shot it again, firing at it till it sank and the gun was empty. Cursed that too. He stood then and unzipped and relieved himself of some of the beer. They had to listen to that. To know that about him. To endure that, unprotesting.

Back and forth on shore the other one ranged, restless. He lit another cigarette. He coughed. He called, "Hey! They got away, man, that's all. Don't get your shorts in a wad. Let's go."

"Yeah." He finished. He zipped. He stumped back across the planks and leaped to shore, leaving the dock tilting amid widening ripples. Underneath, they waited.

The bike cranked. The other ratcheted, ratcheted, then coughed, caught, roared. They circled, cut deep ruts, slung gravel, and went. Their roaring died away and away. Crickets resumed and a near frog bic-bic-bicked.

Under the dock, they waited a little longer to be sure. Then they ducked below the water scraped out from under the pontoon, and came up into free air, slogging toward shore. It had seemed warm enough in the water. Now they shivered. It was almost night. One streak of light still stood reflected on the darkening lake, drew itself thinner, narrowing into a final cancellation of day. A plane winked its way west.

The girl was trembling. She ran her hands down her arms and legs, shedding water like a garment. She sighed, almost a sob. The woman held the dog in her arms; she dropped to her knees upon the random stones and murmured, private, haggard, "Oh, honey," three times, maybe all three times for the dog, maybe once for each of them. The girl waited, watching. Her granny rocked the dog like a baby, like a dead child, rocked slower and slower and was still.

"I'm sorry," the girl said then, avoiding the dog's inert, empty eye.

"It was him or you," her granny said, finally, looking up. Looking her over. "Did they mess with you? With your britches? Did they?"

"No!" Then, quieter, "No ma'am."

111

When the woman tried to stand up she staggered, lightheaded, clumsy with the freight of the dog. "No, ma'am," she echoed, fending off the girl's "Let me." And she said again, "It was him or you. I know that. I'm not going to rub your face in it." They saw each other as well as they could in that failing light, in any light.

The woman started toward home, saying, "Around here, we bear our own burdens." She led the way along the weedy short-cuts. The twilight bleached the dead limbs of the pines to bone. Insects sang in the thickets, silencing at their oncoming.

"We'll see about the car in the morning," the woman said. She bore her armful toward her own moth-ridden dusk-to-dawn se-curity light with the country grace she had always had when the earth was reliably progressing underfoot. The girl walked close behind her, exactly where *she* walked, matching her pace, matching her stride, close enough to put her hand forth (if the need arose) and touch her granny's back where the faded voile was clinging damp, the merest gauze between their wounds.

Dreams of Sleep

JOSEPHINE HUMPHREYS

There are certain animals, usually small, scraggly creatures, that don't build their own homes but take over the abandoned burrows of other species. *We live like that now,* he thinks, *making our pitiful nests in these grand houses, dwarfed by the high ceilings and enormous rooms; the cornices and ceiling medallions and wainscoting are mere curiosities to us now.* Claire's place is a carriage house behind a tall Victorian mansion that has been cut up into twelve apartments. Will parks his car on the street and walks back down the unpaved driveway, under the leaning, scrawny trunks of Japanese plum trees.

No one will notice him. Or his car. No one will come to a window and say with suspicion, "Who is that guy?" because strangers are familiar here.

The Japanese plums grow right up out of hard gray dirt and a rubble of brick, stucco hunks, mortar chips. The plants that thrive in this town are those that don't need rich black soil, plants that can find nutrients in the mixed ruin of fallen walls, burned houses. Japanese plums are tough trees. The long, serrated leaves are stiff and make a clatter when he walks through them. So what if anyone hears? The apartment people don't know him, even after three years. Still, the rattle of the dry leaves disturbs him.

In the early-evening shadows some of the apartment lights are on in the big house. Through a third-floor window he can see a refrigerator. Surely anyone with the bad luck to live here must count on someday living somewhere else: in a house with the refrigerator on the ground floor, things in the normal places. No one could think of this place as a permanent home, but would always have to be trusting in something better coming up.

Once this whole house was the home of one family. Is this how things fall apart, then? Not in sudden collapse, but by slow fragmentation. Houses turn into apartments, estates into subdivisions. We can't sustain the things we used to sustain: dynasties, clans, big families; we can't even maintain their monuments. Statues are losing their noses, tombstones their letters.

Growing up in an old city, you learn history's one true lesson: that history fades. Nothing sticks together for very long without immense effort. His own strong house is in a constant process of disintegration. He calls workmen to come repair the roof, paint the porches, replace sills; but even this work has no permanence, it will have to be done again in four or five years. Is this noble activity for a man? Patching, gluing, temporizing, begging for time?

Near his back door a lump of stucco fell from the wall after a heavy rain, leaving a round wound of exposed deep-brown brick. The bricks are still solid but the mortar between them is a fine powder that he can gouge out with his finger. Now he has to decide how far to go with repairs, whether to tear off more stucco and find out how extensive the damage is, even take out bricks and re-lay them or just cover up the wound and try not to think about what's underneath, as he must do with some patients.

Claire's carriage house is nicer than an apartment. It's small but at least it is a house with its own walls and roof. He has a key. He lets himself in and calls her. The shower is running upstairs; she doesn't answer. Her philodendrons and ferns are all bunched up in a semicircle around the small bay window. She used to have a cat, but when it died she bought more plants instead of another cat. He looks closely at the philodendron; he touches one of the leaves. Claire actually shines them, rubbing each leaf with wet cotton. They seem to have a sharp green smell after they've been rubbed.

Or maybe that is his imagination. There is something here, something like a scent, that makes his hair stand on end and makes poetry fly into his brain. He likes to walk in and see her unmatched oak chairs, plants huddled together, the thinning Oriental rug, the strange way light streams into her windows without lighting the dark, shadowy corners of the room. Everything here is thin and clean and private as a closet. There is no evidence of a man; it is a single woman's place, and being in it is like being inside her thoughts. He is the only man who comes here. He knows the place well. Here's her forlorn bookcase, the titles reading like a list for a desert island life: *Norton Anthology, Outline of Western Thought, Lives of the Composers*. She actually reads these books because she's sure everybody but her is thoroughly familiar with Verdi's life or the categorical imperative or Theodore Roethke. Nobody knows this stuff, he tries to tell her. Even if they heard of it in college, which is unlikely, they have forgotten it. But she's unconvinced. She stays up late reading Janson's *History of Art*, which she can hardly hold up at a readable angle. Now, looking over the neatly arranged shelf, he realizes her life with him *is* a desert island.

He sees a new book, a slim red volume, wedged down there between two paperback Shakespeares. He takes it out, leafs through it. Poems. *Love's Meter*, "an anthology of the greatest love poems in the English language." Why did she buy this? He puts it back on the shelf but not soon enough: it has spoiled his reverie, the sense he had of being a familiar intruder. He never saw that book before. It is one he would have chosen for her. But the day when he gave her love poems is gone.

The cramped kitchenette is so small they always bumped into each other when they cooked. He used to stand behind her and bother her while she worked, press against her behind and reach around to touch her breasts while she was chopping parsley. The

115

little refrigerator and stove are so old their white finish has deepened to a rich cream. He loves this kitchen. Its diamond-paned
cupboard doors reaching to the ceiling, its deep old sink and mis-
matched faucets—it is like the good old kitchens, not the new
magazine kitchens. He grew up in a house with the same refrigerator in its kitchen for twenty years, same stove, sink, bread-
box, can opener on the wall. Now a kitchen isn't good for more
than five years, the styles change. You had to have harvest gold or
avocado. Then those were out and some new color was in, cop-
pertone. Stainless steel. Almond. His mother's new kitchen is
almond, with an island in it, and in the island a processing center, with attachments that screw in and chop or slice or grate your
food. Cuisinarts make people think life is eternal. Marcella whir-
ring up a puree in that gleamy dazzly almond kitchen has not an
inkling of what really is the end of all that preparation. But
here—here in Claire's dark old kitchenette a shiver of recognition
dances across his shoulders, the rich dark thickness of time moving toward an end.

He unpacks the bag of food that she has left out on the counter.
Her groceries are pitiful, a quart of skim milk, a big can of V-8,
celery, Cup-A-Soup envelopes. But then down at the bottom he
finds a package of two thick filets and a basket of unblemished
white mushrooms. The first good sign of the day. His spirits soar.
She used to love to cook and eat with him and then make love.

He hears the shower turn off upstairs; the pipes rumble behind
the walls of the kitchen. She dries herself inside the shower stall
so that water won't drip on the wooden floor of the bathroom.
Then she wraps the towel around her waist and steps out carelessly, not even thinking of her breasts. If he were there she would
be self-conscious. She thinks her breasts are too big. He knows
how she moves. Slowly. When he hears her bare feet on the floor
above him, the soles of his own feet itch, just as they did when he
was a boy climbing a roof or a tree, and the itch was a combination of exultation and fear. Then her footsteps stop. Maybe she is
bending forward, shaking out her curly black hair, her breasts

jiggling with each toss of her head. She twists the towel around her head, straightens up, and (he's seen her do this before, he is not making it up but remembering now) arches her back, her hands resting behind her hips, elbows bent. He knows how she moves.

But it is reverence for his old passion that brings him here now, not passion itself. He is hanging around the way pilgrims haunt the site of an old miracle, not hoping to see it again really but honoring it, needing its memory. The first time he slept a whole night through with Claire he kept waking up in nervous agitation, like a man who has a rash. His brain ticked with the continuing knowledge that the woman next to him was an unfamiliar size, a new shape. Her feet kept touching his; Alice's never did. After the fourth or fifth waking he pulled her underneath him and made love to her again, as a kind of certification. In his arms, half-asleep, she was moving with him, making a soft, loving noise, and he was ashamed to be thinking of Alice. Why, when he could go for days hardly remembering her existence, would she come to him then, shaking his heart? He could not forgive her that immanence. To spite it he made a harder, rougher kind of love to Claire, and it took hold of him. He couldn't stay away from her. After that first night here, his life seemed new, *he* seemed new. He was crazy. What risks he took! Once he spent three days here with her, telling Alice he was in Colorado. Claire used to laugh at him, surprised by his delight and its depth. Her own was something different. In the act of lovemaking she was agile and undistracted, dolphinlike, arcing above him in that night ocean with an abandon he did not know a woman could be lost to; but immediately afterward her mind flooded with irrelevant thoughts, memories of childhood, worries. She rolled away from him and gasped, "Oh God, my father's birthday is tomorrow," or, "What can I do about the bats?" The attic of her house was full of bats; some had gotten in under the eaves and reproduced. You could hear them scratching around, tweeting up there. But he would stroke and rub her legs until her fretting

117

subsided and she could stretch out and doze or sleep. Then she was like a cat, close to purring. He could see that he made her happy.

She didn't seem to mind, back then, the position this love put her in. Perhaps the danger wasn't visible then. She didn't seem to mind when he told her she would have to be a brave girl (he used just those words, in a joking way) and not press him for what he could not give. She understood, and only once had she disobeyed: after an abortion. Danny Cardozo made the arrangements and did the abortion in the hospital. No one knew, not even the OR nurse, who thought it was a diagnostic D & C. He wanted to stay with her, but he couldn't do it again, witness the death of a child of his; and he couldn't explain that to Claire or Cardozo. He was frightened by the apparent tendency of his life to replicate its own past. How many times would love bring him the loss of a child, the grief of a woman whose bravery mocked his cowardice? He waited in the doctors' lounge, then drove her home and sat in a chair next to her bed while she slept off the Pentothal.

When she woke up he touched her cheek and pale mouth. Her eyes were still big and woozy. She said, "I love you." Her mouth was cracked at the corners, the skin dry and split. Her face was discolored, with hollows under her eyes as dark as if she had been hit.

She said, "Come on, say you love me. You do." She reached up to his ear and held his earlobe and tugged at it. He leaned down and kissed her forehead. She laughed. She said, "Sometimes it's not having a baby that locks people together." She was right. He had already felt it, driving her home, as she sat rigid on the seat next to him and her fingers, folded over the armrest, were white from gripping it so hard. He helped her down the driveway and inside, got her into bed. When she played with his ear, he pulled back. He saw her stretched out, her soft blue nightgown, her breasts overfull, sloping outward. Her bare feet stuck out

118

from the nightgown; her toes, he realized, were very much like his mother's, long and fingerlike.

"Tell me you love me," she said.

"Don't."

"I was thinking about you. My main thought was, what a waste. I know you love me, Will, I can tell you do. You touch my arm and you stare at me and you get sad when I'm not around. You want me to sit in your lap. Last month when I had that bad cold you were so worried! It was just a cold!"

"I know."

"I'm not asking you to leave your family or something earth-shaking. Just to say you love me."

"You're exhausted, Clairy." Her looks frightened him. Her eyelids were swollen and her eyes had the deep wet shine of fever. Her hands moved across her stomach.

She said, "One time we stayed up all night and slept the next day. You wouldn't go. Then I kept saying, 'You'd better leave,' and you'd pretend to be asleep, you wouldn't let go of me. You wouldn't leave. You said you couldn't leave me."

"I couldn't."

"Then please. Oh, it's so *easy.* It isn't hard!"

She sounded so sure of it. And probably he did love her. The difference between love and no love is slight, anyway. People are fooled every day about whether they have it or not. So he picked up her hands and leaned down close to her.

"I can't do it!" he cried out in anguish, surprising her, surprising him. . . . He was thinking of the depletion of his resources. For Alice the passion lasted, say, five years, for Claire one year; and with that record he could look forward only to meager affairs, matters of months, weeks: pitiful spurts of passion.

"Don't ask me to. I can't." He turned away from her, knowing she'd cry now, and then what would he do? She cried easily. When the cat died she cried for days—it had crawled up into his car engine one night to get warm, and when he started the car

something broke the cat's back and flung it out onto the pavement. She blamed him for it. She cried when patients miscar-
ried; she cried when she saw *Kramer vs. Kramer.* One time he
found her crying in the office because she had been thinking
about Alice and said she knew how Alice would feel if she found
out he was unfaithful.

But that night as he stood looking out of the low window onto
the dirt driveway, and the leaves scuttled across the ground like
crabs, and a child had been lost, that night she did not cry.

He had sat by her bed until midnight, without ever turning on
the lights. The sun dropped low, colored the sky, set; the room
grew dark slowly. They listened to the news and sports on the
radio. Before he left he gave her a Demerol, and set another one
for her on the table next to a glass of water.

That night was more than a year ago, but something about this
darkening evening has reminded him of that one. The leaves in
the wind, the dark house—it is time to turn lights on but he is
reluctant to do it, he wants to see night come.

He could have been wrong about the pilgrims. Secretly they do
hope for a return of the miraculous. They only pretend not to
because they don't want to get their hopes up; they don't want to
make fools of themselves.

Her footsteps cross the floor again.

He knows why artists have always loved to paint "the Bath."
When is a woman ever more desirable? Warm and pink from hot
water, her skin is tight, soap-scented. Tendrils of her hair are wet.
Her face is clean and childlike and sure of privacy. That's the one
common quality of all the bathers of Renoir, Degas: the woman is
preoccupied, she bends, trusting her solitude, intent on some
detail of her bathing—and all the while the voyeur lurks with his
palette in the shadows, peeping. In the quiet instant just before
violence he savors a pure guilt, all his own, none hers. Between
what Degas's crouching bather thought and what Degas knew,
what a world there was, and half an explanation of love.

He would wish it that way now—he would climb the steps without making this creaking noise, which certainly alerts her; he would like to sneak up on her. But as he comes up through the stairwell he meets her eyes, locking onto his as if they had been trained to the exact spot where he would emerge, waiting for him. She has on an old velour robe that has lost its shape, faded unevenly from purple to dull red. She's shaving her legs. Toward him from the opening in the velour rises one long naked leg, its foot resting on a chair.

"You're late," she says.

"I wanted to surprise you."

"You did." He can see to the top of her thigh. The slender length of her leg takes his breath away. She leans over and shaves her calf.

"You do that without soap and water?"

"No, I shaved in the shower but I missed a spot."

"Here?" He moves to her side, touches her ankle, rings it with his thumb and finger, just above the anklebone. She tries to pull her leg back but he holds it tight. He has her off balance.

"Untie your robe," he says.

"No. Let me get dressed now."

His left hand moves under the robe. She pulls back in earnest one last time, but then his hand reaches her belly. He lets her foot slip from the chair, keeping a grasp on her thigh to hold her foot just off the floor. She unties the robe without taking her eyes from his. Then he lets go of her in order to step back and see her. Behind her the light of her small lamp fails to reach to the spot where they stand; there is only a glow in the corner. More light comes from the window, the reflected pink of a sun already below the horizon, the rays glancing to clouds and bending back to earth, to neck, breasts, hips. Someone in the yard could see. If he were she, he would not allow it; she permits him to endanger her.

"You're pink and gold. Look." He pushes the robe back off her shoulders, and uncurls her fingers from the handle of the razor.

Her eyes are closed.

121

"I've loved you a long time," she says.

"Years and years."

"Longer. I loved you before I loved you." She turns to him, leans into him and the twist of the body into his is familiar, a recognizable instant in the turn; she should stop here, they should make love. But she keeps on turning and is turning away from him, out of his grasp completely. She is pulling on the robe, tying it tight around her waist, tough as a nurse again.

"I really have to talk to you, Will."

"Let's hear it, then." He should never have let go of her, he should never have let her regain her balance. She turns on another lamp, pulls down the window shade.

"This is going to be real hard," she says.

"Why don't we skip it, then."

"It's serious."

"Are you pregnant? Say so right away if you are. Christ. I can't stand stalling, Claire. Say it."

Tears fill her eyes, her nose turns red, exactly like when the cat died.

"There are worse things than being pregnant," she says.

"Well, I don't want to go through it again."

"We didn't go through it the first time." She tries not to cry but the words bring sobs out with them. "Anyway, I'm not. But I want to be. I don't want to waste away."

"Is that all? Is that what we have to talk over? Is that it?" But she is crying too hard to talk. He says, "I'm sorry. Claire, I am sorry. Listen," he says to comfort her. "Don't be sad. I know how you feel."

"You don't."

"Yes, I do."

"I'm going to get married, Will. Danny and I are going to get married."

A man can lose his leg and not know it. His brain can't handle the enormity of the loss. At first Will hardly hears what she says, it makes so little sense. Then his sense of direction fails, he feels his face turn hot.

She takes a green dress from the closet and underwear from the bureau drawer. The underpants and bra are iridescent white, shiny. They're new.

"What do you mean?"

Her voice breaks, her lip trembles. "We're going to get married."

"You and who?"

"Oh, please. Please, Will." She's still holding her clothes. "I love you. But this is the end of it. I came to some kind of end."

"And in stepped the good doctor Dan."

"I can't talk to you about him."

"No, I guess not."

"Don't be bitter. He's been worried sick about this, he really has, he doesn't know what to do. He tried to get you to go into practice with him. He doesn't want you to be left alone."

Will sits on the edge of the bed.

"What is it?" she says.

"How long have you been seeing him?"

"That doesn't make any difference now."

"The hell it doesn't! It makes all the difference. How long?"

"Look, I said I would not discuss him with you."

He leaps from the bed and grabs her by the arm, so suddenly that she gasps.

"Tell me," he says.

"I—we've been friends for maybe a year."

"Friends."

"Yes. That's all. That's what we've been."

"But you did hide it. You deceived me."

"Deceived you?" she says.

"Yes! You deceived me. You betrayed me. Both of you."

"Let me go."

"Oh God. Yes, I'll let you go. I should have let you go sooner."

"Will, I have to get dressed."

"Go ahead." He turns away while she dresses behind his back. Silently he conducts an inventory of her furniture: the bed, the dresser, the chairs. He loves her furniture. He doesn't want to give it up.

Especially not to Danny. Claire bends toward the low mirror on her dressing table. She puts lipstick on the way a little girl might, slowly, squinting her eyes, and the whole action, usually unattractive, is endearing.

"Why Danny?" he says after a while.

"He's nice to me."

"That's a reason to marry him?"

"Yes. He's that nice. He loves me, he likes how I am. He thinks I'm pretty."

"I've always thought you were pretty."

"He says it."

"I said it."

"Twice. The first time was the first night you slept here. The second was when I went home for my mother's funeral and you felt sorry for me. I looked terrible. So what, anyway. You don't want to marry me. But just for the record it was only twice. You are very mean, you know." She says it without malice, it's a simple statement he can hardly argue with.

"Danny's mean, too," he says. "Danny's just like me, Claire. Is that why you're going to marry him?"

"He's not like you at all."

"He's like me in all the ways that have driven you crazy."

She looks at him sharply. "You're wrong. He cries for me. Can you imagine that? He cries out loud asking me to marry him, saying he can't live without me."

"I don't believe you."

"Is it so incredible?"

Of course she would be impressed by that. A man who weeps for a woman either loses her immediately or binds her to him forever, depending on what kind of a woman she is. Claire is the kind who, having lived her whole life unaware of the possibility of men's tears, is utterly won by them when they come.

"He's cracking up," Will says.

"Get out."

"I mean it. He told me. He's having all kinds of problems."

"Get out, Will. Get out now."

"Listen, Claire. I'll marry you."

"Sure you will."

"I will. I want to. I can't give you up." Sitting on her bed he reaches for the hem of her dress, holds it between his thumb and fingers.

"How could you marry me?" she says.

"It's done all the time. Divorce."

"Divorce Alice? You would divorce Alice?"

Oh, don't say her name, don't make it sound so real. He would never divorce Alice. He can't even hear it said.

"Yes. It wouldn't take too long. I could go to Haiti or somewhere and get a divorce in a day."

"You would do it?"

"Yes." *Liar! Deceiver of women, and of the dwarfish, unspined self behind these eyes!* He lies enormously and pointlessly, yet can't confess a half-true love that might once have done Claire good.

Claire stands looking at him for a long time.

"I don't know if I believe you or not," she says slowly. "But even if I did, I wouldn't say yes. Six months ago I would have. Not now. Everything's changed now."

"Well, just tell me how the hell everything could change so fast without my knowing? I've seen you every day. If you were changing shouldn't I have had some hint of it? Shouldn't I have noticed something?"

"Yes, but you didn't."

"Okay, then, what was I supposed to notice? How was I to tell you were falling in love with someone else? You didn't exactly cut me off. We did a lot of fucking, Claire. Were you fucking him, too?"

She starts to cry. "No, I wasn't." She puts a finger under her bottom eyelash to steady her contacts, and he realizes that all this while, despite his suffering, she has been dressing for Cardozo. Those are Cardozo's goddamn steaks downstairs.

He pulls her down to the bed and wipes the tears from her face, holds her the way she likes it when she is sad, with her head against his chest, his hand smoothing her hair. He unzips the green dress and helps her take it off, and her white underwear, and after a while she stops crying; he can hear only her sharp breaths against his ear as she holds on to his neck and shoulders. It is nothing like what he wanted; it is a desperate, cornered loving, ungenerous. He zips up his pants and lies next to her. He loves her, after all, that's the ironic part. She lies naked, unmourning, next to him.

After a while he pulls the sheet up over her.

"When are you going to get married?" he asks.

"I don't know. We thought about it last Wednesday but a patient delivered early."

"Last Wednesday! My God, Claire. This isn't something you can just run down to the corner store for. You have to make plans. You have to get a license and a place to live."

"We have a license. We have a place to live."

"Not at his place. And not *here*. This place is mine."

"Oh, Will. Listen. I do want to help you, but you have to make an effort. Don't torture yourself."

"*Help* me!" He laughs.

She says nothing.

"Well, where *are* you going to live? Or is it a secret?" he says.

"We don't know."

"It's here, isn't it?"

"I said we don't know."

"Please don't use the plural pronoun. Please just speak to me

126

as one person, just yourself if you can. I know it, anyway. I know it's here. God." He wants to ask her for a souvenir—a book from the bookshelf, a fork, a towel. He kisses her forehead and gets up from the bed.

"You need me to go now. Isn't he coming?" he says.

"Not until eight."

"It's almost seven-thirty."

"I know." She stares at the ceiling.

"I'll marry you," he says, passing her the underwear, the green dress.

"I know." She doesn't reach for the clothes. He lays them next to her, careful not to crease the dress.

He stumbles down the stairs, or at least he thinks he stumbles, falling out into the evening air, stupidly and clumsily fleeing the carriage house and its gridded rectangles of golden light, like some little house in a forest, the humble home of a woodsman and his good wife, shrinking behind him as he runs down the driveway. He is panicked at the thought of meeting Danny coming in. Claire is the most truthful person he has ever known, but he can't really believe that Danny Cardozo ever wept for her or wants to marry her. Danny will never marry Claire. Goddamn him for deceiving her.

Out in the street there is no light left, and he drives home through accomplished darkness. There may be stars, but in a car you don't feel stars. Turning onto his block he spins the wheel a fraction too far and his wheels bump up over the curb on the right; he recovers, but the jolt shakes his plans. He does not stop at his house. The lights are on in it, but they are not lit for him, and he does not stop. He telephones his wife from the office, wakes her up in order to lie to her. He spends the night on the vinyl sofa, and the room is so closed off that no external sound or light can reach him, only the rackety and shifty figures of his dreams.

127

Come Back, Lolly Ray

BEVERLY LOWRY

The sun and river were to the west, back over their shoulders on the other side of the levee. The main street of town—along which they waited, impatiently—dead-ended there, at the foot of the levee. Holding on to one another for support, they leaned out over the curb to see if she was coming yet and some even stepped into the street and stood hands cupped over their eyes in the middle of it, looking for a sign of her . . . until someone else shouted for them to get themselves back up on the sidewalk where everybody else was. Children, hot, played chase in and out of their parents' legs and pulled at their clothes and, wanting to get on with what they came for, gave notice if she wasn't here soon they were going home. Though by the calendar autumn had arrived, the day was still and hot, and no breeze at all came to dilute the heat pouring thick and heavy down on them. Even now, late afternoon, the sun persisted. Low, resting on the levee's crest like a sleeping baby's head, it seemed to want to see her too, and refused to sink behind. There was no sign yet of the north wind predicted to blow in that day and cool things off.

She wore a gold suit. Because the music was too far behind her, they would not hear it first, but awaited another clear and familiar signal. When the sun's light butted headlong into the bright gold thing she wore and was reflected off it: that quick flash of light. They watched for it. And just about the time the kids' squirming started turning into fistfights, the word passed that it had happened, the light had flashed and she was coming; she was on her way. Children screamed and pushed at each other for places to see from. The adults did not scream, but pushed. They couldn't see her distinctly at first because of the light bouncing back and forth. When she turned the corner at Hawthorne and came down Main toward them, all they could make out was a waving gold flash moving alone down the center of the street, boldly into the sun; as hot and bright as it was, braving it; coming down Main toward them and the river, directly into the Friday afternoon sun. The backs of their necks dripped with sweat as they kept their heads turned toward her.

At her middle, there were, in addition to the sun's reflection and her dazzling gold suit, yet two other bright things but these were silver, and moving. And when one of them went suddenly up to her face then past her head, people leaned out even farther and did what they could to help themselves see: they made awnings of their hands, or put spread fingers palm-out in front of their eyes, peering between them as if through blinds. The children pointed as the silver thing went farther and farther up over her, and screamed as it held there, a gleaming disc of silver which soon became pulled out into a starlike shape by the light of the sun. Heat waves rose up around her ankles and her body swam and turned under the silver star, like a goldfish in a pool of heat. Then as the silver started to come down, they held their breaths and followed it, waiting to see if it hit the street, wondering if it would, hoping it would, at the same time believing it would not, caught up in the excitement of both possibilities. Either way, they would have the exhilaration they came for. Then when it did not hit, when she stopped it at her waist where the other one was and moved them both one after the other quickly in succession behind her, around her, under her leg, around her neck, and finally back up over her so high the tallest old oaks lining Main could not with their topmost branches reach it, then the people released their breaths, sighed, clapped proudly, pounded their children on their backs, and said among themselves, "That Lolly . . . that girl! She never misses!"

She was their twirler, both in her time and after it, *the* town twirler, a title she could claim as surely as if she had been crowned, no matter who else was twirling while she was or continued to after she was through, because Lolly Ray Lasswell's name and legend would be passed on from generation to generation as the town of Eunola's own. Like Graham, the town drunk, like Booth Oates, the town idiot, and Alberta, the town whore, and even, though he was long gone, Sexton Cunningham, Eunola's comical and self-styled historical figure, Lolly would not be deposed by time, as they had not, the tales of their accomplishment now having been established outside time and ordinary human considerations. By the time Lolly was twirling, Sexton had been dead fifty-six years and Graham, seven. But Graham was still the town drunk, even though people in Eunola were a drinking community, and except for the hard-shelled Baptist refugees from Texas and the hills (those who always seemed to be squinting, sun or no, who waited Fridays not for Lolly but the band behind her), everybody thought it was all right to do it and most did. But there was not and had never been as far back as anybody could remember a drunk like Graham, who was above every other consideration in his life a drunk, who never merely *drank* but shaped his drinking as if it were an art: until it was his life itself. His capacities were sublime; his legend established; his place, unshakable. Because he transcended ordinary notions of ordinary limitations, he was exalted, and Lolly was no different from Graham. She was that kind of twirler.

As she got closer to the big crowd (which gathered about halfway up Main toward the levee because the big front-porched houses down toward Hawthorne and the railroad tracks were Eunola's oldest, and their inhabitants, also Eunola's oldest, prized their roses and camellias and didn't care for parade watchers trampling up the Bermuda grass), and they could see her better, their excitement grew. They became quieter, concentrating strictly on her now, unwilling to risk even a glance away in the chance it might be the moment when she did a special trick or, as noteworthy, dropped her baton. The promise of either kept them on edge, anticipating. She was shining now, coming closer, like a piece of the sun. Her uniform was made entirely of dime-sized solid gold overlapping sequins, each of which was attached at the top only so that when she moved the sequins shifted and swung a split second later and it looked as though either she was moving twice every time or that the uniform as it caught the sun and gave it back to them was moving on its own. It was a one-piece, sleeveless, legless costume, designed and made by Lolly herself, elasticized as far as it went, which in length was just far enough that arcs of her butt slipped out when she high-stepped. Her boots were silver up to her knees, tight, zippered, with two-inch heels and three gold tassels in a row swinging down the front. She was tiny, and thin. Her skin was pale; her hair the color of deep wet mud with an overlay of rust, glittering as the river was now with the sun almost in it, bouncing on her shoulders as if it had springs. As the band was still not in sight, she came alone, prancing by herself, though the sound of drums could now be heard approaching.

As she neared the last of the oak trees before the commercial part of downtown, the crowd, having waited so long, grew edgier. Children's screams thinned to squeals. They could see her face. People said . . . especially majorettes and majorettes' mothers . . . she was not *pretty*, not really. She was too pale, too thin, her features too large for the size of her face. And her nose . . . ! (Majorettes doted on the shape and length of Lolly's nose, which instead of turning up in the popular fashion, pointed down.) Curls of her thick coarse hair draped heavily about her face and half-covered her eyes, which, cool and blue, focused on something her fans could never determine the exact location or nature of. Certainly she never looked at them. Just like her daddy, some said. Never gives anybody the time of day unless he's pinned down and asked it.

She had two batons, which she turned like wheels in front of her, her arms straight out. Suddenly, about half a block from where they waited, she slapped them one over each arm and pranced straight ahead in a kind of goosestep, her arms in absolute and unshakable rhythm with her feet. As one baton went straight up beside her head, the other reached its position alongside her thigh. Alternating. Up . . . thigh, arm, baton . . . down. Locked in. Up . . . catching the sun again and again.

In the middle of the intersection just before the crowd's edge she stopped dead still, square in the center under the traffic light which blinked on and off, red, for the parade. Each thing she did was absolutely distinct from the next so that if afterward you had been asked you could have said she did this-then-this-then-this in clear succession with no overlap. She raised both arms, batons east-west, perpendicular to her arms, and pointed one toe toward the levee and one back toward the railroad tracks. Keeping her knees still and her head straight, her chin out toward the sun, she started easing her way down, sliding into a full split. And very slowly the batons began to turn in time with her sliding. The closer she got to the street, the faster the batons turned, until, when the tops of her thighs were within the heat of the concrete and she had thrown her head back, her eyes were facing the blinking light above, the tips of her hair were grazing her butt and the batons were speeding like crazy. She looked up . . . at the batons? The light? The sky? They wondered but could not tell. People in back leaned down on shoulders in front of them to see her going down and to try to figure out what it was she saw, for Lolly never gave them everything they came for. As natural a dream as those that come in sleep, she let them grope for their own endings and explanations and slid on down then as easily as if on slick glass and when she was all the way down sat as if it were natural to be split apart one leg due east and one due west, naked

132

against the hot street, facing the awful sun, toes pointed hard as street signs, her head still tilted.

On the sidewalk a little girl marched like Lolly's shadow, turning a circus baton in imitation. She, too, was on the concrete with her legs spread and as Lolly hopped gracefully back up on her feet and started off again, the little girl struggled to her feet. Unlike Lolly, the child acknowledged the applause and cheers. Lolly's eyes, still abstracted, disregarded them. But she did smile. Her teeth were large and straight, and with her head back shining, the smile held out promises.

About that time the band turned from Hawthorne down Main and the gaunt women in plain belted dresses, the teetotaling Baptists who had not looked at Lolly, or if they had, had looked quickly away as if it were sinful, clapped one hand stiffly against the other in recognition of the band's approach.

The line of majorettes across the front of the band (and no one referred to Lolly as a majorette except the majorettes themselves, who said the only difference between them was that Lolly wore a different uniform and could do a few more tricks) in their heavy chin-strapped, plumed tin soldier hats and standard white majorette boots and mid-thigh satin uniforms came red-faced into the threatening sun, marching as instructed, knee up groin high, toe pointed, to the music, keeping the line straight, and when the people got around to turning back and as an afterthought applauding them, it was little consolation. Being accompaniment for Lolly not only infuriated them, it made them even hotter in the afternoon sun than they might have been. And they could not, hard as they marched, catch up with her. Perspiring beneath the long sleeves of their white satin uniforms, the top fatty wedge of their thighs chafed and raw from constantly rubbing in the same place . . . same place . . . same place . . . against one another, they marched like hot little soldiers, trying not to see Lolly way ahead of them floating back and forth free as a dream, her hair shining and loose, jiving up and down and over and across potholed half-cobblestoned old Main Street, turning, flipping,

133

kicking, leaping, twitching, sashaying her butt in their faces without a stumble or fall in her body.

Two Eunola residents were not at the parade, had in fact seen Lolly perform only one time on a Friday afternoon. Her father, Frank Lasswell, was back at the high school in his car, her school clothes draped over the seat next to him, waiting for her to get finished so he could take her home for dinner. Her mother was home in the trailer watching the last daytime television serial of the day.

"Can you believe it?" Sid Strunk said as if for the first time when Lolly passed his furniture and appliance store. "That girl was raised in a trailer house!" He said it every time she passed, every Friday of football season repeated those exact words. Part of the legend being the establishment of the language which, once done, remained impeccably unchanged. Part of the dream the astonishment that where she came from had not determined her destiny. That she had not become—like every other girl from the trailer park—a trailer tramp. That in his time as well Graham, a Cunningham, had rejected family advantage to go into the business of keeping a drunk on. That Booth Oates's family was a severely quiet and respectful one, who had yet produced one son, an idiot. Who, because he was *their* idiot, the town took care of. That their whore, Alberta, put on her hat and shopped with the best of them, demanding proper service, which was unhesitatingly given. All four outside regular social considerations, outside family and church . . . *outside.*

Two blocks before the levee, at the Delta Theater . . . known for its rats, B-grade black and white movies, and a pervert who sat against the left-hand wall waiting for colleagues and strangers . . . somebody yelled to Lolly to throw up her baton. She and the little girl on the sidewalk both did, and as Lolly leaned toward one knee, keeping a perfect balance between the strain of her body on the street and the silver stick moving against the force of its own inertia, she found her focus. Not on the baton itself but its aura, that stream of silver that when the baton was going fast enough caught up with itself and made a solid round of silver in the air. That dazzling exhaust; it kept her attention. Pure chance, from pure perfection. She thought concentrating on it would take her past where she was now, past all the ribbons and trophies she had already won, past being the substantiation of a dream for a town she disdained into being . . . the Lolly Ray Lasswell . . . of the *world*, somehow. She caught the baton and moved on, and the man who had called out for her to throw it beamed as if he had done it himself.

Behind the band another group turned from Hawthorne to Main. The Homecoming Court. It was Homecoming, and the queen and her six maids also trailed Lolly.

At the end of Main in front of the levee, the city had erected a statue in honor of its World War II dead. Some city fathers designed it, which, to Eunola's chagrin, was exactly what it ended up looking like, a statue designed by a committee. It was supposed to represent a warship. And you could tell it was a ship all right, but it looked more like one a child might draw than what any adult would design: trapezoid with top line longer than bottom, straight line sticking out the top, square attached to line, stars and stripes inside the square. If a child drew that, you'd say good, fine. But as a memorial, it was a monstrosity, an embarrassment. Which everyone saw every time he or she drove down Main toward the levee. It was made of white tile bordered in blue, and across the top of the memorial just under the border it had said for years now "TO T OSE WHO PROU LY ERV D IN ME RIAM." The missing letters had either fallen or been stolen and since the war by now had been pretty much relegated to past history and nobody wanted to fool with that memorial anyway, they had not been replaced. Listed under that message were the names of every white Eunolite who died in World War II.

When Lolly got close to the memorial, she tossed her hair out of her eyes and looked, for the first time, into the crowd. The statue stood directly in front of the levee, and as the levee blocked off the sun a little when she got close enough to it, she could look straight into the faces there. She was actually searching for a name on the memorial, Cecil Cyril DeLoach, against which he usually leaned. When she found it, he was not there. But he had never missed. Then she saw his wings glint, on the other side, to the left. There. He had moved; he was directly in front of Morris Leon Grizzanti, leaning on the second z. Morris' brothers and sisters now ran a pizza place near the trailer park. And the smile flooding over Lolly's face then was as pure as a baby's. Unclouded joy spread like a blush. He wore mirrored sunglasses and silver wings on his air force shirt, both of which picked up what sunlight they could from that angle and flashed it at her, just as she was flashing to the crowds up and down the street. That was what had caught her eye the first time, and while she hadn't been able to see his eyes for those strange silver glasses—and still hadn't— he had signaled her with a cocky two-finger salute, which, combined with the way he grinned at her and the slouchy way he leaned against the memorial, had established him in her mind as a collaborator. He knew what she was up to, it seemed, her contrivance and plans, and saw beyond what the others did. And saluted her for it. After that first time she looked for him every Friday there and acknowledged his presence with—besides that spectacular smile—a special heel-toe jiving dance step and an over-the-baton jump before turning left down River Road toward Court where she would turn left again and head, sun behind her, toward the high school she had started from.

Above the wings, though Lolly couldn't see it, a blue plastic tab announced her compatriot's name, which was Lt. James Blue. Lieutenant Blue came to see Lolly every Friday and never waited to see a single majorette.

Once the sun gave up and started sinking into the levee, the air cooled off a little and people felt a little easier standing on the concrete. Still, those lining Court had to look into the half-sun's blurred glow to see Lolly, and the majorettes still squinched their eyes up as they neared the end of Main. Lolly's performance never let up, but because the people on Court were a little less fanatic than those on Main, whose compulsion was not only to see her but to see her *first*, she gave them less. Some of the Mains came over to Court, however, and on the corners where they shouted to her she did a special trick, like bending herself backward until her head came down between her feet and all they could see was half her body with its head between its legs and two silver sticks turning beside it. Others went on home, some to prepare dinner and return to the stadium behind the high school, where she would twirl again at halftime. As it was Homecoming, crowds would be heavier than usual.

Frank Lasswell waited patiently for his daughter. From the sun's near disappearance he knew she'd be coming soon. Smoking, easing ashes off the end of his cigarette with his middle finger, he gave the impression of a tough and leathery, unapproachable old man. Parked over the railroad tracks in front of the school, he would see her just before she climbed the hump the tracks ran on, one split second where Court Street curved, then would lose her behind the hump. When she got high enough he would see her again, coming up like fireworks.

He neither understood nor liked what Lolly did. She had little idea what she risked, stirring people up, and little notion what they were capable of, once aroused. He didn't watch her in the parades because he couldn't stand to. He was vulnerable where she was concerned, and inside his stony chest his heart leaped and fell with her tricks and stunts. But she had worked so hard. He had seen her day after day from the time she was ten years old, turning first a broomstick then a baton around and around until her fingers ached. And when he had asked if she wanted to go to twirling camps and classes and she had refused and said she didn't need them, he had understood. Doing it on her own made her proud. It enabled her to have what she had worked for for herself, setting her off from the town. And so he said nothing of his skepticism, and helped her every way he knew how.

When he saw her on the tracks, her chin high, he thought she looked like Lucille . . . though Lucille had never done anything remotely similar to twirling a baton. When she hit the top of the tracks she turned around on one toe then stopped stock still between the ties. Her eyes were on Frank, her chin was out and up and long, her shoulders were back, and from up there she was looking out as if over a countryside that belonged exclusively to *her*. At that moment, she had the look of a Peavey. His wife's people. That fierce and uncontainable pride that bordered on hatred. If, that is, a Peavey had ever in his life owned anything to overlook besides his own delusions. It unnerved Frank.

At home, Lucille stirred the stew and checked the cornbread, which she was warming from lunch. Although she was not watching it, the television set filled the trailer with sounds of cartoon characters. The table was set for three, and every now and then Lucille ran a hand through her long curly graying hair and moaned softly. Her head hurt again.

After Lolly did her turn atop the railroad tracks, she was through . . . the act was over . . . and when she ran like a child to her father and asked if she could please drive home, it was as if a mask had been taken off.

"No," he said briskly, "get in; we have to hurry." Not meaning to be short with her but still off-balance from seeing the Peavey in her.

But when she rounded the front of the car and coyly stuck her tongue out at him, looking across the car hood from the sides of her eyes, his face uncrinkled, he shot out a loving hand urging her to come take his place, and, bewitched, slid across.

She patted his leg softly when she got in, then pulled away from the curb. When they turned the corner just before the tracks, the majorettes were cresting the hump, perspiration running like rain from beneath their hats. Lolly glanced at them but did not wave or speak, and neither did they.

Behind the band and the Homecoming Court, the sun had finally dropped from sight. Only its fierce red and gold afterglow remained, its last gasp before sinking into the river and yielding to the north wind, which drew near. Clouds which had all day puffed and billowed themselves about like soap bubbles were now stretched out thin, and with the sun's light coming up through them their whiteness had turned into bright, hard colors, red, orange, and a violent pink. Like cheap teasing dimestore scarves they discreetly covered the sun's decline.

Lucille was sitting at the table waiting for them, angry. Dinner was on the table, the bowls on cardboard pads to protect the maple finish; the iced tea was poured, the ice melting; the cornbread still in the oven, which she had neglected to turn on.

She liked to be in the trailer alone. Days she didn't have headaches she was quite happy there, wandering room to room all day, sniffing out corners, going through Lolly's belongings, watching television games and serials. She resewed sequins on Lolly's gold costume and polished her silver boots; mended her clothes, washed and ironed them expertly; tasted her daughter's life the only way she knew how or was allowed to, like a burglar. But Lolly took good care of herself and had so little need for her mother that Lucille sometimes invaded the neatness of her daughter's room, put it in disarray, and came back later on in the day to survey the disorder and set about straightening it.

They were late, she thought, again. They were always late.

She got up and took the cold cornbread out of the oven, and, back at the table, stared at the door they would come through.

She expected they were afraid to ask what she did all day alone, either that or they didn't care; at any rate they never asked, which was just as well. If they knew how content she was, how well she operated there . . . if they saw her even smile occasionally at the antics of some TV clown when they had not seen her smile in years . . . they might think her capable of getting on better with them and with others, they would expect more of her, and she could not take on anything other than what she was handling now. There was a sign outside the trailer, pushed into the ground next to the steps, that said "Lucille Lasswell, Sewing," but nobody ever came with work for her to do any more. She used to

139

sew, not scratch sewing, nothing new, only alterations, lifting and lowering hems, taking in, letting out, patching, turning collars, until one day the seams in front of her merged like cracks in the earth turning this way and that going nowhere, and she had run the machine up and down somebody's dress and ruined it. From then on nobody came. Well, she thought, it was just as well. It was all she could do to get through the afternoon serials—they sometimes depressed her so—which ran from noon to four. By the time Frank and Lolly got home at four-thirty, she would have retired to bed to prepare herself for the night with them. Lying there staring at her hands, pushing back the cuticles, admiring her long slender fingers, the skin taut and shiny across the knuckles . . . beautiful hands, a piano teacher had once told her, talented fingers . . . running a palm gently against those knuckles, she felt fine and peaceful actually until she heard the trailer door unlocked and opened. Her footsteps came first, rapid and clicking in those clickety shoes she bought with pennies slid into slots above the arch. Strange shoes, Lucille thought, to have slots in them for pennies. Then his, heavy, solid, from his work boots, with the silver plates across the toes . . . dirty, no doubt. And the door, the terrible sound she had never gotten used to, after all the years living in a trailer. Like the door to a meat locker, it echoed metallic sounds, clasps, locks, buttons, aluminum frames . . . a terrible *clunch* sound . . . the closing of an airtight container, all that was inside now sealed up. It took her breath away to think of it. And since windows were never opened because of their fancy central air conditioning and heat, everything inside stayed inside.

A trailer house was simply not substantial enough for her, who when she walked the earth felt it tremble beneath her, who feared in a light wind the threat of a tornado. For one who trusted neither nature nor life itself, a trailer was simply not secure enough that she could ever feel comfortable in it.

She became a mad sullen woman then, outraged, crazy, as heavy as a stone. With the closing of the door, the rage which ruled her life moved up and encased her and her night began. It was as though a dark hood had descended. It would not come off again until they were gone again the next morning and she was alone, free to work inside her own rhythms and reality. The rage fed her and kept her in a day-to-day cycle she could manage. Anger kept her going; bitterness was her solace. Without either, she'd have taken to her bed and not got up.

Fridays, however, were different. Frank had asked if during football season she could possibly manage to have dinner ready when they got home on Fridays after the parade and she had said she would. And so every Friday she was sitting at the table waiting for them when they arrived, dinner cold, having been ready half an hour before they got there, even though she knew what time they would come. She sat leaning on one elbow, the table meticulously set, napkins folded in half beneath the forks, spoons to the right of knives, glasses perspiring into coasters, glaring at them when they walked in, as if to say, I have done what you have demanded of me and now you are late . . . late. *Why are you doing these things to me?*

FROM

July 7th

JILL MCCORKLE

At the far end of Main Street there is a boarding house, a two-story brick structure with old time windows framed in lumber, a porch that wraps around the front and sides and supports the various creeping vines which over the years have reached all the way up and neatly entwined the two upstairs windows as though it had been planned that way. Once when this was a central location in town it was a very fashionable tourist home, and in the summers the gray-planked flooring of the porch creaked under rocking chairs, feet gently pushing an old glider, a swing. Now it is at the edge of town, separated from the bottoms only by a broken-up and overgrown railroad track. What little brick is left unexposed by the creeping vines is dark with age, and it seems at a glance that it could all crumble down with the slightest tremor, yet the brick is very strong, its texture intact, only the appearance has changed.

  Now a yellow light illuminates the porch where there is an old chipped-up kitchen chair propped against the wall, cigarette butts along the cement steps, an empty Coke bottle propped between the spindles of the railing. Moths hover around the light, beat themselves against the bare bulb without venturing into the dark recesses where the vines fall like curtains. There is a small pair of jeans hung on the ledge of the upstairs window on the left. They belong to M. L. McNair, who is six years old and lives in this room with his grandmother, Fannie McNair. Earlier in the day she had washed out his jeans as she always does and hung them there to dry. Now she has forgotten them. Now she can be seen in the dim light of her window like the pupil of a large tired eye, as she sits in her overstuffed chair, a reading lamp behind her casting a glow that clings to the sweat on her dark forehead where her knotty hair is pulled tightly back and bobby pinned in a straight line. The radio is turned down low, just low enough that she can still hear it but so low that it doesn't wake M.L., who is curled up on his side of the low double bed in the corner. Fannie McNair spends all of her evenings this way, just sitting and listening to the gospel music that plays after midnight, even though she could fall asleep at any given moment. It is her time to "think and pray," as she always tells M.L. when he stirs over there in the darkness and calls out her name. This is what she is doing now, thinking of her husband Jake, wondering where he might be, if he's still alive, if he's living with some other fool woman, if he's sprawled out dead as a doornail in the alley of some big city street. It'd serve him right, God knows it would, but no, Jake deserves as much hope as any other body. And it wasn't always bad, not always.

There was that rainy Thanksgiving when just the two of them were together and he surprised her with a radio that he bought at Sears, the very one that she's listening to now, and they had stayed in bed near about all day listening to the radio and the rain and hadn't even eaten their hen and stuffing until nine-thirty that night. There was something special about that day, special because she has always been certain that that was the very day her daughter took root inside of her. It was just like Elizabeth in the Bible, because she was thirty-five years old and had just about given up on having children other than those that she was paid to keep. God, it was a happy time when that second month had passed without a trace of bleeding. Then her stomach got to where it was pushing out and she had to go to work with her skirt

143

unfastened. It was a miracle, truly it was, and she had more energy than she could ever remember having, wasn't sick a day, and kept right on working and going about her life. She was sitting right there on the front pew of Piney Swamp Baptist Church on a day that was just about as hot as yesterday was, when her water broke. There was so much commotion and jubilation in that building that she just stood up and clapped and yelled with the best of them and made her way out of the church without anybody even noticing what had happened. She caught a ride with a farmhand who went back inside the church to find the doctor, and off they went to hers and Jake's house which stood just on the other side of the tracks where there is now a warehouse. It wasn't much of a house, but that day it seemed like it was, especially when she opened her eyes and heard that cry. "His name is John," she had said, releasing the grip she had held on the edges of the mattress, "and he's a Baptist."

"You'll have to wait for the next one," the doctor said and held up that wrinkled little baby.

"Elizabeth, then."

Jake didn't have much to do with Elizabeth, looked at her, pulled out a bottle of liquor and then disappeared for about three days. All those years he had blamed himself for them not having children, and had spent years worrying about Fannie finding a man who could give her what she wanted. Now that Elizabeth had come, he had somehow come to think that it was all Fannie's fault, and she thought he must have spent a lot of time thinking about all the seeds he could have planted elsewhere. Fannie knows it probably was her with the problem, it probably was some sort of miracle that she should even have had a baby. But Jake had spent all those years believing what most people always have believed, that black women are just like watermelon vines and once one gets ripe, there's another right behind it. She reckoned Jake was for the first time proud of his manhood, and took it out on her that he had doubted himself all those years. Before Elizabeth was even a year old, Fannie was already having to unfasten the

144

tops of her skirts. It didn't seem like such a miracle that time, because Jake was gone before she even got to wearing big loose frocks with no waist to them. She named that child Thomas because it was all that doubt and resentment that had brought him to her.

She tells herself that there were some blessings to come out of it all, that she has forgiven Jake for leaving the way that he did, forgiven Elizabeth for going to New York and leaving M.L. with her to raise from the time he was a year old. She tells herself that her children deserve better if they can find it, though she's proud of her life, proud of the fact that she is sixty-five years old and gets up and goes to work every day, cooking and cleaning for the Fosters who live in one of the big houses out in what she still calls Piney Swamp even though it has been given a fancy name that she never can remember. One day M.L. will have himself a fine house with a long table set with matching dishes and silverware. M.L. might just be a doctor and that would be fine, but for Fannie McNair, the most important thing is that M.L. grows up to be decent and proud, hard working and loving, not fighting to prove he's something that he ain't like Thomas, who lives somewhere right in this town but hardly ever comes by. M.L. ain't gonna sit and watch his mailbox for the government to send some kind of check.

She goes over now and leans down close to M.L. where his face is buried down in the stomach of an old stuffed monkey that he calls F.M. after her, and she can feel the warmth of his breath against her cheek. This is a ritual that she performed with her own children and did with M.L. before he was even left there with her, and now, with the assurance of his measured sleep, she goes back to her chair for a few more minutes of thinking. Her gnarled fingers work in and out while she hems the dress that Mrs. Foster is going to wear to a party tomorrow night that is being given for a couple about to be married. It's a pretty dress, green and silky, cool to Fannie's fingers as she slides the material around. The dress smells like Mrs. Foster, clean and a little spicy like those crumpled-up dried flowers that Mrs. Foster has in little bowls in the bathroom. It smells like the Fosters' house and it makes Fannie feel for a minute that Mrs. Helena Foster is right there in the room with her, though of course she's not; Mrs. Foster has never been inside of this room or right out front on the street, or if she has Fannie doesn't know it. Mr. Foster picks her up in the mornings and brings her back home, or if he is out of town, Mrs. Foster gives her taxi money the day before. That's the way it is, Fannie tells herself, though there have been times when she would have liked for Mrs. Foster to come up here and see her home, see the quilts and afghans that Fannie has made, because Mrs. Foster is real interested in homemade things like quilts, rugs, bread and jelly, though as far as Fannie knows Mrs. Foster has never made a thing in her life, probably not even a bed.

It makes Fannie smile just to think of how that whole house would fall apart if she wasn't there to keep things right. But she likes Mrs. Foster. Sometimes she just likes to look at her because it's so hard to believe that a woman getting close to forty with two children could look that way, that frosted blonde hair that she pulls up in a loose bun, those long nails always glazed in clear polish, those bright plaid pedal pushers that she wears around the house or to the grocery store. It is something, the way that Mrs. Foster looks like she's always about to go somewhere even when she isn't. She wears earrings every day of the week.

Fannie breaks off the thread and carefully hangs the dress back on its hanger and carries it into the bathroom to hang it on the shower rod so that nothing will happen to it. She pulls out the skirt and lets it rock back and forth like a ghost dancing there. She does like to think and wonder about the Fosters, to think of how Mrs. Foster's voice changes a little when she has company, how she doesn't spend much time with Fannie when other people are there. Mr. Foster is real quiet most of the time and Fannie never has been able to decide if he's mad or if he's just a soured person. He isn't even smiling in that wedding photograph that Mrs. Foster has on her dresser.

146

Fannie goes back to her chair and now that that dress is out of the room it's a little easier to forget about the Fosters. She will be back with them soon enough, back with Billy Foster locked up in his room all day long, asleep till noon and before she can get in there to make his bed, he's already back on it, just sitting on top of rumpled covers and playing his record player full blast. He reminds Fannie of a scrawny little chick who goes around acting like a bantam rooster till somebody crosses him and he goes crying to his Mama. M.L. ain't that way. M.L. don't act a bit bigger than what he is and he isn't a crybaby, never has been. But that Billy Foster is something. Fannie can't quite figure it out. How did such a cute little boy grow up like that, except that he's spoiled rotten. He has all these posters on his walls, of people with their faces all painted up like some kind of freak show. "Kiss," it says below these awful faces. Fannie McNair wouldn't touch one with a ten foot pole, let alone kiss one. Fannie supposes that he comes by this sort of taste for pictures naturally, though. Just the other day, Mrs. Foster called Fannie away from her cooking to come into the living room and see the new picture. "It's a Primitive," Mrs. Foster said. "We got it at an auction. Isn't it wonderful?" Fannie nodded like she was agreeing, but she thought that it was more than primitive; she thought it was downright scary with that head too big for that child's body like some kind of poor dwarf. Mrs. Foster talks about all these things like she knows something about them, but Lord knows, she don't know too much. She doesn't know a thing about the history of Marshboro; she didn't even know that her house is just a hop and a skip from where Piney Swamp Baptist Church used to be, and even though the Fosters are members of a church in town, Fannie has not once heard them discuss a service and has never heard a hymn sung in that house, until she herself began singing while she works.

Sometimes it makes Fannie feel proud that she works in such a fine house with all that silver to polish, like she owned it all or something since she's the one to care for it. But other times, she feels guilty for thinking that way, for forgetting herself and wishing that M.L. had his own bathroom with a little towel with his name on it like Parker Foster, who is only twelve years old and has everything that most grown-up women don't even have. Sometimes it goes on and on until that pride turns a little to doubt and resentment and she can't help but remember being a young woman and going to the movies, having to sit in the balcony where it said "colored," using a bathroom that said "colored," and it makes her feel a fever deep in her body, the same fever, she is certain, that Thomas McNair has felt every day of his life.

There is a soft rapping at the door and Fannie realizes that she's been thinking about the Fosters again, thinking about all those old sad things that have happened in her life. She tiptoes across the old hardwood floor, her stocking snagging on a small splinter. "Who's there?" she whispers, though she's certain it's Corky Revels from across the hall.

"It's me, Fannie," comes the voice so she takes off the chain and opens the door. Corky is standing there in a blue cotton gown that reaches her thin calves; she has one foot curled around the other. "I saw your light beneath the door. I didn't wake you, did I?"

"No, honey, you know I sit up late as I can stand it." Fannie motions for Corky to come in and then closes and locks the door. Corky goes over and sits on the footstool in front of Fannie's chair. "I just couldn't get to sleep," she whispers, her large pale eyes magnified by the dark circles below them, her light hair slipping from the ponytail on top of her head and falling around her face. She waits for Fannie to settle back into her chair. "I guess I just wanted to talk for a minute."

"You've got to get some sleep." Fannie leans forward so that she can talk without waking M.L. "Don't you work in the morning?"

"I go in at seven." She seems to relax a little, stretching her feet out towards Fannie's chair.

"It's well after one, now," Fannie whispers. "Can I fix you something to eat?" She is hoping that Corky will say yes because she's as thin as a rail but she just shakes her head and the tears well up in those large sad eyes.

"No thank you," she whispers and then she just stares out the window. Fannie doesn't mind Corky coming over in the late hours; she does it often and Fannie never knows exactly what to do except to sit there. Corky told her one time that that's what she needed, to be with somebody.

"Are you frightened?" Fannie whispers. "Cause you can get right over there and sleep with M.L., you know you can." Corky blinks those long lashes and the tears roll down her cheeks while she shakes her head. "Are you all right?"

"Yeah, yeah, really I am," she says and pulls the neck of her gown up to wipe her cheeks. "I know, Fannie, tell me about the house where you work."

"Well, what part of it?" Fannie has been over that house with a fine tooth comb with Corky. Corky could probably make her way around the Fosters' house blindfolded and she has never even set foot there.

"Tell me about that bedroom suit that they have that is as old as George Washington." Fannie is not sure if that's right or not. Mrs. Foster had told her that it was just like what George Washington slept on, but she tells about it again, and the bedspread and that dressing table with the skirt on it and the big wooden mirror with brass-covered lamps on either side. She talks on and on until Corky's eyes start looking heavy and she gets off of the footstool and stretches out on the rag rug.

"Come on, honey, come get into bed with M.L." Fannie shakes her shoulder and Corky sits up. "Come on, you're tired."

"I think I can sleep now," she whispers. "I'll go on home." She gets up from the floor, marks from the rug on her cheek and arm, and tiptoes to the door. "Thanks, Fannie," she says and kisses her on the cheek, and Fannie watches until she has let herself into her room across the hall. Fannie goes over and cuts off the light, pulls off her thin bathrobe and lays it at the foot of the bed. She believes that things are the way they are for a reason; she believes

that one day it will all make sense, why her life is hard sometimes, because the God that she prays to wouldn't have it any
other way. She thinks of Corky and the way that she comes over
here to cry late at night, Corky, with hardly no family at all. She
prays silently as she eases herself onto the bed and the words flow
through her mind like the words to a song. She doesn't close her
eyes or bow her head but stares over at M.L., a dark little bundle
beneath the sheet, because he is what she is thankful for, every
day and every night, he is the blessing of her life, the reason that
she keeps on going and she repeats this to herself over and over,
her lips barely moving, her eyes tired and heavy, with no thought
of the pair of jeans hanging limply on the window ledge without a
trace of breeze to stir them.

Drawing Names

BOBBIE ANN MASON

On Christmas Day, Carolyn Sisson went early to her parents' house to help her mother with the dinner. Carolyn had been divorced two years before, and last Christmas, coming alone, she felt uncomfortable. This year she had invited her lover, Kent Ballard, to join the family gathering. She had even brought him a present to put under the tree, so he wouldn't feel left out. Kent was planning to drive over from Kentucky Lake by noon. He had gone there to inspect his boat because of an ice storm earlier in the week. He felt compelled to visit his boat on the holiday, Carolyn thought, as if it were a sad old relative in a retirement home.

"We're having baked ham instead of turkey," Mom said. "Your daddy never did like ham baked, but whoever heard of fried ham on Christmas? We have that all year round and I'm burnt out on it."

"I love baked ham," said Carolyn.

"Does Kent like it baked?"

"I'm sure he does." Carolyn placed her gifts under the tree. The number of packages seemed unusually small.

"It don't seem like Christmas with drawed names," said Mom.

"Your star's about to fall off." Carolyn straightened the silver ornament at the tip of the tree.

"I didn't decorate as much as I wanted to. I'm slowing down.

151

Getting old, I guess." Mom had not combed her hair and she was wearing a workshirt and tennis shoes.

"You always try to do too much on Christmas, Mom."

Carolyn knew the agreement to draw names had bothered her mother. But the four daughters were grown and two had children. Sixteen people were expected today. Carolyn herself could not afford to buy fifteen presents on her salary as a clerk at J. C. Penney's, and her parents' small farm had not been profitable in years.

Carolyn's father appeared in the kitchen and he hugged her so tightly she squealed in protest.

"That's all I can afford this year," he said, laughing.

As he took a piece of candy from a dish on the counter, Carolyn teased him. "You'd better watch your calories today."

"Oh, not on Christmas!"

It made Carolyn sad to see her handsome father getting older. He was a shy man, awkward with his daughters, and Carolyn knew he had been deeply disappointed over her failed marriage, although he had never said so. Now he asked, "Who bought these 'toes'?"

He would no longer say "nigger toes," the old name for the chocolate-covered creams.

"Hattie Smoot brought those over," said Mom. "I made a pants suit for her last week," she said to Carolyn. "The one that had stomach bypass?"

"When PeeWee McClain had that, it didn't work and they had to fix him back like he was," said Dad. He offered Carolyn a piece of candy, but she shook her head no.

Mom said, "I made Hattie a dress back last spring for her boy's graduation, and she couldn't even find a pattern big enough. I had to 'low a foot. But after that bypass, she's down to a size twenty."

"I think we'll all need a stomach bypass after we eat this feast you're fixing," said Carolyn.

"Where's Kent?" Dad asked abruptly.

"He went to see about his boat. He said he'd be here."

Carolyn looked at the clock. She felt uneasy about inviting Kent. Everyone would be scrutinizing him, as if he were some new character on a soap opera. Kent, who drove a truck for the Kentucky Loose-Leaf Floor, was a part-time student at Murray State. He was majoring in accounting. When Carolyn started going with him early in the summer, they went sailing on his boat, which had "Joyce" painted on it. Later he painted over the name, insisting he didn't love Joyce anymore—she was a dietician who was always criticizing what he ate—but he had never said he loved Carolyn. She did not know if she loved him. Each seemed to be waiting for the other to say it first.

While Carolyn helped her mother in the kitchen, Dad went to get her grandfather, her mother's father. Pappy, who had been disabled by a stroke, was cared for by a live-in housekeeper who had gone home to her own family for the day. Carolyn diced apples and pears for fruit salad while her mother shaped sweet potato balls with marshmallow centers and rolled them in crushed cornflakes. On TV in the living room, *Days of Our Lives* was beginning, but the Christmas tree blocked their view of the television set.

"Whose name did you draw, Mom?" Carolyn asked, as she began seeding the grapes.

"Jim's."

"You put Jim's name in the hat?"

Mom nodded. Jim Walsh was the man Carolyn's youngest sister, Laura Jean, was living with in St. Louis. Laura Jean was going to an interior decorating school, and Jim was a textiles salesman she had met in a class. "I made him a shirt," Mom said.

"I'm surprised at you."

"Well, what was I to do?"

"I'm just surprised." Carolyn ate a grape and spit out the seeds. "Emily Post says the couple should be offered the same room when they visit."

"You know we'd never stand for that. I don't think your dad's ever got over her stacking up with that guy."

"You mean shacking up."

"Same thing." Mom dropped the potato masher, and the metal rattled on the floor. "Oh, I'm in such a tizzy," she said.

As the family began to arrive, the noise of the TV played against the greetings, the slam of the storm door, the outside wind rushing in. Carolyn's older sisters, Peggy and Iris, with their husbands and children, were arriving all at once, and suddenly the house seemed small. Peggy's children Stevie and Cheryl, without even removing their jackets, became involved in a basketball game on TV. In his lap, Stevie had a Merlin electronic toy, which beeped randomly. Iris and Ray's children, Deedee and Jonathan, went outside to look for cats.

In the living room, Peggy jiggled her baby, Lisa, on her hip and said, "You need you one of these, Carolyn."

"Where can I get one?" said Carolyn, rather sharply.

Peggy grinned. "At the gittin' place, I reckon."

Peggy's critical tone was familiar. She was the only sister who had had a real wedding. Her husband, Cecil, had a Gulf franchise, and they owned a motor cruiser, a pickup truck, a camper, a station wagon, and a new brick colonial home. Whenever Carolyn went to visit Peggy, she felt apologetic for not having a man who would buy her all these things, but she never seemed to be attracted to anyone steady or ambitious. She had been wondering how Kent would get along with the men of the family. Cecil and Ray were standing in a corner talking about gas mileage. Cecil, who was shorter than Peggy and was going bald, always worked on Dad's truck for free, and Ray usually agreed with Dad on politics to avoid an argument. Ray had an impressive government job in Frankfort. He had coordinated a ribbon-cutting ceremony when the toll road opened. What would Kent have to say to them? She could imagine him insisting that everyone go outside later to watch the sunset. Her father would think that was ridiculous. No one ever did that on a farm, but it was the sort of thing Kent would think of. Yet she knew that spontaneity was what she liked in him.

154

Deedee and Jonathan, who were ten and six, came inside then and immediately began shaking the presents under the tree. All the children were wearing new jeans and cowboy shirts, Carolyn noticed.

"Why are y'all so quiet?" she asked. "I thought kids whooped and hollered on Christmas."

"They've been up since *four*," said Iris. She took a cigarette from her purse and accepted a light from Cecil. Exhaling smoke, she said to Carolyn, "We heard Kent was coming." Before Carolyn could reply, Iris scolded the children for shaking the packages. She seemed nervous.

"He's supposed to be here by noon," said Carolyn.

"There's somebody now. I hear a car."

"It might be Dad, with Pappy."

It was Laura Jean, showing off Jim Walsh as though he were a splendid Christmas gift she had just received.

"Let me kiss everybody!" she cried, as the women rushed toward her. Laura Jean had not been home in four months.

"Merry Christmas!" Jim said in a booming, official-sounding voice, something like a TV announcer, Carolyn thought. He embraced all the women and then, with a theatrical gesture, he handed Mom a bottle of Rebel Yell bourbon and a carton of boiled custard which he took from a shopping bag. The bourbon was in a decorative Christmas box.

Mom threw up her hands. "Oh, no, I'm afraid I'll be a alkyholic."

"Oh, that's ridiculous, Mom," said Laura Jean, taking Jim's coat. "A couple of drinks a day are good for your heart."

Jim insisted on getting coffee cups from a kitchen cabinet and mixing some boiled custard and bourbon. When he handed a cup to Mom, she puckered up her face.

"Law, don't let the preacher in," she said, taking a sip. "Boy, that sends my blood pressure up."

Carolyn waved away the drink Jim offered her. "I don't start this early in the day," she said, feeling confused.

Jim was a large, dark-haired man with a neat little beard, like a bird's nest cupped on his chin. He had a Northern accent. When he hugged her, Carolyn caught a whiff of cologne, something sweet, like chocolate syrup. Last summer, when Laura Jean brought him home for the first time, she had made a point of kissing and hugging him in front of everyone. Dad had virtually ignored him. Now Carolyn saw that Jim was telling Cecil that he always bought Gulf gas. Red-faced, Ray accepted a cup of boiled custard. Carolyn fled to the kitchen and began grating cheese for potatoes au gratin. She dreaded Kent's arrival.

When Dad arrived with Pappy, Cecil and Jim helped set up the wheelchair in a corner. Afterward, Dad and Jim shook hands, and Dad refused Jim's offer of bourbon. From the kitchen, Carolyn could see Dad hugging Laura Jean, not letting go. She went into the living room to greet her grandfather.

"They roll me in this buggy too fast," he said when she kissed his forehead.

Carolyn hoped he wouldn't notice the bottle of bourbon, but she knew he never missed anything. He was so deaf people had given up talking to him. Now the children tiptoed around him, looking at him with awe. Somehow, Carolyn expected the children to notice that she was alone, like Pappy.

At ten minutes of one, the telephone rang. Peggy answered and handed the receiver to Carolyn. "It's Kent," she said.

Kent had not left the lake yet. "I just got here an hour ago," he told Carolyn. "I had to take my sister over to my mother's."

"Is the boat O.K.?"

"Yeah. Just a little scraped paint. I'll be ready to go in a little while." He hesitated, as though waiting for assurance that the invitation was real.

"This whole gang's ready to eat," Carolyn said. "Can't you hurry?" She should have remembered the way he tended to get sidetracked. Once it took them three hours to get to Paducah, because he kept stopping at antique shops.

After she hung up the telephone, her mother asked, "Should I put the rolls in to brown yet?"

"Wait just a little. He's just now leaving the lake."

"When's this Kent feller coming?" asked Dad impatiently, as he peered into the kitchen. "It's time to eat."

"He's on his way," said Carolyn.

"Did you tell him we don't wait for stragglers?"

"No."

"When the plate rattles, we eat."

"I know."

"Did you tell him that?"

"No, I didn't!" cried Carolyn, irritated.

When they were alone in the kitchen, Carolyn's mother said to her, "Your dad's not his self today. He's fit to be tied about Laura Jean bringing that guy down here again. And him bringing that whiskey."

"That was uncalled for," Carolyn agreed. She had noticed that Mom had set her cup of boiled custard in the refrigerator.

"Besides, he's not too happy about that Kent Ballard you're running around with."

"What's it to him?"

"You know how he always was. He don't think anybody's good enough for one of his little girls, and he's afraid you'll get mistreated again. He don't think Kent's very dependable."

"I guess Kent's proving Dad's point."

Carolyn's sister Iris had dark brown eyes, unique in the family. When Carolyn was small, she tried to say "Iris's eyes" once and called them "Irish eyes," confusing them with a song their mother sometimes sang, "When Irish Eyes Are Smiling." Thereafter, they always teased Iris about her smiling Irish eyes. Today Iris was not smiling. Carolyn found her in a bedroom smoking, holding an ashtray in her hand.

"I drew your name," Carolyn told her. "I got you something I wanted myself."

"Well, if I don't want it, I guess I'll have to give it to you."

"What's wrong with you today?"

"Ray and me's getting a separation," said Iris.

"Really?" Carolyn was startled by the note of glee in her response. Actually, she told herself later, it was because she was glad her sister, whom she saw infrequently, had confided in her.

"The thing of it is, I had to beg him to come today, for Mom and Dad's sake. It'll kill them. Don't let on, will you?"

"I won't. What are you going to do?"

"I don't know. He's already moved out."

"Are you going to stay in Frankfort?"

"I don't know. I have to work things out."

Mom stuck her head in the door. "Well, is Kent coming or not?"

"He *said* he'd be here," said Carolyn.

"Your dad's about to have a duck with a rubber tail. He can't stand to wait on a meal."

"Well, let's go ahead, then. Kent can eat when he gets here."

When Mom left, Iris said, "Aren't you and Kent getting along?"

"I don't know. He said he'd come today, but I have a feeling he doesn't really want to."

"To hell with men." Iris laughed and stubbed out her cigarette. "Just look at us—didn't we turn out awful? First your divorce. Now me. And Laura Jean bringing that guy down. Daddy can't stand him. Did you see the look he gave him?"

"Laura Jean's got a lot more nerve than I've got," said Carolyn, nodding. "I could wring Kent's neck for being late. Well, none of us can do anything right—except Peggy."

"Daddy's precious little angel," said Iris mockingly. "Come on, we'd better get in there and help."

While Mom went to change her blouse and put on lipstick, the sisters brought the food into the dining room. Two tables had been put together. Peggy cut the ham with an electric knife, and Carolyn filled the iced tea glasses.

"Pappy gets buttermilk and Stevie gets Coke," Peggy directed her.

"I know," said Carolyn, almost snapping.

As the family sat down, Carolyn realized that no one ever asked Pappy to "turn thanks" anymore at holiday dinners. He was sitting there expectantly, as if waiting to be asked. Mom cut up his ham into small bits. Carolyn waited for a car to drive up, the phone to ring. The TV was still on.

"Y'all dig in," said Mom. "Jim? Make sure you try some of these dressed eggs like I fix."

"I thought your new boyfriend was coming," said Cecil to Carolyn.

"So did I!" said Laura Jean. "That's what you wrote me."

Everyone looked at Carolyn as she explained. She looked away.

"You're looking at that pitiful tree," Mom said to her. "I just know it don't show up good from the road."

"No, it looks fine." No one had really noticed the tree. Carolyn seemed to be seeing it for the first time in years—broken red plastic reindeer, Styrofoam snowmen with crumbling top hats, silver walnuts which she remembered painting when she was about twelve.

Dad began telling a joke about some monks who had taken a vow of silence. At each Christmas dinner, he said, one monk was allowed to speak.

"Looks like your vocal cords would rust out," said Cheryl.

"Shut up, Cheryl. Granddaddy's trying to tell something," said Cecil.

"So the first year it was the first monk's turn to talk, and you know what he said? He said, 'These taters is lumpy.'"

When several people laughed, Stevie asked, "Is that the joke?"

Carolyn was baffled. Her father had never told a joke at the table in his life. He sat at the head of the table, looking out past the family at the cornfield through the picture window.

"Pay attention now," he said. "The second year Christmas rolled around again and it was the second monk's turn to say something. He said, 'You know, I think you're right. The taters *is* lumpy.'"

Laura Jean and Jim laughed loudly.

"Reach me some light-bread," said Pappy. Mom passed the dish around the table to him.

"And so the third year," Dad continued, "the third monk got to say something. What he said"—Dad was suddenly overcome with mirth—"what he said was, 'If y'all don't shut up arguing about them taters, I'm going to leave this place!'"

After the laughter died, Mom said, "Can you imagine anybody not a-talking all year long?"

"That's the way monks are, Mom," said Laura Jean. "Monks are economical with everything. They're not wasteful, not even with words."

"The Trappist Monks are really an outstanding group," said Jim. "And they make excellent bread. No preservatives."

Cecil and Peggy stared at Jim.

"You're not eating, Dad," said Carolyn. She was sitting between him and the place set for Kent. The effort at telling the joke seemed to have taken her father's appetite.

"He ruined his dinner on nigger toes," said Mom.

"Dottie Barlow got a Barbie doll for Christmas and it's black," Cheryl said.

"Dottie Barlow ain't black, is she?" asked Cecil.

"No."

"That's funny," said Peggy. "Why would they give her a black Barbie doll?"

"She just wanted it."

Abruptly, Dad left the table, pushing back his plate. He sat down in the recliner chair in front of the TV. The Blue–Gray game was beginning, and Cecil and Ray were hurriedly finishing in order to join him. Carolyn took out second helpings of ham and jello salad, feeling as though she were eating for Kent in his absence. Jim was taking seconds of everything, complimenting Mom. Mom apologized for not having fancy napkins. Then Laura Jean described a photography course she had taken. She had been photographing close-ups of car parts—fenders, head-lights, mud flaps.

"That sounds goofy," said one of the children, Deedee.

Suddenly Pappy spoke. "Use to, the menfolks would eat first, and the children separate. The womenfolks would eat last, in the kitchen."

"You know what I could do with you all, don't you?" said Mom, shaking her fist at him. "I could set up a plank out in the field for y'all to eat on." She laughed.

"Times are different now, Pappy," said Iris loudly. "We're just as good as the men."

"She gets that from television," said Ray, with an apologetic laugh.

Carolyn noticed Ray's glance at Iris. Just then Iris matter-of-factly plucked an eyelash from Ray's cheek. It was as though she had momentarily forgotten about the separation.

Later, after the gifts were opened, Jim helped clear the tables. Kent still had not come. The baby slept, and Laura Jean, Jim, Peggy, and Mom played a Star Trek board game at the dining room table, while Carolyn and Iris played Battlestar Galactica with Cheryl and Deedee. The other men were quietly engrossed in the football game, a blur of sounds. No one had mentioned Kent's absence, but after the children had distributed the gifts, Carolyn refused to tell them what was in the lone package left under the tree. It was the most extravagantly wrapped of all the presents, with an immense ribbon, not a stick-on bow. An icicle had dropped on it, and it reminded Carolyn of an abandoned float, like something from a parade.

At a quarter to three, Kent telephoned. He was still at the lake. "The gas stations are all closed," he said. "I couldn't get any gas."

"We already ate and opened the presents," said Carolyn.

"Here I am, stranded. Not a thing I can do about it."

Kent's voice was shaky and muffled, and Carolyn suspected he had been drinking. She did not know what to say, in front of the family. She chattered idly, while she played with a ribbon from a package. The baby was awake, turning dials and knobs on a Busy Box. On TV, the Blues picked up six yards on an end sweep.

Carolyn fixed her eyes on the tilted star at the top of the tree. Kent was saying something about Santa Claus.

"They wanted me to play Santy at Mama's house for the littluns. I said—you know what I said? 'Bah, humbug!' Did I ever tell you what I've got against Christmas?"

"Maybe not." Carolyn's back stiffened against the wall.

"When I was little bitty, Santa Claus came to town. I was about five. I was all fired up to go see Santy, and Mama took me, but we were late, and he was about to leave. I had to run across the courthouse square to get to him. He was giving away suckers, so I ran as hard as I could. He was climbing up on the fire engine—are you listening?"

"Unh-huh." Carolyn was watching her mother, who was folding Christmas paper to save for next year.

Kent said, "I reached up and pulled at his old red pants leg, and he looked down at me, and you know what he said?"

"No—what?"

"He said, 'Piss off, kid.' "

"Really?"

"Would I lie to you?"

"I don't know."

"Do you want to hear the rest of my hard-luck story?"

"Not now."

"Oh, I forgot this was long distance. I'll call you tomorrow. Maybe I'll go paint the boat. That's what I'll do! I'll go paint it right this minute."

After Carolyn hung up the telephone, her mother said, "I think my Oriental casserole was a failure. I used the wrong kind of mushroom soup. It called for cream of mushroom and I used golden mushroom."

"Won't you *ever* learn, Mom?" cried Carolyn. "You always cook too much. You make *such* a big deal—"

Mom said, "What happened with Kent this time?"

"He couldn't get gas. He forgot the gas stations were closed."

"Jim and Laura Jean didn't have any trouble getting gas," said Peggy, looking up from the game.

"We tanked up yesterday," said Laura Jean.

"Of course you did," said Carolyn distractedly. "You always think ahead."

"It's your time," Cheryl said, handing Carolyn the Battlestar Galactica toy. "I did lousy."

"Not as lousy as I did," said Iris.

Carolyn tried to concentrate on shooting enemy missiles, raining through space. Her sisters seemed far away, like the spaceships. She was aware of the men watching football, their hands in action as they followed an exciting play. Even though Pappy had fallen asleep, with his blanket in his lap he looked like a king on a throne. Carolyn thought of the quiet accommodation her father had made to his father-in-law, just as Cecil and Ray had done with Dad, and her ex-husband had tried to do once. But Cecil had bought his way in, and now Ray was getting out. Kent had stayed away. Jim, the newcomer, was with the women, playing Star Trek as if his life depended upon it. Carolyn was glad now that Kent had not come. The story he told made her angry, and his pity for his childhood made her think of something Pappy had often said: "Christmas is for children." Earlier, she had listened in amazement while Cheryl listed on her fingers the gifts she had received that morning: a watch, a stereo, a nightgown, hot curls, perfume, candles, a sweater, a calculator, a jewelry box, a ring. Now Carolyn saw Kent's boat as his toy, more important than the family obligations of the holiday.

Mom was saying, "I wanted to make a Christmas tablecloth out of red checks with green fringe. You wouldn't think knit would do for a tablecloth, but Hattie Smoot has the prettiest one."

"You can do incredible things with knit," said Jim with sudden enthusiasm. The shirt Mom had made him was bonded knit.

"Who's Hattie Smoot?" asked Laura Jean. She was caressing the back of Jim's neck, as though soothing his nerves.

Carolyn laughed when her mother began telling Jim and Laura Jean about Hattie Smoot's operation. Jim listened attentively, leaning forward with his elbows on the table, and asked eager questions, his eyes as alert as Pappy's.

"Is she telling a joke?" Cheryl asked Carolyn.

"No. I'm not laughing at you, Mom," Carolyn said, touching her mother's hand. She felt relieved that the anticipation of Christmas had ended. Still laughing, she said, "Pour me some of that Rebel Yell, Jim. It's about time."

"I'm with you," Jim said, jumping up.

In the kitchen, Carolyn located a clean spoon while Jim washed some cups. Carolyn couldn't find the cup Mom had left in the refrigerator. As she took out the carton of boiled custard, Jim said, "It must be a very difficult day for you."

Carolyn was startled. His tone was unexpectedly kind, genuine. She was struck suddenly by what he must know about her, because of his intimacy with her sister. She knew nothing about him. When he smiled, she saw a gold cap on a molar, shining like a Christmas ornament. She managed to say, "It can't be any picnic for you either. Kent didn't want to put up with us."

"Too bad he couldn't get gas."

"I don't think he wanted to get gas."

"Then you're better off without him." When Jim looked at her, Carolyn felt that he must be examining her resemblances to Laura Jean. He said, "I think your family's great."

Carolyn laughed nervously. "We're hard on you. God, you're brave to come down here like this."

"Well, Laura Jean's worth it."

They took the boiled custard and cups into the dining room. As Carolyn sat down, her nephew Jonathan begged her to tell what was in the gift left under the tree.

"I can't tell," she said.

"Why not?"

"I'm saving it till next year, in case I draw some man's name."

"I hope it's mine," said Jonathan.

Jim stirred bourbon into three cups of boiled custard, then gave one to Carolyn and one to Laura Jean. The others had declined. Then he leaned back in his chair—more relaxed now— and squeezed Laura Jean's hand. Carolyn wondered what they said to each other when they were alone in St. Louis. She knew with certainty that they would not be economical with words, like the monks in the story. She longed to be with them, to hear what they would say. She noticed her mother picking at a hangnail, quietly ignoring the bourbon. Looking at the bottle's gift box, which showed an old-fashioned scene, children on sleds in the snow, Carolyn thought of Kent's boat again. She felt she was in that snowy scene now with Laura Jean and Jim, sailing in Kent's boat into the winter breeze, into falling snow. She thought of how silent it was out on the lake, as though the whiteness of the snow were the absence of sound.

"Cheers!" she said to Jim, lifting her cup.

Storyteller

LEWIS NORDAN

It was Wiley Heard talking and cooling his coffee at the same time. "You heard about all them grain elevators blowing up in Kansas, didn't you?" Wiley was a short, wiry one-legged man with a red face and white eyebrows. He was retired head coach of the local football team. He stopped blowing across his coffee and took a long, slurping pull, then held up the heavy cup, like evidence, so everybody could see. One or two of those standing around moved in closer to the marble counter and were careful not to overturn a spittoon. They poured cups for themselves and lay their change on the cash register. "See this?" he said. "It's the best cup of coffee in the entire state of Arkansas. Right here in Hassell's Blank Store. Used to be called Hassell's Drug Store, long time ago. Back before any you boys would remember." They tried not to notice Coach Wiley pour a nip of Early Times into his coffee from a flat bottle he slipped out of his jacket pocket. "Yessir," he said, "Gene Hassell sold the wrong drugs to the wrong man. Two men, in fact. Federal agents pretending to work on a truck for two days across the street, out yonder by the railroad tracks, before they come in for pills. On account of which old Gene's pharmacy license got taken away. And so did Gene, come to think of it, down to the Cummins penitentiary. Couldn't get him in Atlanta. It was all full up that year, I think was the

166

trouble. His wife, poor thing, Miss Eva, I swan. She just painted out the word *Drug* on the sign and held a shotgun up under her chin, bless her time. It was that old twelve-gauge of Gene's that kicked so bad, real old gun, belonged to his daddy and ejected shells out the bottom. Remington, I think it was. She pulled the trigger and shot off her face. The whole damn thing from the bottom up, jaw, teeth, nose, and eyes, and broke both her ear-drums. Terrible sight to see, even after the skin grafts. No face at all. Can't see, hear, smell, or taste, just keep her alive in a nurs-ing home down in Arkadelphia, feeding her through tubes, and not one pellet touched her brain. It's a sad case, boys. It would break your heart. We been calling it Hassell's Blank Store ever since, and him still in jail, I guess, or dead, but you say you did hear about them grain elevators, didn't you?"

Somebody said he had. Everybody else agreed.

"I know you did," said the coach. "You heard about it on the Walter Cronkite Show, didn't you? They had it on the TV every night for a month, seem like. But I bet you forty dollars you didn't hear what happened the other day over in El Dorado, did you? Just outside El Dorado, I ought to say, over close to Smack-over. A dog food factory blew up. That's about like El Dorado, ain't it? Ain't nowhere but El Dorado, and maybe parts of north Mississippi, they going to blow up a dog food factory. But you never will hear that one on the Walter Cronkite Show, nayo-siree, and don't need to. The longer they can keep El Dorado, Arkansas, off the national news, or Smackover either one, the better for everybody, is what I say. Hound Dog dog food factory— and three men are missing, so they tell me. Might of been mule skinners, mightn't they? I think they was, in fact. If any you boys are looking for work they going to need somebody to skin them miserable old horses before they can put them in a can. Over this side of El Dorado actually, up close to Smackover. But that was years ago Gene Hassell went to jail. You boys wouldn't remember him, years ago. Hell, he may not be dead now, all I know. Proba-bly is, though. Probably is dead now he can't drink no more of that paregoric. He probably died his second day off that paregoric, didn't he? He'd been drinking it for twenty years. He's been constipated that long. He probably didn't know what to think, did he, down there in Cummins behind them bars, or out on that hot scrabble farm chopping him some prison cotton, when he felt that first urge to go to the bathroom. Hell, he probably died right off, didn't he? Didn't even have to call the dispensary. He probably got him a shit fit and the blind staggers and keeled over with his eyes rolled up. His old crazy paregoric eyes probably looked like the rolled up window shades of Miss Dee's whorehouse on Sunday morning, he was so happy. But not Miss Eva, that's his wife, she's not dead. She's still over to Arkadelphia at the Wee Care Nursing Home, got a married daughter out in California, or is it granddaughter, pays the bills. That little red brick building with the neon sign saying Wee Care out on the old airport road, real nice place, and expensive too. But Jerry Rich down in Prescott, out beyond Prescott really, just this side of De-light, he's the one owns this place now, Hassell's Blank Store. He's owned it for years. Poor old woman had to sell out right away, of course, after she lost so much face here in town trying to kill herself, and her husband in the pokey. The daughter had to sell, I mean. And no face at all, Miss Eva, and never did have much personality to speak of. But old Jerry, he doesn't get up here much any more, long as there's a quail in them cornfields and one old sorry dog in the pen. Not even to change the name on the front of the store. Painting out Gene's name would be a piss-pore way to remember a good man, though now wouldn't it? Lord, but his wife was a boring woman, even back when she had a face. It was three of them missing, though, three skinners, all of them white men, I believe it was, I'm not real sure about that. Dog food factory over in El Dorado, outside El Dorado really, out close to Smackover, Hound Dog dog food factory."

Wiley was still talking. "They used to feed dog food to circus animals. Sounds awful, don't it? But it's true. It'd make them crazy, too. It'd make a trained beast turn on his master, so I hear. Nothing to be done about a bitch elephant once they turn on their keeper. Bull elephant's a different story, trustworthiest old wrinkled buggers you ever want to meet, but not a bitch, you can't trust one with a nickel change once she gets sour on life, might as well save yourself the trouble."

"Why's that, Coach Wiley?" The coffee drinkers turned and looked. It was Hydro, a gawky young man with a broom and a large head.

"Nobody knows," said the coach, "and don't ask no more questions, Hydro. Godamighty. You get on done with that sweeping before you start asking so many questions. But it happened one time over in Pocahontas. One two y'all might be old enough to remember it. Your daddies'd be old enough. Some little off-brand circus or other. Clyde Beatty or something. Naw, not even that good. They had two old scrawny lions that hollered half the night they was so hungry from eating that dried dog food they give them. Probably Hound Dog dog food, when they was looking for meat, like that place blew up over past El Dorado, except that factory wasn't there till ten years ago, so it must have been some other brand the lions had to eat, but nobody ought to feed dog food to a lion and get away with it. King Jesus jump down. It'd take a worthless sumbitch to do that, now wouldn't it? Worthless as a whistle on a plow, as my poor old dead daddy used to say. Daddy he was a funny little quiet man with rusty hair and deep eyes. Housepainter and paperhanger, and a good one too, and a handful of elephants with their nose up each other's ass like a parade and some scrawny old woman in a little white dress and bleached-out hair riding on top of the first elephant, when this baggy old gray African elephant went kind of crazy. *Commercial Appeal* said she was in heat and real nervous. That's when they dangerous. Some old boy name of Orwell, from West Memphis or Forrest City or somewhere, was quoted as saying that was right. He claimed to know all about elephants, though I can't say I ever knew a family of Arkansas Orwells. Plenty of them in Mis-

sissippi, of course, Delta people, but none to my memory in
Arkansas. Unless, of course, they come here since the World
War, but I think she was just sick of Pocahontas and circus food.
That'd be me. Best thing ever happened to Pocahontas was that
tornado in 1957, tore down half the town. They just about due
another one, if you want my personal opinion. Didn't have many
teeth, my daddy, and had fainting spells on top of that, because
you notice she didn't bother to pick out her own trainer to step
on. That'd be too easy. She had to bring down all hell and her left
front foot on another African, one of her own people, you might
say. She had to step on some little local boy hired on as a handler.
Plez Moore's grandson is who it was, in case some y'all are old
enough to remember Plez. Course my daddy always did love his
whiskey and had a heart enlarged up the size of a basketball, but
the fainting spells commenced long before that come to pass,
who I always liked, Plez I'm talking about, and hated to see anything bad come to him in spite of not especially blaming the
elephant and never could straighten up his back, Plez, on account of getting syphilis when he was just a boy, stepped right on
that poor little child and flattened him out like one them cartoon
pictures when a steamroller runs over somebody. He looked like a
pitiful little black shadow some child lost. But you couldn't
blame the elephant, I couldn't, having to live cooped up in
Pocahontas all week and that terrible sawed-off circus. It wouldn't
do, though, but they had to kill the elephant, and you can see
their point, especially if that Orwell boy from West Memphis
knew what he's talking about, though I still think he was from
somewhere over in Mississippi.

"Anyhow, that's what the mayor and aldermen said, got to destroy the elephant. They was agreed with by the Colored Ministers Association, which has now got some other name and is
joined up with the NAACP. They was quickly agreed with, I
might add, which was the first and last time the Pocahontas town
officials and the colored ministers ever agreed on anything, except maybe last year when Horace Mayhan—you remember him

playing football right here in town and always stunk real bad, before old man Mayhan moved them all to Pocahontas where they'd belonged all along and fit in so good with the paper mill— last year when old Horace won a free trip, so to speak, to Washington, D.C. He had to testify before a senate subcommittee on the subject of who cut them eyeholes into the sheets the FBI found in the trunk of Horace's car, that cream-colored Mustang with the rusted top and STP stickers on the front bumper. That boy gave new meaning to the word *white-trash*, not to mention who sawed the stocks and barrels off all his shotguns and enough dynamite to provide every man, woman, and child in Arkansas fish dinner every night for a week. But the trouble was, of course, that nobody in Pocahontas had a gun big enough to kill an elephant, not even a hungry old scrawny elephant that probably needed killing."

"Shoot him in the eye." The words were totally unexpected, but the minute they were in the air everybody knew it was Hydro again and that he was in trouble. He had forgotten that the coach told him to stay quiet. It was obvious from his enormous face that he thought he had made a good suggestion. The coach stopped talking and looked at him. Everybody else looked at the floor and tried not to breathe. They wanted to become invisible. "Hydro, my man," Coach Wiley said, with a chill in his voice that galvanized every gaze upon the floor, "I always kind of liked you, boy. And I know you got your own problems. But listen here. Don't you never interrupt me again. Not now, and not never. Not till you get smart enough to know a whole hell of a lot more about elephants than shoot him in the eye."

"Or," said a voice with an unnatural cheeriness, "maybe you could just shoot him up the butt." It was Hydro again, and he had missed the fury underlying the coach's tone. If any of those standing around the coach in the Blank Store had not been too embarrassed to think of it, they might have hated Hydro, and themselves, and they might have hated God for making Hydro so damn dumb. Nobody thought of it. Nobody knew why they depended on Wiley Heard's approval, and dreaded his disapproval. "It's bound to bust something loose up in there," Hydro said, still pleased as he could be to help.

The coach became more deliberate. For everybody but Hydro, breathing was out of the question. Some of this began to dawn on Hydro.

"Hydro," said Coach Wiley Heard, "I am going to say this one more time. Now, boy, I mean for you to listen. Are you listening?" There was no need for Hydro to answer. He had caught on now. "Shoot him in the eye and shoot him up the butt will not do. Not to interrupt me telling a story, nawsir. And neither will anything else do, to interrupt me telling a story. Are you listening, Hydro? Not nothing that you or anybody else that's going to come into Hassell's Blank Store is likely to think up is going to do to interrupt me. So just forget about interrupting me, boy. At any time, or for any reason whatsoever, with shoot him in the eye or shoot him up the butt or anything else. Now do you understand what I am saying?"

Hydro was quiet and miserable. He said, "Yessir," in a tiny whispery voice. He recognized his chastisement. The act of breathing started up again. Throats got cleared, and feet were shifted. Some of the little crowd looked up.

When the coach finally spoke again, it was not to them, not at first, not exactly. His voice was low and deep and coarse and gravelly, and there was a snort of a humorless laugh behind it. "Shoot him up the butt," they heard him say, almost soundless, and they heard the low, snorting laugh. A few of them laughed a little too; they tried it anyway, the laughter, not loud and not self-confident, and when they heard it, they found no pleasure in its sound. For a few more seconds he let the silence continue. He sweetened his coffee again with Early Times, and they made sure they didn't notice.

When he began again, the tone of his story was immeasurably darker. There were no more self-interruptions, there was no more marshaling of irrelevant detail. The story had become deadly serious and even most of the errors of grammar had disappeared from his speech. If the story were told again, or if it had been told without Hydro's interruption, each person in the store could have imagined it as wonderfully comic, the dark, laughing comedy that underlay every tale he told. But it was not comic now. The elephant, he said, would have to be killed. It would have to be killed by hanging. Some let out sounds that might have passed for laughs, but none of them were proud to have done so.

"By now the elephant was quiet," he said. "I saw her led to town by her trainer, a dirty man and sad-faced. The bleach-haired woman was with them, too, wearing a maroon suit and low-heeled shoes, the one who rode the elephant in the parade. The railroad crane and log-chain were on a flat car. The chain was made into a noose and put around its neck. The giant gears started creaking, the crane was lifting. I remember a blind fiddler was in the crowd and a little Indian boy with blue short pants and no shirt high up on the top of a locomotive. The elephant's feet were like the feet of a great turtle. The hind feet brushed the air a scant inch above the cinders of the station yard. When she was up, hanging there, choking, she lifted the wrinkled old trunk straight up and trumpeted one time, one blast to heaven, before she was choked dead. Her back feet, her gray old big turtle feet, were just an inch above the cinders, a little inch."

Those who listened stood, silent, and held their coffee cups without drinking. One man, whose son stood beside him, lay an unconscious hand on the boy's arm and pulled him a little closer to his side. No one knew what to say, or do. For a moment, during the silence, they forgot that Coach Wiley Heard was in charge, in control of the pause. He allowed a few more seconds to pass. They thought of the beast's trumpeting. They did not imagine, even for a second, that the coach's story might be untrue, that he might have made it all up, or adapted it from an older tale, and now maybe even believed it was all true, that it had all really happened on a certain day, to a certain people with bleached hair or sad faces or blind eyes or Indian blood, or any other hair and face and eyes and blood he chose to give them, and that it all happened in a station yard in eastern Arkansas, in a town called Pocahontas. If disbelief crept in, it came like a welcome brother into their company. They poured it a cup of coffee and showed it the sugar bowl and treated it like a friend too familiar to notice. They thought only of the gray feet and the cinders, the little inch between.

Then it was over. The coach released them. With a sudden, unexpected cheeriness, and maybe even a wink, he said, "You not going to forget what I told you, now are you, Hydro?"

"No sir," Hydro said, certain he would not, but still a little uncertain how to act. The coffee drinkers were able to love Hydro again, and pity him and feel superior to him. He shifted his broom and looked at its bristles. Everybody felt confident and happy. Everybody smiled at Hydro's innocence and at his need for forgiveness.

"Shoot him up the butt!" the coach roared suddenly, merry and hilarious and slapping his good leg. "Shoot him up the butt! Great godamighty!" Now they could laugh. They did laugh, uproarious and long. The coach slapped Hydro on the back and called him son and hugged him roughly against him and shook him by the shoulders. "Shoot him up the butt!" he said again. "Got damn, Hydro, I'm going to have to tell that one on you, now ain't I!"

When the laughter was over and the coach had wiped a tear from each eye with a clean handkerchief, he spoke to Hydro in a voice a little different from the one they had been listening to for most of the day. He said, "Let me tell you about my daddy, son. You'd of liked him. He had to walk on crutches all one winter, he had tonsilitis so bad." They knew now that they could stay and hear this story if they wished, but they knew also that it would not be told to them. They envied Hydro. They wished they were Hydro. They wished they were holding his broom and feeling the coach's warm, alcoholic breath on their faces. "Daddy always

174

smelled like turpentine and Fitch's shampoo," they heard the coach say, as if from a distance. "It's the only place I ever smelled the two in combination. It breaks my heart to remember." There was a pause, a silence of a few seconds. "He carried this little nickel pistol with him," the coach said, thoughtful. "I'll show it to you sometime. A little nickel pistol, with walnut handlegrips."

Hydro was happy. Everybody could see that. There was no reason for anybody else to hang around, though. They eased out by ones and twos.

FROM

A Short History of a
Small Place

T. R. PEARSON

On the Tuesday after Miss Pettigrew's funeral Mr. Conrad Rackley returned to Neely in a rented truck the cab of which he shared
with a pair of Masseys who we did not know for Masseys right off
but who we recognized as relations on account of a common
chinlessness, which is apparently the predominant Massey trait
in the West Virginia end of Kentucky. Now the Neely Masseys,
and there are eight altogether, are adequately chinful people, but
each one of them can catch rainwater in his ears without ever
tilting his head. Daddy says there is probably some jackrabbit in
the family somewhere. So nobody was even guessing Massey
when Mr. Conrad Rackley turned off Scales Street onto the boulevard and proceeded to Miss Pettigrew's house. There was, however, some speculation that it was possibly Newsomes, who go
almost direct from the bottom lip to the neck without any distrac-
tion, but most folks figured Newsomes to be strictly a local phe-
nomenon and did not consider it prudent to make such a serious
accusation against total strangers.

This time Mr. Conrad Rackley pulled up alongside Miss Pettigrew's wrought iron fence without ever stopping off at the Gulf
station to find out how, and he left both the Masseys in the truck

while he went himself to the front door and beat on it and kicked it and beat on it again before backing off the porch and into the yard to holler at the cedar clapboard, and I do believe Aunt Willa stood in the doorway for a full two minutes and listened to him yell before she brought herself out into the sunlight where he could see her.

"I come for some things," Mr. Rackley said, and Aunt Willa just stared at him. "I's here before," he told her, "and I come back for some things. Conrad Rackley, you remember me." But still Aunt Willa just stared at him and did not nod or twitch or even blink either, and Mr. Conrad Rackley looked to his left and looked to his right and then glared at the sky straight up over his head. "Shit woman," he said and made a vigorous exhalation, "I ain't got time to mess with you. Get on out the way, I come for some things." And he motioned to the Masseys who bailed out of the truck cab and followed him up the steps, across the porch past Aunt Willa, and on in through the doorway, and by all reliable reports the younger Massey had not hardly disappeared into the foyer when he came out again creeping backwards across the porch and searching for the top step with his right foot. It seems he got as far as the apron, which put him abreast of Aunt Willa, when the older Massey who turned out to be the younger Massey's daddy came out through the doorway frontwards and suggested to the younger Massey that he drag his butt directly back on into the house. "I ain't," the younger Massey told him, "I ain't about to as long as that gorilla's running loose," and he continued to probe for the top step with his foot.

"That monkey won't hurt you," the older Massey told him, "now get back in here."

"I ain't, Daddy, I ain't about to," the younger Massey said, and what chin he had was all aquiver.

So the older Massey turned his attention to Aunt Willa and asked her would she please bind up her monkey somehow or another and Aunt Willa stepped into the house long enough to fetch Mr. Britches back out with her and carried him down the steps to the flagpole while the younger Massey looked on with some considerable attention. And once he was satisfied that the monkey could not work free of his tether, he commenced to back across the porch towards the doorway and eventually vanished into the foyer.

Mr. Conrad Rackley and the two Masseys rummaged throughout the house for a spell independently of each other, and the assortment of people who had collected along the wrought iron fence on account of the truck and on account of the monkey and on account of the combination of the truck, the monkey, two Masseys, and a Rackley all watched the various window sashes on the front of the house fly open in an agitated and violent sort of way so as to allow the older Massey or the younger Massey or Mr. Conrad Rackley himself a breath of untainted air. And I do not believe the first piece of furniture saw daylight until the entire Pettigrew mansion had been all opened up and cross ventilated like a Swiss cheese and even then it was only an endtable that Mr. Conrad Rackley dragged outside, inspected on the lawn, and promptly carried on back into the house. He did not reappear for the best part of a half hour afterwards and neither did the younger Massey or the older Massey or Aunt Willa either, so the folks along the fence had to amuse themselves with the monkey, who was not hardly a danger to them any longer on account of his pressure problem and consequently was not hardly amusing to them either, even in his plaid sportcoat and his porkpie hat and with his lips turned inside out. Mr. Britches's bladder trouble had gone a ways towards deflating the thrill of monkey watching in Neely. Naturally, then, people were growing noticeably edgy and annoyed in the absence of Mr. Conrad Rackley and the accompanying Masseys, and there was mounting the threat that some one or two of the spectators might go on about their business when at last the air was filled with a kind of syncopated thud-thumping like maybe somebody was dribbling a piano down the inside stairway, and the noise had just barely left off echoing across the front lawn when the Masseys came trotting through the doorway on either end of a bonnet-topped highboy with Mr. Conrad Rackley close behind them cheering them on but not really carrying anything. He directed the Masseys straight to the truckbed, selected a spot for the highboy, and encouraged them to put it there. Then he drove them on back up the front steps and into the house in the most amiable sort of way. They were gone maybe five minutes this time when from out of the foyer came a tremendous splintering crash which seemed to indicate that Mr. Rackley and the Masseys had gotten together and decided to dispense with the dribbling and had simply tossed whatever it was off the second-floor landing. At length the Masseys passed through the doorway carrying between them a kind of a dressing table that was lovely, delicate, and complete except for three legs and Mr. Rackley encouraged them to set it off to one side of the porch.

After that the Masseys did not dribble any furniture and did not launch any either but did carry a great variety of items across the front yard to the truckbed under the cheerful direction of Mr. Conrad Rackley who did not dribble any furniture himself and did not launch any and managed to avoid carrying any also. I suppose all in all Mr. Rackley, with the invaluable assistance of the two chinless Masseys, made off with an even dozen end-tables, five or six highboys, a matching pair of cedar wardrobes, countless whatnot shelves and several boxes full of countless whatnots, two pine hutches, one overstuffed leather chair, a ponderous oak bedstead, three pair of andirons, one stackable walnut barrister's bookcase, four Tommy Dorsey albums, two sets of silver service, and one very large gilt-framed portrait of an excessively grim individual who was not then and has never since been verifiably identified though Mrs. Louise Tullock Pfaff, who got the best look at it, insisted it was Jefferson Davis. And all throughout the hauling and the loading and the stacking Mr. Conrad Rackley persisted in his undying encouragement except for the brief few minutes he spent against the wrought iron fence talking to Mr. Mickey Roach sr. and Mr. Covington from the Gulf station and Mr. Russell Newberry and one of the wispy white Tallys along with two of the standard-sized Frank Lewis negro Tallys. As Mr. Newberry told it, Mr. Rackley wiped some accumulated perspiration off the top of his bald head and said, "Gentlemen, this furniture here is awfully heavy."

"Yes sir," Mr. Mickey Roach sr. replied, "I bet it is."

"Awfully heavy," Mr. Rackley said, and dabbed at himself. "We sure could use some extra hands to help carry it."

"Yes sir," Mr. Mickey Roach told him, "I bet you could." And that was about all of it except for the hard looks followed by some general chortling on the part of most everybody but Mr. Conrad Rackley. So the Masseys continued to carry out the furniture alone and continued to suffer the singlehanded encouragement of Mr. Conrad Rackley until at last the truck was packed full and the door was lowered and latched and the older Massey and the younger Massey each were rewarded with a coffee cup full of tapwater. The departure was exceedingly uneventful to a point. There were no fond farewells, not even a solitary civil goodbye, just two Masseys and a Rackley in the cab of a rented truck which backfired when the engine turned over and then went off from the curb in a cloud of grey smoke. And I suppose the departure would have been entirely uneventful if Mr. Britches had not been startled enough by the backfire to urinate on account of it, and though it was not a thick and masterful stream it was a sort of arc nonetheless and drew a riotous ovation from the onlookers.

Daddy said that was that monkey's last hurrah though we didn't know it at the time and surely that monkey didn't know it either. I suppose only Aunt Willa knew it since she had gone ahead and called the zoo in keeping with the specifications of the deceased, and the people in charge there had immediately agreed to drive the width of the state from Ashboro to Neely if only to pick up a dilapidated, bladder-plagued chimpanzee with a court record. You see, the zoo was a fairly new undertaking at the time and was understandably scant of resources. There weren't any elephants just then or giraffes or zebras or tigers or crocodiles but just a few deer, one reasonably tame black bear, and enough corn snakes to start a Bible society, so I do believe the zoo would have flown a man halfway across the country to fetch back a housecat not to mention hopping over to Neely for a legitimate monkey. Consequently, someone came for Mr. Britches right away, or anyway came for him two days after Aunt Willa had called, which was about as right away as you could hope for from a state-supported institution. Aunt Willa had him dressed to travel in his porkpie hat and his handsome blue blazer and his black Keds sneakers, and Mr. Britches was squatting comfortably atop his flagpole when the green station wagon from Ashboro pulled out of Scales Street onto the boulevard and made direct for the curbing in front of Miss Pettigrew's house. The driver got out and stretched himself. He was dressed in khaki from the feet up, kind of like Jungle Jim, but I do not believe he possessed much of a natural instinct for chimpanzees since he passed through the gateway, along the sidewalk, and climbed the steps to the front porch without ever noticing just what it was that had been run up the flagpole, but when Aunt Willa came out of the house and commenced to reel in the tether that fellow did some extremely serious noticing and in fact could not seem to stop himself from gawking at the porkpie hat and the blazer and the sneakers and the entire monkey in general. He did not appear willing to catch up Mr. Britches in his arms when Aunt Willa offered him the chance to and he did not appear willing to take Mr. Britches by his hairy hand when that opportunity presented itself. Instead he seemed to prefer simple gawking and he persisted in it as Aunt Willa hauled Mr. Britches up the front steps and then turned around and hauled him back down again along with his suitcase, or anyway that's what the man from the zoo called it though it was really not anything but a little canvas valise.

"What's in that suitcase?" he said.

"Clothes," Aunt Willa told him.

"Monkey's clothes?" he said.

And Aunt Willa moved her head just enough to indicate yes.

"Ma'm, our animals don't wear clothes," he said.

And Aunt Willa did not move her head any and did not open her mouth any but just stood where she was about as animated as a treestump.

"They don't wear anything," he said.

And Aunt Willa watched him with one of her most accomplished bloodless expressions.

"Nothing at all," he said.

And Aunt Willa continued to exhibit all the liveliness of a cinderblock.

"Not anything," he said. "Nada. Zilch. You got me?"

And he glared at Aunt Willa who watched him watch her but did not move her head and did not open her mouth.

"Lady," he said, "we're running a zoo, not a supper club. Now get this monkey naked and bring him out to the car."

So Aunt Willa set the valise down on the sidewalk and helped Mr. Britches out of his sneakers and out of his blazer and out from under his porkpie hat and then carried him through the gateway to the back of the station wagon, where she attempted to give him over to the man from the zoo who did not show any more of a natural inclination towards monkeys than he had previously, and consequently Aunt Willa herself deposited Mr. Britches in the steel hound cage and latched the door and shut the tailgate, and I do not believe much of anybody saw him off except for her and except for Jump Garrison who gassed up the station wagon and then stood by the pumps holding the nozzle as he watched Mr. Britches go away down the street with his little hairy fingers around the bars of his cage.

And that was about all of Miss Pettigrew except for the odds and ends and she had lived sufficiently long enough to accumulate a vast assortment of them which Mr. Conrad Rackley and the two chinless Masseys had not even begun to deplete, so Aunt Willa contracted with Mr. Ellis Spainhour of Yanceyville who primarily handled cattle and tobacco but took on estate work when it came his way. The announcement arrived a week and a day after

Mr. Britches's departure and it was addressed Occupant so was mine to open since Daddy got all the Mr. Louis W. Benfield sr. mail and Momma got all the Mrs. Inez Yount Benfield mail and since Aunt Sadie did not ever send me five dollars on my birthday anymore which excluded me from any sort of postal involvement except for a monthly *Boy's Life* and that wasn't even in an envelope. So Momma set aside all the Occupant mail for me along with the occasional Resident flier from the grocery store and in the evenings just before supper me and Daddy would sit down in front of the television and open our mail together. He generally got the significant items like bills and bank statements and requests for donations to the Waccamaw Boy's Home while I generally got pizza coupons and sample boxes of catfood, but a week and a day after Mr. Britches's departure I opened up the auction announcement and read it out loud to Daddy, who called Momma in from the kitchen and had me read it out loud to her. It was surely the most vital piece of Occupant correspondence I had ever received.

We do not get too many auctions in Neely. We do not even have a regular flea market, and most usually furniture out on a front lawn means an eviction and not a yard sale. Consequently news of the Pettigrew auction touched off some noticeable local fervor, and even those folks who cannot hardly make the mortgage from month to month began to discuss and debate and speculate over just precisely what portion of the estate they would purchase. Of course there was not a tremendous amount of estate left since a goodly part of it had already been hauled off to the West Virginia end of Kentucky, but there was a sufficient assortment of furniture, kitchen utensils, and personal effects for people to get venomous over. The auction itself was held about noon on the Saturday of the Labor Day weekend, which gave everybody a full ten days to tap their noses and tug at their ears and scratch their topnotches and just generally brush up on various bidding techniques, and Mr. Spainhour and his assistants had arrived early enough to haul the auctionable items outside so by the time a crowd began to collect in earnest it looked like the house had gotten sick and thrown up all over the front yard. There were little bits and pieces of the estate everywhere, loose and in boxfuls and stacked on top of each other and strewn across tabletops and draped over shrubbery and canted up against tree-trunks and piled all roundabout the wrought iron fence, and people swarmed in through the gate and covered over the yard and they picked up this and poked at that and fiddled with one thing and studied another. I'll be the first to tell you there were certainly some grand items to be had. I recollect an upright piano in passable condition and a brass coattrack with all sorts of colorful bends and twists to it and an oversized pitcher and wash basin—what Momma called exquisite spongeware—and some kind of mahogany monstrosity with lion's feet that I could not purely decipher a purpose for but which was entertaining to look at nonetheless and a solid silver fruit bowl and a handsome mantel clock with a clipper ship etched into the glass of it and a table lamp made from a wagon wheel hub and a velvet upholstered divan, Daddy called it, which was pretty enough to look at but did not seem the sort of thing you could watch TV from. However, most everything else was not grand and was not especially appealing but was just old and mildewed and dusty and termite-eaten, and all the books and dishes and clothes and framed pictures and tables and chairs and boxfuls of bric-a-brac lay scattered across the front lawn like they had been turned up with a grubbing hoe. There was not anything that did not have some grime to it, and since there was not anything that did not get touched or picked up or otherwise handled somehow the grime circulated freely onto fingers and palms and subsequently onto shirtfronts and necks and faces and pantlegs. So by the time Mr. Ellis Spainhour called for the auction to commence and drove us into a corner of the front yard, we carried a good part of the available filth with us and looked for all the world like a band of refugees.

The auction got underway promptly at noon and Mr. Spainhour started things off with the upright piano. Mr. Rollie Cobb pinched his nose, pulled at both his ears, and snapped his fingers twice in an attempt to bid ten dollars for it, but Mr. Spainhour told him the bidding would start at two hundred and fifty dollars instead and Mr. Rollie Cobb put his hands in his pockets so as to avoid any sort of temporary bankruptcy. For a spell afterwards there was not any pinching or pulling or snapping to be seen from anybody, but once Mr. Spainhour had provided us with an extremely flattering and altogether fictitious description of the instrument followed by a second and then a third request for two hundred and fifty dollars, a man on the sidewalk outside the fence waved his arm at Mr. Spainhour, a man in a floppy tennis hat and sunglasses and green plaid pants, a man from somewhere else who obviously had a far more refined understanding of pianos than any of us did. But just as soon as Mr. Spainhour had his two hundred and fifty dollars, he wanted two hundred and seventy-five and straightaway he got that from a woman midway back in the crowd who looked like some sort of exotic variety of Oregon Hill French but turned out to be a High Point Pembroke. So the man from somewhere else was pressed to three hundred dollars and then to three hundred and twenty dollars and when it looked like he would own a piano at last Mr. Wiley Gant scratched underneath his hat and drove the price up higher which I do not believe he intended or was ever aware of and which seemed an extraordinary thing for him to do seeing as how he had no right arm after the elbow. The High Point Pembroke got back in at three hundred and thirty-five and her and the man from somewhere else were joined by a distinguished grey-haired gentleman in a blue suit who Mrs. Phillip J. King said was a senator. The three of them together were responsible for all of the rest of the bidding except for a brief interruption by Mr. Wyatt Benbow who wrestled most mercilessly with his chin until he got recognized at $372.50, but much to his apparent relief he was immediately passed by the senator who gave way to the High Point Pembroke, who was vanquished at length by the man from somewhere else. The whole business grew a little tedious at the end so we were all pleased to see the piano going, going, and then finally gone though Mr. Wyatt Benbow shook his head and tried to look sick about it.

The lion-footed mahogany monstrosity got dispatched with next. It went to the High Point Pembroke after some furious bidding, and I think she was fairly pleased to have purchased it although it did not seem to me she had any clearer conception of exactly what it was than the rest of us did, so I suppose by way of consolation she bought the mantel clock also since its purpose was not in any way mysterious or indecipherable. The senator made off with the silver fruit bowl and the wagon hub table lamp while Mr. Estelle Singletary succeeded in buying the exquisite spongeware under what appeared to be a threat of death. Mrs. Mary Margaret Vance Needham got the brass coatrack, and in an exhilarating display of financial abandonment and serious chin-yanking Mr. Wyatt Benbow came away with the velvet upholstered divan. Daddy said it was just the thing for a grocery store magnate to rest his hams upon. And that was the last of the truly grand items though a few marginally grand items did show up here and there in the midst of the innumerable ordinary odds and ends that remained, but after the divan went to Mr. Benbow all the nose pulling and ear tugging and head scratching seemed to lose some of its novelty. So I did not pay much attention to the auction for a time and instead retired to the wrought iron fence with Daddy and Mr. Russell Newberry and Mr. Phillip J. King and Mr. Bobby Ligon of Draper, who all smoked together and spat and then launched directly into a vigorous discussion of the higher sciences. What touched it off was Mr. Phillip J. King's terrier, Itty Bit. Mr. Phillip J. King had her with him on a leash and, being the nervous and thoroughly idiotic creature that she was, Itty Bit passed the time in barking fairly persistently at nothing much in particular. We'd all grown somewhat accustomed to the aggravation of it, so nobody paid any attention to Itty Bit except for Mr. Bobby Ligon, who was sitting on his heels just to her backside, and he spent a full minute and a half in devoted contemplation of Itty Bit's rearend, tilting his head first towards one shoulder and then towards the other.

"You know," he said at last, "I wish you'd just look how that little dog's shithole opens up every time he barks."

And Daddy looked at Mr. Russell Newberry and Mr. Russell Newberry looked back at Daddy and then the two of them together looked at Mr. Phillip J. King who said, "What?"

"I said," Mr. Bobby Ligon told him, "I wish you'd look how that little dog's shithole opens up every time he barks."

"Every time she barks," Mr. Phillip J. King replied.

"Yes sir," Mr. Bobby Ligon said, "every time."

Naturally we all looked at Itty Bit's shithole, and sure enough every time she barked it popped open which was a matter of great wonderment to all of us until Daddy commenced to explain it away. He said the activity at Itty Bit's rear section was simply an illustration of one of Mr. Newton's laws of nature, a law that had not been formulated specifically for terriers' shitholes but would work there as well as anyplace else. According to Daddy it was all a matter of balanced thrust. The barking tended to knock the dog backwards and the shithole kicked her forwards so the both of them served to cancel each other out. "Now if Itty Bit could just work her shithole without working her mouth," Daddy said, "why then she could skim along the ground like a jet."

"No!" Mr. Bobby Ligon exclaimed.

"Yes," Daddy replied, and Mr. Russell Newberry and Mr. Phillip J. King shook their heads yes also.

"Ain't that astounding," Mr. Bobby Ligon said.

"It truly is," Daddy told him.

And I do believe it was sometime during the course of what Daddy called his shithole disquisition that Momma made her purchase since not me or him either saw her make it, blinded as we were by the marvels of nature. She bought an oval hand mirror, not a very fashionable little implement but useful enough. The glass was noticeably aged and discolored around the edges but otherwise highly reflective, and the casing and stem were done up in tiny silver-plated rosettes that ran roundabout the whole business on a vine and were joined opposite the glass by Miss Pettigrew's initials, or most of them anyway since the A had fallen off, which left a little M beside a big P beside a brass rivet. So Momma had bought a nice enough item, but she did not seem inclined to show it off and carried it under her arm when she came back to the fence hunting me and Daddy, and when Daddy asked her what she had Momma just said, "A mirror," and did not bring it out for us to see. She had come to tell us she was through with auctions for a spell and would be going home directly, and Mr. Phillip J. King asked her would his wife be going home directly with her, but Momma told him Mrs. Phillip J. King was waiting to bid on the naked sabre and so would possibly be awhile. "Very possibly," Daddy added.

So Momma left us for home and me and Daddy and Mr. Phillip J. King and Mr. Russell Newberry leaned backwards against the wrought iron fence with our elbows through the palings while Mr. Bobby Ligon squatted unsupported on his heels beside us. They all smoked and spat and told stories and made terrier shithole jokes and I spat some myself and partway listened and partway watched the mayor and Miss Pettigrew's belongings get sold off piece by ragged piece. Now that all the grand items had been dispensed with and all the marginally grand items had been taken as well, there was not much of anything left but the shabby, mildewed, termite-eaten stuff, so naturally I was not expecting to see anything of interest when Mr. Spainhour took up by the leg a small upholstered footstool and held it high over his head. Just the sight of it made my ears tingle and straight off I could not figure why my ears should tingle on account of an upholstered footstool; I couldn't exactly figure what tingling ears meant anyway. But shortly I recollected an acquaintance with that footstool which I myself had seen under Miss Pettigrew's very feet in the month of March I am certain of 1977 I do believe. We were selling toothbrushes for the James K. Polk middle school baseball team with the money to go for new uniforms. The old uniforms

188

had developed holes in all the crotches and Coach Mangum did
not think it seemly to turn a squad loose in them, so we were
attempting to generate funds with Pepsodent toothbrushes in an
extraordinary assortment of colors. The coach reasoned they
would be easier to move than magazine subscriptions or seventy-
five-cent nut clusters, and as it turned out they were fairly easy to
move. I sold two to Daddy and three to Momma. Mr. Phillip J.
King bought a red one as a gift for Mrs. Phillip J. King. The
Reverend Richard Crockett Shelton purchased a pair following
one of Momma's sleepy meatloaf dinners. My barber Mr. Lacy
went in halves on one with his partner. I inflicted two yellow ones
and a blue one on Mr. Russell Newberry, who soaks his teeth at
night in a dish. And Miss Pettigrew bought up the remaining half
dozen, which is precisely where the footstool comes in.

Of course I had not intended to sell any toothbrushes to Miss
Pettigrew; it seemed to me Momma and Daddy and Mr. and Mrs.
Russell Newberry were good for four or five more between them.
But Momma suggested I drop by her house, and when I resisted
the first suggestion she made another one and when I resisted that
one too she gave me two bottles of damson preserves in a basket
and showed me the door. I guess I circled Miss Pettigrew's lot for
forty-five minutes trying to convince myself that Miss Pettigrew
was as regular and ordinary as Momma believed her to be. I'd
heard at school she'd cut off your feet and stew them in a pot,
which had seemed ridiculous at the time but was commencing to
weigh somewhat heavily on my imagination as I passed around
the house from the frontside to the backside to the frontside
again. However, at length I reasoned it was best to risk my feet,
the danger seeming altogether remote and improbable, than to
return home with the damson preserves and surrender up my
backside. So I went in through the gateway, along the sidewalk,
up the front steps, and onto the porch, where I beat on the door
with the fleshy part of my hand and then put my ear to one of the
panels and heard the flooring in the foyer creak and pop.
Straightaway the deadbolt shot back, the doorknob jiggled, and

the heavy front door swung open to reveal Aunt Willa in her usual smock and scowl ensemble, and she invited me on into the house if you can call a jerk of the head an invitation. "Hello," I said once the door shut tight behind me, "my name is Louis Benfield and I'm selling toothbrushes for the baseball team at James K. Polk middle school," and then I raised up and sought out some eye contact. Coach Mangum told us eye contact was an essential facet of good salesmanship. But my pupils were still fluctuating on account of the sudden and general gloom so I could not find Aunt Willa's eyes or any other part of her to focus in on which turned out to be understandable since I was by myself in the foyer except for an umbrella jug that did not seem in the leastways interested in toothbrushes. And me and the umbrella jug had not hardly struck up a meaningful acquaintance when Aunt Willa came back and led me out of the foyer before I could even begin to tell her I was Louis Benfield from the James K. Polk middle school.

I followed her down a short, dark hallway, across two broad, dark sitting rooms, and to the door of what looked to be a closet which when opened gave onto a tiny den where Miss Pettigrew sat by the lone window with a book in her lap.

"Hello," I said.

"You are Louis Benfield," Miss Pettigrew told me, "Inez Benfield's boy, and you've come bearing gifts and toothbrushes."

I forgot myself momentarily and put the inside of my mouth on exhibition.

"You see," Miss Pettigrew said and smiled at me in the most delightful sort of way.

And I told her, "Yes ma'am" out of sheer reflex and politeness though actually I did not see much of anything at the time.

"Please sit down, Louis Benfield," Miss Pettigrew said, motioning me to a chair, and I closed my mouth and took it. "You have something for me?" she asked.

"Yes ma'm," I said and leaned forward to give her the basket and the preserves.

"How nice, how very nice." Miss Pettigrew held one of the bottles up to the window and looked through it. "Lovely. Tell your mother they are simply lovely."

"Yes ma'm," I said.

"Beautiful preserves," Miss Pettigrew added.

"Yes ma'm," I said.

And as Miss Pettigrew rearranged the preserves in the basket prior to setting it on the rug beside her chair, a great surge of vigorous activity commenced on the floorboards overhead. It sounded to me like a herd of squirrels in a footrace and had set in so suddenly I near about leapt straight out the window without so much as a goodbye.

Apparently Miss Pettigrew noticed my anxiety because she put her hand to my wrist and told me, "It's just him," and then she rolled her eyes upwards the way apostles used to.

"Yes ma'm," I said, "just him," and I tried to sit back and be comfortable.

Miss Pettigrew soothed me somewhat with a few very bland and harmless remarks of the sort adults are generally prone to, and by the time she got around to exhaling a pair of well-well's, which is what they all get around to eventually, I was feeling sufficiently bold to seek out some eye contact. But I had just barely set in on the crisis at James K. Polk middle school when Miss Pettigrew held up her hand and stopped me. "No need for that," she told me.

"Yes ma'm," I said, "no need for that," and of a sudden the eye contact seemed to me an incredibly bad idea so I made some contact with the floor instead and that was when I first noticed Miss Pettigrew's upholstered footstool. It was sitting flush in the middle of the only patch of sunlight that fell across the rug. There wasn't anything extraordinary about it and I don't imagine I would have even recollected it if not for Miss Pettigrew's feet atop it though more truly on account of Miss Pettigrew's ankles, which were connected to Miss Pettigrew's feet which were resting atop the upholstered footstool. I had never before seen and never hope to see again such astoundingly white skin on a living human. It was not your regular old folks white skin all pale and waxy and eat up with blood vessels, but was more in the line of your stately princesses white skin, what people call fair, and best as I could determine it was about the color of fatback. I don't imagine there was anything whiter anywhere else in the house and I do not even suppose there was another patch of skin so pure and unfreckled for three city blocks roundabout. I tell you they were the most unpuckered, ungathered, unbesmirched ankles I've ever been witness to and were a matter of considerable wonderment to me, considerable wonderment, and I'm generally not the sort to get worked up over girls and such, especially over old women, especially over old women's ankles. Occasionally I'll find myself hypnotized and somewhat nauseous on account of a fuzzy open-toed slipper, but usually it is the vitality of it that affects me, and Miss Pettigrew's ankles did not possess any vitality to speak of. They were altogether stationary and lifeless. I just suppose in a place where everything else is scarred and spotted and interrupted all over it's pleasing to find even two ankles' worth of purity and perfection.

So I watched Miss Pettigrew's ankles in a highly discourteous and unforgivable sort of way, and I do believe Miss Pettigrew thoroughly wore out her stock of polite observations before she finally resorted to addressing me directly. "Louis?" she said.

"Yes ma'm?" And I drew off from the footstool to look Miss Pettigrew in the face which was hardly so striking a thing as her ankles and seemed worn and ancient and inhumanly weary everywhere but the eyes. Miss Pettigrew's eyes were not in the leastways antiques.

"Louis, tell me," she said, "do you ever look at the stars?"

"Ma'm?"

"Do you ever go out in the summertime and lie on you back in the grass and look up at the sky?" Miss Pettigrew said, and turned her head towards the lone window, which gave onto a very slight portion of the backyard.

"Yes ma'm," I told her, "sometimes. I mean I used to, I used to when I was little but I don't much anymore."

"When you were little?" Miss Pettigrew said, and of a sudden pondered me straight on until I could not look at her any longer.

"Yes ma'm," I said.

"And how old are you now, Louis?" she asked me.

"Thirteen, ma'm. But I'll be fourteen in June."

"Ah," Miss Pettigrew said, "my apologies."

She watched me with those eyes of hers until I wanted to seep off into the cellar through a crack in the floor, and only after a prodigious and excruciating silence did she fetch up a little brass bell off the windowsill and ring it sharply. "Good day, Louis Benfield," Miss Pettigrew told me. "Do give my regards to your people." And I bowed at the waist for some reason I have yet to decipher since it is not and has never been my habit to bow at the waist, after which I followed Aunt Willa into the foyer where she paid me cash money for a half dozen toothbrushes, mostly blue ones.

I left that place in an excessive hurry. I don't know precisely why now, but at the time it seemed the circumstances called for an excessive hurry so I provided one. I did not bother with the front steps but left the porch for the sidewalk and exited through the iron gateway at the height of my stride. As I recollect it now, I ran hard for three blocks, trotted two more, and then walked the rest of the way home, where Momma was waiting for me on the glider in Daddy's grey sweater and with her arms wrapped around herself.

"Did you see her?" she asked me almost before I could get into the front yard.

"Yes ma'm," I said.

"How did she look?" Momma wanted to know, and she got up off the glider and met me on the top step.

"She looked old, Momma. She looked old and tired."

"Well, did you talk to her?" Momma asked me.

"Yes ma'm. I talked to her."

193

"And what did she say?" Momma wanted to know.

"She asked me did I ever lie on my back in the grass and look up at the stars."

"Did she?" Momma said.

"Yes ma'm," I told her, "she did."

Machine Dreams

JAYNE ANNE PHILLIPS

The Secret Country: Mitch

I was born on the farm in Randolph County, 1910, lived there until I was six. Then went to Raynell with my aunt and her husband. He was a conductor on the railroad—big business then, everything went by rail. It was a new job for him and not traditional in the family; they had all been household farmers and worked the mines. Mines weren't like they are now. Then, there was no automation, mostly crawlspace, and the coal hauled out by mule. Three of the brothers died in the mines, including my father, but I never really knew him, never even remember seeing him. I know he was there sometimes in the summer, because there are photographs.

My mother lived at the farm during her confinement and left right after I was born. The birth certificate gives her name as Icie Younger, but no one ever told me anything about her. Her people were from down around Grafton and she went back to them. When I was selling road equipment for the State I used to travel through there. Asked after the family several times but no one had ever heard of them.

I grew up living always with one or another of the sisters. In the beginning there were twelve kids in that family, seven boys and five girls; and the farm was five hundred acres. Bess was the youngest, twenty when I was born, and she took care of me. The boys, my uncles, worked all over the county once they were grown, but the sisters stayed home until they married. Even after, they came home in the summers—the sisters and the wives of the brothers, with all the children. The men came for a few weeks and made repairs, helped the old man. They grew their own food but didn't farm much on the rest of the land—too mountainous and rocky—but all those hills were rich-timbered. The family had already started selling timber to the Eastern businessmen, who came in and clear-cut and paid a fraction of what the trees were worth. Later the mineral rights were sold as well. Hampsons had been in that valley a hundred years with just their neighbors, and didn't understand much about business.

The farm was beautiful, two big white frame houses cross-pasture from each other, the smaller a guest house, and a plank sidewalk built up off the ground so the women wouldn't dirty the hems of their dresses on Sundays. The houses had full circular porches with fancy trim, and a black iron fence to keep the barn animals out of the yard. The women held church socials and picnics. They picked berries near the barn and used their big hats for baskets, then were all day making pies.

Church was the only social life, and Coalton Church was a half hour's wagon ride away; in warm months there was something going on nearly every night. Don't ask me what. But my uncles had built that little church for the town, and the family gave the land for the graveyard. It's still called Hampson Cemetery, and most of them are buried there: the grandparents, the parents, all the brothers but Calvin, who left home at seventeen and disappeared out West, and all the sisters but Bess, who is ninety now and the only one left living after Ava died.

Ava died at a hundred, think of that. You remember her funeral. That was the old family plot. Snowing so hard no one could drive past the gate and they had to walk the casket up. Bess took the death hard. The old house was just down that road, out the Punkin Town turn-off. Foundation still standing, but that trail is steep mud in bad weather.

All those winters the family stayed put, just ate food they'd dried or put up in pantries, and venison the old man shot. They kept one path shoveled through the snow to the barn, and the walls of the path were as high as a man's shoulders.

I know all this because I heard about it, growing up—I was too small to remember, really. Just a few things.

I was lying in the grass and watching my uncles hammer slate on the barn roof. They were all big men dressed in broadcloth shirts. They swung the hammers full circle, from the shoulder, as they drove the nails. Tall pine ladders lay against the barn walls and thick yellow ropes hung down. The slates were shining like mirrors.

And once I looked out a window at snow. Snow as far as you could see, pasture fences covered and trees gone, so their top limbs fanned out of the snow like spikes. Nothing but snow. Snow like an ocean.

In the winter, I was the only child.

I was with Bess at first. We were in the big house by ourselves, except for the old parents, and at times the brothers stayed a few days. The wagon was hitched on Sundays, and not even then in January, February. Snow too deep for the wheels. When Bess was a girl, she'd gone to finishing school for a year in Lynchburg, so she'd been farther from home than any of the other women. She was the youngest, and pampered. The older sisters would tell a lot later how she'd been sent away to learn to ride a horse like something other than a savage.

Bess had been married once before; she was young and it was kept secret in the family. Divorce was rare then. The first husband? He wasn't from around here. Seems to me his name was Thorn. She probably came back from finishing school and had big ideas at eighteen, nineteen. Left with this Thorn and went out West; I don't think she knew him very well. Just within a month or so, she wired home from St. Louis—he'd taken off and left her out there. It was my father, Warwick, went to get her. He was closest to Bess in age and had warned her against leaving in the first place. They booked passage back on the train, but it was near Christmas and a winter of bad blizzards; they were weeks getting home.

Afterward Warwick was very protective of her. All this was before I was born and no one ever talked about it. Why would they? What's the difference, it don't matter.

Bess stayed there on the farm for seven years then, and helped—putting up food, companion to her mother. Maybe she felt chastised, but the family would not have said a word to her. She was like a mother to me.

The brothers all had parcels of the land but were twenty, fifty miles distant. They farmed or mined and drifted by the homeplace every few weeks, on horseback, alone; women and children didn't travel in the winter. My father, Warwick, was the only brother worked in towns a while and wore a suit. Later he went back to the mines, but then he was a wholesaler for a dry goods company. Just a few weeks after he brought Bess home from St. Louis, Warwick brought this bride of his to the farm and moved her in. Then he left, as Bess tells it, and was only back twice the months the girl was there. She was a girl he'd met in his work, a working girl. She never gave any facts about herself, Bess says, and went away after I was born. Went away as soon as she could travel, and sent no word to anyone again. *Warwick paid for a wet nurse half the winter, but there is more to a baby than feeding it.* I never saw my father, not really. *You did see him, you don't remember. He had the new wife, but by then you were accustomed to us. Then he died when you were still in skirts.* . . .

They gave the impression it was his new wife didn't want me, but I knew it was him. I don't remember what he looked like, except from pictures. I just remember him yelling at me once or twice. He never did a damn thing for me, never noticed me. One summer—I was real young, at the farm—I had a baby coon. My father had his rifle and was standing over me. It was out at the edge of the fields, away from the house, where the grass was tall. He said go into the field and let that coon go, you can't keep a wild creature. I held the coon and walked in. The grass was over my head, deep and high. He started shooting. The gun made two sounds, a big crack from behind, like thunder, and a high zing close by, like a stinging fly close to your face. The grass was moving and he was shooting where the grass moved. I stayed still for a long time. I don't know what I thought. Years later I asked Bess about it and she said wasn't Warwick did that at all, was a neighbor man, because it was a danger to have coons when there was rabies in the county.

I don't know. He was well liked. There is an old homemade album Bess must have pasted together. The pictures are taken outside the old house, and everyone is dressed in their best. My father is wearing a woman's big hat and posing like Napoleon.

They had his funeral there at the house. The brothers made the casket out of pine board, and the lid was kept shut. That was the practice in that country; if a man died in the mines, his coffin was closed for services, nailed shut, even if the man was unmarked. They would have put Warwick's coffin on the long table in the parlor, the best room. The window shades in that room were sewn with gold tassels. Silk tassels, and children weren't to touch them. The parlor was seldom used, but it was dusted everyday, spotless, and the floor was polished once a week with linseed rags fastened onto a broom.

It was soon after Warwick's funeral Bess left the farm.

She came to Bellington because it was the closest good-size town, and started working as secretary to Dr. Bond. Bess would have been in her late twenties, an old maid. She met Clayton because he was Doc Bond's younger brother.

Doc Bond and Doc Jonas were the only two doctors here besides the veterinarian. Clayton was in the construction business, always was, so the three men started the hospital. Bought two houses; Bess and Clayton lived in the smaller and built onto the bigger one. Knocked down walls inside, built wards. The modern addition that stretches out from the back now wasn't there then; the place was much smaller. Didn't need to be so big; most people birthed and died at home. And Bess has lived here, in this house across the alley, for sixty years. She sold the hospital twenty years ago, but they still get mail addressed to her. She learned a lot about nursing by working for Doc Bond, keeping the office, helping with examinations. Doc Bond died a few years after the hospital got going, and Clayton was building roads, so Bess ended up doing most of it herself—ran the hospital, the kitchen, hired nurses, did the books. Katie Sue and Chuck grew up running back and forth between the house and the hospital.

There was so much talk about Doc Jonas in the later years that Bess didn't like to let him use the hospital, but for a long time hers was the only one in town and she couldn't turn his patients away.

Some swore by Jonas, others said he was a scoundrel. I grew up with his son, Reb, who we always called Doc after his father. Doctors' sons then became doctors as well, inherited their fathers' patients same as another boy would inherit a farm or a storefront. Reb never cared much for doctoring, but he liked being called Doc and he liked not having to go to war when the time came. He and I had some scrapes, all through high school while I was living with Bess and Clayton.

But that was later. Right after Warwick died, I was sent to live with Ava, my aunt ten years older than Bess, and her husband, the train man.

I lived with Ava and Eban eight years but was gone every summer, to the farm, to one cousin or another. Eban was a railroad porter, then a conductor. We lived at Raynell, down near the Kentucky border. That town has nearly disappeared now, but when the trains still moved goods and passengers, Raynell was a big junction for Southern Rail. There was a pride about the railroad then—a railroad uniform in the '20s had almost as much respect as military dress. Eban wore blue trousers, suitcoat and vest, and a visored hat trimmed in braid. He wore white shirts with cuffs that Ava was always ironing. She would stand at the ironing board, a broad wooden one, while the iron heated on the stove.

If Bess was the youngest and prettiest of those Hampsons, Ava was the most stubborn. She was spirited and tall, a handsome woman even if her face was plain. Knew her mind and fought plenty with Eban. They had two little girls, just babies when I went there. Ava kept me out of school all she could, to watch them and help her do the garden. Train ran right back of the house, right the length of the town. Houses shook when the train passed. Kids always played on the tracks, tag and roughhousing. Ava had a fear about her kids getting too close to the trains. The younger girl was slow, never said a word till she was three or four, and collected things the way blackbirds will, shiny things. That was my cousin Emily. She would always be going down to the tracks to pick up pebbles or bits of glass. She never really learned to talk but would sit and stare at anything bright, a gas light or a coal fire. That child died young. Just took sick and died suddenly. They stood her coffin up against the wall; the box wasn't very big, about as high as a man's waist, and it was narrow at the foot the way homemade coffins were. The church at Raynell gave a velvet altar cloth, deep red, to put inside.

Ava arranged the flowers all around. Seems to me she asked the children who lived near to come to the service and sing a hymn. Yes, she did, and the shortest ones were in the front, closer to the coffin; I was nearly ten years old by then and stood in back.

Ava was distracted for weeks. A neighbor woman came in to look after the other daughter and me.

Near that time the B&O Railroad discovered they had employed a leper and, for want of any other plan, deposited the man on forest land by the tracks near Raynell. Townspeople were alarmed. It was said this man was a Chinese known as Li Sung, banished by his own government because of his disease. He had a brother in Washington, D.C., who was a tailor, and he traveled to that city to work in his brother's shop. He wore gloves to cover the lesions on his hands, but somehow his brother discovered the secret. Or maybe Li Sung confessed. Anyway, he was turned out and wandered for a time, then finally got a job maintaining track for the B&O. The railroad often hired laborers who didn't speak English, and paid them very low. Li Sung never removed his gloves and co-workers became suspicious, so the rail superintendent sent him to a doctor well-known in that area. The leprosy was confirmed. B&O had no policy for such a case, so they isolated Li Sung in a boxcar at the rear of the train and transported him all over the state, asking privately after hospitals. No hospital would accept him, and passengers began avoiding the railroad. B&O lost workers on all lines, since no one knew which train pulled the car where the leper was kept. Finally it was decided to put Li Sung in some isolated place with supplies and make him stay there. The railroad sent the B&O surgeon and a caretaker out to prepare a site near Raynell. They found a grassy knoll near the river and put up a World War I army tent with a stout pole in the middle, then camped to await the leper's arrival. The B&O brought him in by night. Employees stood aside as Li Sung was ordered to the tent, then they burned the boxcar and left on the train.

The surgeon stayed behind in the town to arrange for Li Sung's meals, and offered a small subsidy to any widow willing to prepare his food. The food was to be delivered once a day in disposable wooden trays provided by the County, and Li Sung himself was to burn the trays at his campfire.

Ava had done nothing for weeks but mend and starch all the dead child's clothes, smoothing each piece and packing them away in clean boxes. She'd ironed even the handkerchiefs and undergarments, but it was all done and now she volunteered to cook for the leper. Eban tried to talk her out of it, but for the first

202

time she seemed more herself, so he signed a paper saying he allowed the endangerment of his wife and family and would not hold the railroad accountable.

In just a day, the County delivered six months' supply of wooden trays and stacked them like firewood on the south wall of the porch.

The appearance of the trays got the town talking. There were fears Li Sung would bathe in the river and contaminate the water. The railroad surgeon walked with Ava and me to show us the route to the tent, ten minutes' walk along Ransom's Ridge. We put the tray (bread and cow cheese and cold grits, as it was a warm day) on a stump fifteen feet from the site. And the surgeon yelled for Li Sung to come out.

He did, and stood by the tent pole, barefoot, dressed in a white button-collar shirt, suspenders, and the wool trousers of a winter rail uniform. The trousers were too large for him and he wore bulky work gloves, tied to his wrists with twine. He was slight and looked younger than Ava, who must have been in her late thirties then. Not many people in those parts had seen an Oriental. His black hair was long like a woman's and hung in one thin braid down his back. His eyes were slanted, almost like slits, and hid any expression. He stood politely and waited for us to talk. The surgeon yelled—as though the leper was deaf—not to go into the river or touch the water, to fill his bucket by holding to the handle and dipping the bucket in, and to burn all his trays and the paper used to wrap his food. He was told to eat with his fingers, as no one could solve the problem of utensils. To each instruction, the leper called back, "Yes, yes," in an accent. Anytime I heard him talk, he had a tone of question in his voice. He understood some English. The surgeon said, "Do you see the bucket?" and the leper pointed to it.

The first month, Ava put up his food every morning and carried it out herself. She would be gone about an hour and watched to see that the leper ate. She spoke to him a bit and he talked back, though sometimes only repeating what she'd said to him.

He was cheerful and often waiting outside the tent when she arrived. She took him a tin coffeepot, a supply of tea and coffee, a mirror, scissors, needle and thread, and a comb. She gave him some of Eban's old clothes, but Li Sung never wore them; he wore only his railroad uniforms, which he laundered himself with soap provided by the railroad. After Li Sung's death, it was discovered he'd saved Eban's shirts and trousers and sewn them layered onto his blankets during the cold. But that was later.

Early on, Ava tried to give him a dog for companionship, but he chased the animal back to her as though afraid he would infect it.

He was grateful for the smallest kindness; the railroad men must have been very brusque to him. I took no liberties and addressed him as "Sir" or "Mister." I would put the tray down and back up to the edge of the woods; he would nod and bow, pick up the food, and then sit cross-legged by the tent, eating. He seemed to feel he showed thanks by eating in silence with great concentration. I went closer again. Later we spoke briefly or sat without speaking. He knew some words but understood the ideas behind many more.

I hadn't been outside my house in weeks. Early mornings in the woods were so quiet and green, all the wildflowers blooming and the sounds of the river so cool. The clearing was like a church, the sky arched over and deeply blue. I think I talked aloud because I knew he didn't understand all I said. I told him my little girl had died and showed him in motions. She was . . . this tall, etc. He knew someone had died and folded his hands, then pointed to his eyes and touched his cheeks. When I describe these simple gestures, I don't mean to give the impression he was not smart. I believe he was quite intelligent, and wishing to comfort me. He gave me to understand that he also had children, two, in his homeland. He would not see them again. I explained he might send letters, messages, but he said, "No, no," holding his finger to his lips.

I wanted him to see Emily so badly that I took him a photograph of her, knowing once he touched it I could not take it back. I put the picture on his tray. He understood at once and looked at the image carefully; then he bowed his head to me in gratitude and put the picture in his breast pocket. He placed his hand there and said, "Yes, safe. Safe." "Yes," I said to him, and knew she was, when before I'd felt only the injustice.

Safe. He knew that word because the railroad men had said it loudly, many times, about the woods and the tent, and where they were taking him.

By July Ava was much improved and began keeping house again. I was sent with the trays; Ava went with me on Sundays. She told me always to call out to the leper and make a remark or two that required answer. This was important, she said. The man could go crazy if he never spoke with anyone.

Some boys from the town tormented Li Sung that summer, but he didn't know they were making fun. A few threw apples at him and he picked them up, nodding his head like the fruit was a present. If anyone came too close, he stood in the door of his tent, holding his arms over his head and calling out in his accent, "Unclean, unclean!"

Winters were hard in that country. A lumber company donated wood, and some rail workers arrived in September to build a shack. Li Sung sat at a distance and watched the work. The old tent was burned where it stood after the leper transferred his belongings, and a low fence was strung around the shack. The people of Raynell donated a wood stove, feather tick, and ax, and allowed the leper to gather and chop his own wood from near the shack in early morning.

Snow was deep for five months. I walked out once or twice a week, pulling a sled of provisions. Ava sent a cache of preserved foods, canned vegetables, jams, and meat jerky. The leper constructed a rabbit trap and used it with some success.

He got through the cold weather but wouldn't talk anymore in the spring. I came with the trays every day again; he would only look out and pull away. Ava was concerned and walked out with me. She had dressed as though on a social call and stood talking in front of the shack. *Mr. Li Sung? I know you are listening. Won't you come out?* He never answered, so we hid in the woods to watch for him. He looked just the same, though shabbier, peering from the door. Then he walked out and stood beside the tray. He stood for a full five minutes, looking down the ridge like he was trying to see trace of us in the distance.

Ava insisted I keep talking to him even if he didn't talk back. I felt damn stupid standing in front of that shack every day and yelling. I had nothing to say and was in a hurry to get to school, so I would call out whatever was on the tray, tell him the weather according to the almanac, and say the date. Since I never saw him, I started being afraid of seeing him.

In May he didn't pick up the tray at all, and Ava sent word to the railroad doctor. He found Li Sung dead in his cot. Heart attack, the doctor said, but I doubt he examined the body very close. Some men from Raynell, Eban among them, went out to put an end to the whole thing. They wore kerchieves over their faces, dug a grave, filled a casket with quicklime, and raked the leper into it. They covered the casket with lime and dirt. The shack was doused with kerosene and burned, and the ashes covered with lime. The men camped out there the whole day to be sure no one stumbled onto the contaminated ground unawares. It was the first time Eban had seen the leper or the leper's house. He wouldn't say anything when he came back home, though some of the other men talked around the town. They said it gave Eban a start to see his long-worn clothes sewn on those blankets, the sleeves of the shirts and the trouser legs spread out like one body on top of another and another.

Bess and Clayton let me come to Bellington when I was thirteen so I could go to high school there in the town. Bess seemed a lot older when I saw her again, and I called her Aunt. Clayton probably didn't want me at first, but I became an older brother to their kids. Katie Sue was a pretty little girl and Chuck was moody like Clayton, thin as a rail—they were just tykes. The town looked like a big city to me. It was prosperous in 1924: several lumber mills were going, and the Methodists had started a college. Most people had automobiles, and the streets were paved with bricks.

That first day, Clayton took me for a ride in his Studebaker, up Quality Hill past the Jonas house, and he stopped to talk to the Doc. That old house is a wreck now, broken up into cheap apartments, but it was pretty then—a big white elephant on the hill back from the street. All those round cupolas in white shingle and a circular drive planted with boxwood. The drive went right up past the front porch under a latticed arch. There was Doc Jonas in his white rocker, and there was Reb, with green eyes like a snake's. Fourteen, and drove his father's car like a bat from hell. Brand-new Pierce Arrow coupe. You could see yourself in the running board. Reb tended that car like it was living, and thought of it every minute. His father said he was love-struck.

In those days most people didn't bother to get a license, just bought a car and drove. Cars were like toys; nobody thought they were dangerous except people who couldn't afford them. There had been a few wrecks in the town, but no one ever killed or hurt bad. Streets were wide. Seldom more than a few cars on any one at a time, and nobody went very fast by today's standards. Reb and me would tow the mark in town anyway, because everyone was looking.

But after dusk you could get outside the city limits and go like the wind—not meet a soul. Road between here and Winfield wasn't paved, but in the spring it was smooth dry dust that flew up behind like a cloud. . . .

. . . .

Fourteen years between high school and the war. Time passed like lightning.

Why didn't I ever get married? Having too much fun, I guess, wasn't ready to settle. And it was the '30s too. A peculiar time. You worked for nothing. Everyone did.

I went to college a year and dropped out, then worked in construction with Clayton. He got me on at Huttonsville. Maximum-security prison there used to work chain gangs and they needed foremen. I worked crews awhile. Those were rough men, but I never had trouble, never held a gun on them. Worked all but a few without leg irons and never had a man run. Prison labor was an accepted thing in this state for many years. But I did better working on my own—lived in Morgantown, Winfield, working for various companies. Clayton and I didn't start the cement plant until after the war. Earlier I traveled a lot and stayed in boarding houses, moving with the work crews on the road jobs. Between times, I stayed at Bess and Clayton's in Bellington, in my old room. It was good to have a man there: Bess was busy at the hospital and Clayton was gone a lot; I helped with the kids in his absence.

Every spring we went out to the cemetery at Coalton. Even after the land was sold and deeded to the mining companies, Bess insisted on taking the kids every year. *Our people are there and as long as I'm breathing those graves will be tended. It's anyone's duty. One day we'll be lying there ourselves, miles from anything.* Clayton was away, working at Huttonsville most likely. Bess had Katie Sue and Chuck ready. We were in a hurry, wanted to get there before the heat of the day came up, and Katie cut a fit. She got sick in cars when she was little and dreaded riding any distance. Seven or eight and high-strung as an old lady. She hid in the house and wouldn't answer us. I got damn mad and switched her with a birch switch. Don't you know I regretted it for years. Only hit her a couple of times across the legs but she hollered like she was killed. I guess it bothered me too that these kids didn't care anything about the farm—to them it was just a deserted old place. I still liked to go there. House and land were empty, but otherwise it was all the same—mining companies didn't work that property till after the war.

I went to the farm before enlisting, one of the last things I did. Took a good look. Went out with Reb. We sat on the porch of the old house and drank a few beers. I wasn't real happy about the army, but they were going to draft me. Reb had a wife and children, but they wouldn't have helped if he hadn't been a doctor. He said if all the docs in town hadn't signed up on their own, he'd have paid them to enlist so he could stay home and deliver babies.

The farm looked pretty, wintry and frosted and quiet. I enlisted in March—March 2, '42—so must have been late February. Grass in the fields didn't sway, didn't move in the wind. Everything was chill and clear. Reb finally said it was time to leave and not sit any longer in the cold like fools.

The war swallowed everyone like a death or a birth will, except it went on and on. I was gone three years. They dropped the atom bomb on Japan as our troop ship steamed into Oakland harbor. No one really understood what had happened at first; soldiers got on the trains and went home.

I had my thirty-fifth birthday on the train—cake with candles, and ice cream. Red Cross girls kept all that information on us, must have been their idea to celebrate. They were nice girls. The men got a kick out of it and joined in with the singing. The train was hitting rough track about then, and one of the girls (she was from Ohio, I believe) came walking down the aisle carrying a big square cake, lurching from side to side and trying to keep the candles lit. The way the car was jolting and shaking made me think of the boat crossing to the Philippines . . . April of '45, how bad that night storm was. Raining and blowing, gusts of wind till you couldn't stay on deck. Not a star in the pitch black and the boat tilting so you couldn't keep food in a bowl. I looked out the train window as they were singing; we were crossing the Southwest. Flat, yellow land, and the sky was sharp blue, blue as it was in Randolph County the summers on the farm. I thought I would go back there even though the farm was gone—just to see it. Go back to look at the fields.

But I didn't go back for a long time, even though I wasn't far away. When I was married and had my own kids I was down that country—selling cranes and bulldozers for Euclid to a strip-mine outfit. The land was all changed, moved around. There were a few buildings left from the Main Street of Coalton, used as equipment shacks and an office. But out where the farm was— almost nothing. Heaps of dirt, cut-away ledges where they'd stripped. Looking at it made me think I'd been asleep a long time and had wakened up in the wrong place, a hundred miles from where I lay down. Like I'd lost my memory and might be anyone. Only thing they left alone was the wooden church, all falling in on itself, and the cemetery.

I walked up by the stones, between the rows of names. Warwick. Eban. Ava.

Icie. What kind of name is that for a woman. You always asked why I didn't try harder to find her. Why should I? She left me.

The cemetery was still and clean, though the grass was ragged. You know I thought of the leper; hadn't thought of him in years.

I never saw the inside of that shack. What did he do all day? No country, no family, no job. No one. Maybe he wasn't sure anymore who he was. He was a secret. I was the only one ever saw him. He could have stopped talking because I didn't seem real either, only another sound he heard in the woods. A sound in his head. During the war I used to dream of him, walking toward me on one of the tarmac landing strips we laid in New Guinea. I'd wake up in a sweat.

I was a secret myself. I used to lie awake nights when I was a kid, before I slept. I grew up in different places: with Bess, with Ava, with cousins at the farm. I'd fall asleep and hear a voice I'd never heard. I was called Mitch, or nicknames like Cowboy. But this voice said, "Mitchell. . . Mitchell . . . Mitchell . . ." with no question, till the sound didn't seem like a name or a word.

Edisto

PADGETT POWELL

The Assignment

I'm in Bluffton on a truancy spree, cutting, we call it, but all you do is walk off the unfenced yard during recess, where three hundred hunched-over kids are shooting marbles. I can't shoot a marble with a slingshot, so I split and go into Dresser's Rexall for a Coke or something, expressly forbidden me by the Doctor because it makes me hyper, she says, but should I drink milk all my life instead or go on now to house bourbon? That is not the point.

Suddenly there she is on a counter stool between me and a cherry Coke, or I'm even considering a suicide—sixteen godoxious syrups in a thimble of soda—but I can handle this disappointment. I could go to the Texaco and have a bottle and talk to Vergil. They even have Tom's peanuts for a goober-bottle rig—you just pour in the peanuts and drink. But Clyde, his pumpman, will try to take off his wooden leg on me. One day I got curious and he unbuttoned his shirt and showed me the network of sweaty straps all over his chest that holds the leg on, and I got closer, and he loosened the straps and took down his overalls, and all of a sudden the leg was off, a small cypress log, and he bounced his stump around on the chair, pecan-colored and hard-looking, and I about fainted. Now I have to beg him to leave it on. When I get pale, Vergil will stop him. "Keep your leg on, Clyde." "Okeydoke," Clyde says, but he still fidgets with the straps and giggles.

But I don't get out of the Rexall unnoticed. She calls me over and introduces me to this gray-headed gent she's with. Now this is what gets me. She says to him, who turns out to be a barrister working land in Hilton Head, she says, "I want you to meet my protégé."

She never includes the detail I'm her son, so I put my name into the dialogue so she might have to mention the relationship. "Simons Everson Manigault," I say to him, stepping up and pumping him a three-pump country shake, squeezing harder than even the old man said to. You say it "Simmons." I'm a rare one-*m* Simons.

So she hatches a "protégé" on the guy and I think I see his face hitch to the floor a hint, as if he had a doubt about her—remarkable, this, because the lawyers I have seen, including my old man, have had better control of facial expression than any actor in the land, and I figure either something twitched him or he doesn't work on his feet. The Doctor has a bit of a reputation, you know, and a suitor outside the college where she teaches can be right skittish. The Negroes call her the Duchess. Anyway, next I look at them he is looking at her legs folded up under her on the chrome swivel stool, bulges of calf flesh pressed out firm as pull candy, so I just drift out of Dresser's—no suicide, but at least not recognized as skipping school either.

Truancy is no big deal to the Doctor anyway, because it's the "material" has her send me to public school, podunkus Bluffton Elementary, when the old man would send me to Cooper Boyd, college-prep academy for all future white doctors, lawyers, and architects in the low country. But the old man cut out some time ago. He gave me a Jack London book and coached me into the best eight-year-old shortstop in the history of the world before the book shit hit. "That kid's supposed to *read* all that?" he said. "I thought that was *your* library." He was shocked by the Plan: the bassinet bound by books, which I virtually came home from the hospital to sleep in the lee of, my toys. Like some kids swat mobiles, I was to thumb pages. Some get to goo-goo, I had to read.

It was something. He (the Progenitor) had actually built the shelves that held the Doctor's training tools, which took me straight away from our after-work grounder clinic and his idea of things. They got in it over this, one charged with sissifying and the other with brutalizing.

I suppose I became my momma's boy, at least she was still *there*, and in fact all this scribbling is directly related to her training program. It's an assignment. I'm supposed to write. I'm supposed to get good at it.

So the day I'm talking about, after leaving the Rexall, I got out of Vergil's without Clyde making me sick, got on the school bus, as usual, and fell out of it racing down the road, as not usual. I looked up from my surprise at not being dead and saw a white face, calm as an ambulance driver, among a whole gawking throng of Negroes. And reading the Doctor's toys for boys is what got me in the predicament.

That's what being a "material" hound will get you: little you who should be up in the front with the nice kids but are in the back listening to Gullah and watching, say, an eight-year-old smoke marijuana like a man in a cell block, eyes squinting toward the driver with each hissing intake of what his grandfather called hemp and took for granted, you trying to orate on the menace of the invading Arabs—"They don't ride camels and carry scimitars, but they are coming all the same; they've bought ten islands, we'll all be camel tenders soon"—when the emergency door flies open and it is not the Negroes nearest who go out and do cartwheels after the bus, it is you who gets sucked out into a fancy bit of tumbling on the macadam, spidering and rolling up the gentle massive cradling roots of an oak tree that has probably stopped many more cars with much less compassion. My tree just said *whoa*. You must see the miraculous thing it is to have avoided death by a perfect execution of cartwheels, rolling over a two-lane highway and partway *up* a tree, to clump down then with only two cracked ribs and no more for medicine than Empirin. The codeine kind not the old-lady kind. I jumped up to tell them I was not dead: Negroes from nowhere, peering at my sleeping little face framed by roots. As I looked at them, before jumping up and losing my breath to the ribs, I saw that one calm light face among them.

Anyway, that's what sniffing out things will do for you, and I was changed by discovering how close the end can be when you don't even think about your being alive, not at twelve, and that same night the one calm face among my coterie of gawkers stepped onto the porch like the process server he was, but with no papers to serve, and I felt the porch sag.

When the ambulance does get there, the Negroes tell the driver, "That the Duchess boy." So he takes me, not that I'm hurt or anything—though I am, sort of, because it hurts when I try to breathe—he takes me to Dr. Carlton back in Bluffton instead of the clinic in Beaufort, and Carlton gives me a ride home. My maternal Doctor has not missed me and has the evening set up.

It gets dark so very gradually it seems pure dark will never descend and I get moody in my new, good-as-dead outlook, walk around the place trying to savor the sudden news that I don't have to be alive, even, and turn on a few lamps. The Doctor clears up the dinner problem by assigning me leftovers, fine with me, and gets a drink and takes up on the wicker sofa, sitting on her folded legs, and drinks her drink.

These are the times that are best: when she is distracted and I am left to whatever I can manage on my own, basically provided for but maybe burning meat loaf or something without a peep from her. These are times when we are least protégé and master. I can feel each drink she pours, each necessary bite of the sour bourbon on her mouth, feel it in a neutral way without any kind of judgment, I am aware is all, by the sounds of glass and wicker, of her evening and she must be as aware that I am going to bed without reading any assignments, just listening to the palmetto and waves and going to sleep.

We are well into that kind of dance this evening when Taurus shows up. Elbows on the drain counter, I am keeping my weight off my ribs and watching the food cook when I see him. You do not know what in hell may be out here on a hoodoo coast and I do not make a move. What follows is not nearly so ominous as I would sound. He don't ax-murder us or anything like that. Yet there is something arresting about this dude the moment you see him. He is shimmery as an islander's god and solid as a butcher. I consider him to be the thing that the Negroes are afraid of when they paint the doors and windows of their shacks purple or yellow. His head is cocked, his hand on the washtub of the Doctor's old wringer, its old manila rolling pins swung out to the side. When he comes up to the screen, I know I have seen his face before.

That's the assignment. To tell what has been going on since this fellow came trying to serve a subpoena to we think Athenia's daughter and scared Theenie so bad it about blued her hair. Before he came I spent most of my time at the Baby Grand—Marvin's R.O. Sweet Shop and Baby Grand, where I am a celebrity because I'm white, not even teenage yet, and possess the partial aura of the Duchess ("The Duchess boy heah!"). And I look like I hold my liquor ("Ain't he somp'm."). The trick there is to accept a new can when anybody offers and let your old one get drunk by somebody else.

And besides playing the freak I can jive a little, too, like the Arab alarum I like to ring. "If it wasn't for the *Marines* down the road, these Arabs'd do more than *buy* this place!" "Shih! Boy *crazy!*" And the dudes there play a tune back, a constant message: Life is a time when you get pleasure until somebody get your ass. And one of the ways to prolong pleasure is to not chop up time with syllables. They go for something larger than words, but no essays. This way nothing large is inaccurate, presumptuous. "Bitch look heavy." "Tell *me.*" Like these James Brown guitar riffs of five notes that run twenty minutes, and then *one* of the five notes goes sharp and a statement is made. A whole evening hums, and then there's a new note—razor out. I still hit the Grand, but less now with Taurus and me doing things.

That night when he stepped on the porch and I was trying to breathe, the Doctor came to the door and stopped short of pushing it open as she would have for an ordinary visitor—he had his hand inside the rim of the wringer tub and his head was slightly cocked off at it as if he were listening to a large conch shell. I noticed then a stack of linen folded—not folded anymore, thrown—by the sink. Some kind of nut is on the porch and I take time out to notice this because now I know something is up.

Because when your Southern barony is reduced as ours is to a tract of clay roads cut in a feathery herbaceous jungle of deerfly for stock and scrub oak for crop, and the great house is a model beach house resembling a pagoda, and the planter's wife is abandoned by the planter, as ours has been, and she has only one servant left (Theenie, who for quarters has only one 10′ x 12′ shack insulated by newspaper and flour on a cold Atlantic bluff), well, that vestigial baroness insists that vestigial slave do her one duty right—"the linen," all that remains of cotton finery. Theenie vacuums the house too, but that doesn't signify as Preserving the South. And the laundry was not in the hall closet (successor to armoire) but flung all over the kitchen counter, which was not right.

If I had not rolled sixty feet at forty miles an hour into an oak tree just hours before, I might have thought nothing of that laundry. But there it was, flopped forlorn on the drainboard, looking a bit like I might have before I stood up to disassociate myself from the dead in that sudden ring of gawkers. There was somehow a connection in all this: my suddenly seeing the linen in the new good-as-dead way of seeing, the linen an embodiment of Theenie and the Doctor's old order and of, somehow, the someone cocking an ear to a sound on our porch, whose discovery stopped the

Doctor mid-track and knocked her into her classroom style, so that she suddenly stood three feet inside the door, straightened up, and spoke as if there were an invisible podium between her and her audience.

"Won't you please come in and let us talk," said the Doctor heavily, as though scanning the line for a student, and she stepped forward and slowly swung open the screen door to a total stranger, who looked young enough and strong enough to be the ax murderer. (Man, several years ago I was all-hours victim to accounts of boogeymen on this windriddled spit of remote earth, one thing that did encourage me to read: you keep reading to stay awake and so get a good jump if the Hook Man breaks in.)

He stepped in. She stepped back. "In the name, it would seem, of paralegal service," she said, and turned and walked away and crossed the living room and sat on the creaking wicker sofa on her legs, "you have done me a *grave* disservice." She said this in her explicatory, cadenced style, punctuated and metered so no idiot could fail to record it in his notebook. The stranger, who had not followed her, then looked at me, evenly and without expression. He came in.

"My maid has quit," she said.

"I have not served anyone yet," the stranger said.

"You wanted her daughter, anyway. I am now without retainer. Do you paralegals make restitution of damages such as retiring twenty-year employees?"

"Do you know where her daughter is?" He sat down.

"Do you want to find out?"

Here they stopped. I could see his back, arms on his knees; he was sitting looking directly at her. She had her drink. She looked over the rim of it at him, sort of looking out the tops of her eyes and hiding her mouth with the drink.

"If you'll tell me, I'll get the other one back," he said.

"No, you won't. You won't even find her."

"Lately I am a professional at finding—"

"You won't find her unless I tell you where she is, and you probably won't find her daughter unless *she* tells you where *she* is."

"Where did she go, then?"

"That's a laid-low to catch a meddler."

"A what?"

"Skip it. I'll tell you what. Since you scared hell out of my maid and my estate is consequently short-handed, you might assist me . . ." She kind of trailed off.

They looked at each other a while.

"If you want to find either of them, you might hang around a bit."

"Hang around?"

"I am short on domestics, it would seem. There's the gardening and the brass polishing, of course, but as a coachman . . . And Simons has just today manifested a problem in his school-bus riding. You could escort him to school and back, and keep up the quarters on the beach, and let me see if I can locate Athenia for you."

"I suppose I might," he said.

"And could you tell me what *is* paralegal service?" She knew what it was. The old man was a lawyer and every joe to take her out since who wasn't a professor was an ambulance chaser or coroner. She was not asking to get an answer, but to know the answerer. This tactic was used when she had brilliant students over, mostly.

The stranger accepted the game. She was still accelerating, ever since the door, and virtually beaming at him over the whiskey, her tawny old Kool-Aid. "That straddles law and law *enforcement*," he said, and I was certain, without any evidence, that he was grinning. He had passed a little test with flying colors—not flinched at all the crap about servants and brass polishing, but accepted her game, and what her game was even I did not know. But I knew something was going on, and if I had not been buzzing on Empirin, I could have told whether it was really going on, or just me, buzzing on Empirin.

"Well," the Doctor said, in her summing-up tone, "there's a cake down there. Send it back with Simons. Can you walk okay, Ducks?"

"Yes ma'am," I said.

I beat him out the door into the trees, leaning with the night wind away from the beach, and headed us for Theenie's shack. It was my birthday and I had a cake.

Here to Get My Baby Out of Jail

LOUISE SHIVERS

The tobacco kept on ripening. The putting-in went on. I didn't go down to the barn for several days. I stayed at the house, keeping Baby as quiet as I could, keeping quiet myself, feeling blank and sick. Every night I'd think that Aaron was going to say something accusing to me, but every night he came in tired and dirty and went to bed as quickly as he possibly could. Jack stayed at the barn.

One morning at the end of the week, Callie slipped up to the house and came right out and asked me why everybody was acting so funny. "It's no fun at the barn, Roxy. We're about to get sick of the whole thing. If I wasn't planning on buying that dress at the Mother and Daughter store I believe I'd just go home."

I didn't know what to say to her. I didn't even try to answer.

I swore to myself every night and every day that I wasn't going to have anything more to do with Jack Ruffin. I was sure the spell he had me under was broken. I wasn't going to do a thing for the rest of my life but be a good wife. If I got too lonesome, I'd just have to stay that way. I kept as busy as I could, cooking and doctoring Baby's sores.

I often wonder what would have happened if Jack had left Tar County right then, if I had tried to make him go.

But after about two weeks like that, just cook, eat and sleep, I started finding it harder and harder to ignore Jack's eyes when he came in to eat, or to have him ignore mine. A little vein in my neck would start throbbing when he walked through the kitchen, but I stayed out of his way and didn't let it be possible for us to be alone for a second, and he stayed out of mine. No music, no joking around while they came in from the fields. Aaron kept a cold back turned to me every night, and in the daytime every time I spoke to him, he'd answer with a loud "What?" that didn't encourage me to say anything else. At night while he'd put up the mules, I'd hear him whistling through his teeth in that way he had.

Baby was getting well fast, and one morning I decided to make a pan of chocolate fudge and take her and it down to the shed. When I started walking down the dirt road to the barns, I heard Callie and Raider let out a big whoop, and I could tell that it was all that they could do to keep from throwing down the handful of tobacco they held. They were almost done with the truck, though, and there wasn't another one in sight, so they hurriedly finished it. I held out the fudge dish, and Raider was the first one to get to it. He grabbed a piece and started rolling his eyes. He ran his tongue around the edge of it, getting the grains of sugar in the corners of his mouth. The plate emptied quickly, and Callie, wanting to prolong the party, said, "Let's get a watermelon, too." She ran out to the edge of the field and got one from the shadiest spot she could find. It was still hot, though, when we busted it and Callie picked up a piece with her black, tobacco-gummy fingers.

"I thought hot watermelon'd kill you," Raider said.

Old Mama spoke up. "That ain't hot watermelon there, that there's *warm* watermelon."

Raider said, "Oh," and bit in. We all broke out laughing. All the tension that had built up had made us silly. When Callie

221

made a face as the bitter tobacco gum on her hands got in the watermelon, I told her to quit eating so fast and stop and wash her hands off with some tomatoes that would cut the gum. I could tell that Old Mama was about to launch into some story about somebody dying from eating hot watermelon when we heard the rumble of the tobacco truck, loud and close to us. I glanced up quickly to see which one it was and looked right into Jack's eyes.

I was sitting, rocking in the kitchen, the wood of the chair pressing against my legs as I sat shelling butter beans from the big aluminum pan that we had bought down at Haw Landing when we first got married. Aaron was stretched out on the day bed that we kept in the kitchen during putting-in time, reading the day's paper. I remembered standing at the front door, watching the mailman put the paper in the box in front of the yard, and not bothering to go take it out, thinking whatever there is in the paper, what has it got to do with me, my life?

Jack had gone on down to the barn to take care of the fires as soon as he'd finished his supper, and Baby was, I thanked the Lord, asleep in her crib in the bedroom.

As I shelled, I glanced over at Aaron. His bare white feet looked so vulnerable; the bones, the little ones going to his toes, were like an ivory fan I'd seen in Ruth's trunk. He arched and moved one foot and then set in motion the nervous twitch I'd noticed that his daddy had, the thump of the big toe against the toe beside it, a motion probably unnoticed by the person doing it but as irritating to the person watching as the steady drip of a faucet. It didn't irritate me right then, though. Since the night before I'd been feeling tender toward him. The night before was as strange as anything that had happened in the last few strange months. Suddenly after weeks of strain, we had become close in the dark, his hands and mouth had searched with a motion and rhythm like silk from evening spiders. We both seemed to be searching over and over, communicating things that words could

222

never say. I saw him again as the clean good boy I had first seen standing at the edge of the cemetery at Cobb Swamp Church.

I looked at his hands and feet for a long time and thought of the time after Baby was born when the doctor had cautioned us to wait six weeks, and in the fifth week, without speaking of it, we had come together and for a while nothing else mattered. How had I come so far from that? How had I let these things happen to me with Jack? Aaron and I had struck a bargain together, and I'd meant to keep it. Had I turned bad because I was lonesome and liked to hear words whispered to me, words like "pretty," words like "smart"?

I kept sitting there looking at Aaron for a long time. I wondered that he didn't feel my eyes on him, didn't know my thoughts. But then I didn't know his, did I? I wanted to, had tried, asked, begged, but there was such a big part of himself that he wouldn't or couldn't share. Maybe all men are like that. I thought of Daddy. Thought of Jack. I looked at Aaron's face, the dark lashes around his eyes. How could I have ever done those things to him? If he could even imagine Jack and me lying in each other's arms the hot nights at the barn when he and Baby lay asleep, and me trying to slip in and wash myself so that he wouldn't notice the cured tobacco smell thick on my skin, what would he do? If he could imagine . . . Could regular people like Aaron imagine such things? I have to stop all this, straighten things out and try again. If me and Baby got lonesome we were just going to have to stand it.

"Roxy—" The word shattered the sound of the ticking clock. Aaron was speaking to me and had startled me out of my thoughts. "There's something Daddy wants me to talk to you about."

He had turned and was sitting on the side of the couch, picking up his shoes and socks. The expression on his face was odd, and he wasn't looking directly at me. My heart jumped, and I felt dizzy and reached for the butter-bean pan for balance. Some of

223

the shells scattered across the floor. I looked at them lying at my feet. They were the best butter beans to come out of the garden all summer. Things might have been bad for us at the house, but the crops took no notice of it. They just kept right on growing.

I waited for him to go on talking—knowing that he couldn't be rushed or prompted, that he would say whatever he had to say in his own good time—but I felt my uneasiness looming up in the room like another person.

"Daddy mentioned something about Jack staying here." Aaron talked fast now, pushing the words out in a rush. "It might be better . . . he said that we ought to get the first tobacco to market and then give him some money and send him on . . ."

I was afraid to say anything, afraid my voice would give out on me. I just kept sitting there, looking down at the hulls on the floor, nodding.

"I've already told him, Roxy, told Jack that after the opening sale we'll be able to manage without him . . . I hated to do it, why don't you tell him too?"

He paused, sat there with his head down staring at his feet, as if he was waiting for me to speak, protest or something, but I couldn't bring myself to say a word. In a way this was what I wanted, for him to make a move to stop the things that were going on and, on the other hand, the thought of Jack's really leaving . . . I couldn't imagine . . . how could I just let him leave . . . ?

"Somebody at the church mentioned to the folks that it didn't look right with you and Jack in the same house all the time . . . that you might start noticing each other . . ." His voice sounded low and embarrassed as he said the last words. In a minute he looked up at me, his eyes solemn, but making an effort to make his voice lighter, he said, "Talk to Jack about it. I hated to tell him. He told me he was counting on staying through the winter. Tell him how it looks for you, Roxy. It might be better."

I sat for a long time after Aaron left the room. I heard him fall into a hard sleep, the sounds coming into the kitchen where I sat rocking and tapping my leg with the fly swatter, trying to think what to do, what to say. I knew I had to go to the barn. I got up, and once I smoothed my skirt and started walking down the dirt path I moved quickly with a purpose. As I walked, I could see little sparks in the smoke going up into the night like drunk lightning bugs, and as I got near the barn the heavy, sweet smell of the curing tobacco hit my nostrils. I could almost taste it—the syrupy, musty smell like bodies making love in the heat. A drug in itself, just the smell of it.

There wasn't a light at the barn. The glint of the lanterns showed once in a while like pictures of a ship, but they weren't lit. The only light was from the fires at the two barns. They crackled and moved and hypnotized me. I don't know anything as spellbinding as a fire except maybe clouds on a day when the wind moves them along so fast that they change shapes constantly and the eye can't leave for fascination.

When I came close enough to feel the heat from the fire, the mosquitoes stopped gnawing at my legs and arms. My eyes made out Jack's form lying on the cot, sprawled out, face down. He didn't speak, but I knew he was watching me and playing possum. He let me get almost up to him, and then with a laugh he lunged up, grabbed me around the waist, boosted me into the air and shook me like a rag doll. We fell laughing into each other. I was laughing in spite of myself, laughing into his chest, forgetting for the moment why I had come to the barn.

I said, "You smell like a tow sack, you smell just like that old tow sack you've been lying on."

He didn't answer, just kept pulling my face into his chest, mashing my words flat against him.

"Jack, Jack . . ."

"Ummm" . . . mocking, teasing.

Pulling me down in spite of my efforts to talk, to protest that I came to talk, to tell him something important; pulling me onto the tobacco-truck bed, covering me with mosquito net, bending over me, holding my face still, putting his fingers on my lips

225

every time I tried to talk. Bending over my face, smoothing the skin of it with tobacco-stained fingers, making me taste the tobacco, making round motions on my cheekbones, tracing the light from the fire on them. Saying, no laughing in his voice, "You, you're the tobacco princess. You're prettier than any Ava."

I couldn't think straight, couldn't help but see how the firelight made the gold colors of his skin glow, couldn't help but think that he was from some other world or time and that nothing else was real except the two of us on the rough bed, lava from an ancient volcano.

I heard him whisper in my ear, "Don't worry, he's not coming down here."

Later we lay still, and I told him what I had gone down there to tell him. We lay there looking at each other. Something unspeakable and strange went between us.

And then early, very early, before the sun was up, I left him, got up and ran up the road, the heavy dew soaking my bare legs and cotton broomstick skirt, ran lightly so as not to disturb the chickens, slipped as quietly as a cowboy from an old-time picture show into the house. I washed myself, combed and wound up my hair and stood in the kitchen in fresh starched clothes, cooking eggs in fried-meat grease when the house woke up. I kept my face expressionless the way I had learned to keep it early in the summer—back inside myself, not reaching out to make things right for Aaron, jealously guarding the secrets inside me from outsiders.

Aaron got up and made his usual morning noises as he washed in the basin in the kitchen, sounds that this morning grated at my nerves. His slow ritual seemed to me to go on and on. I was impatient to see him out the door so I could have moments to myself to lie across my bed and think and collect the night before in my mind and rest a few minutes.

"Did you talk to Jack?" he asked in a matter-of-fact voice.

I had anticipated the words, and I tried to sound as matter-of-fact as he did. "Yes," not "Yes, and he's not going to do it," or

"Yes, and Lord knows what's going to happen now," or "Yes, and now the fat's really in the fire," but just "Yes." And he accepted that and went into the day, and it seemed that it was all taken care of as simply as hitching the mule to the tobacco truck and heading on out to the field.

And that's the way it stayed.

Canaan

CHARLIE SMITH

She woke early because this was the morning she planned to paddle the canoe down to Haven's. The house still smelled faintly of fumigant, a smell like rotten pecans. On the walls were sheets of butcher paper tacked in long strips from the ceiling. On the paper she had written in a felt pen an outline of the history of her life. The red sentences of the history were divided into paragraphs by green lines. Books were stacked along the wall under the paper, obscuring a few of the paragraphs at the bottom. In the top left corner, under a spiderweb which she was careful not to touch, she had written: "I was born on a sunny day in early February, Groundhog's Day in 1920. Whether you believe it or not, the bay was full of sailboats. I can remember the sails which were all white, like the wings of gulls. The people along the Battery thought they were clouds." Between some of the paragraphs she had drawn colored portraits of birds and animals. Above the writing, along the ceiling, she had painted a dark blue strip and dotted it with small white splashes: stars, she explained, a starry night in Charleston, the way the sky looked on the evening after she was born. "I used to gig flounders in the rain" was the next sentence, and she thought as she pushed herself up in the bed and squinted at the strips that it was a better opening than the date of her birth. "I used to fish for flounders in the rain," she said out loud, got up, took her marker from the bedside table and went to the wall. She was halfway down one of the middle strips in the middle of a passage about the Brazilian loafers her father wore when he went out to swim in the pool. They were canvas, the loafers, had thin red rubber soles and were soft as a bird's breast. She had completed a passage that read: "I stole them and hid them in a trunk in my closet. I thought that when I got old enough and my father was dead I would wear them." She stopped; In remembrance of him, she thought, but she didn't write that. She heard a sound outside and crouched down. The sound continued, a scrabbling noise, as if someone were climbing a tree. She went to the closet and got a shotgun, one of a pair of Purdys Haven had ordered for her. She walked through the house to the front porch. Three boys, ten or eleven, were trying to lift the johnboat she and Delight had laid across sawhorses in the front yard. She walked to the top step and pointed the gun at them. The boys froze and the largest one, a child in a red shirt and a blond crew cut, stood up from under the boat. She fired over their heads. The shot cut leaves out of one of the water maples. The boys bolted up the lane along the river. She put another shot into the fair sky above them, broke the breech and sniffed at the wisp of smoke that curled out. "Good morning, world," she said, kicked the shells into the laggard azaleas below the porch and went back into the house. For the life that was in them, she thought, yes, not in remembrance. I didn't want to remember, I wanted to keep. She hummed to herself as she returned to the bedroom, took up her marker and began to write:

Message to the Unnamed Other:
From The Journal of Elizabeth Bonnet Burdette

On the way home from a plantation party one night I drove my father's car off a bridge into the Ashley River. There were four of us in the car: my boyfriend, Estil Johnson; Katherine Vareen; Joe D'Urban and myself. I still couldn't tell you what made me do it. We passed a big field where the moon was shining on the new corn and entered a patch of woods that descended toward the river. We were singing a song, a spiritual about crossing water.

The road curved and we came around the bend through the trees onto the bridge. I wasn't drunk and I didn't have a thought in my head, but halfway across I swung the wheel to the right and we tore through the guardrail and soared out. The car began to turn over back to front, we hit I think on the roof, and sank. The water poured in the windows like we were the floodgates just broken. Estil was knocked out and I had to drag him out the window and swim him to the bank. I dove back in and met Joe who was diving for Katherine. We went down together—the water was a pure blackness—and found her trying to bash her way out the back window which was still intact. She fought us but we managed to haul her to the surface where Joe swam with her to the shallows. The three of them lay in the shallows like old alligators moored to the bank, like bedraggled puppies. I climbed up to a stand of sycamores and looked back down at the river where a faint stream of bubbles rose from the car in the moonlight. I wanted to split the world open and throw everything I hated into the hole. Estil, kneeling in the rank water, looked up at me and said, "What happened?"

"I saw some angels in the trees," I said and sat down. That was all the explanation I ever gave. After a while my friends climbed the bank and I lay with them in the grass until they got their wits back, then we walked a mile to a truck stop where I called my father to come get us.

After my mother's funeral I sat on the back steps with my coat up over my head even though it was spring and hot. Neither warmth nor green life could save me. Everything, not just my mother, was dead anyway. After a while I got up and walked down to the boat pier where a boy in a basketball shirt was fishing. He had lined his string of bass and perch in a row beside his chair. I thought what a sweetness must be in that boy for him to arrange his fish like that, side by side, so he could look at them and marvel. I could have stopped to speak to him, could have touched his pale hair, but instead I picked the fish up and one by one threw them into the water. The boy looked at me with such grievous shock in his eyes, but he didn't say a thing. I walked home thinking, Nobody in the world knows what I know, nobody will ever know.

The first time I saw my husband I thought, Here comes the circus. I thought marrying him might be like joining the rodeo, joining the bucking stock part, I mean.

He had the same moo cow eyes all the other men around me had, but there was something else, there was a depth to them, as if way back inside himself he was anchored to something powerful and permanent. I thought, Here's a bird that will catch fire and won't fly when he burns. He can have me, I thought, he can have me if he is willing to go through what I am going to put him through and that's everything there is on earth. I'm going to take him down to the low places, I'm going to take him to the mountains, up into the sky, away to the desert barrens where people are beyond tears; I'm going to make him understand what it's like to live and die in the same moment, I'm going to make him wish he was never born, make him wish he could live forever.

He appeared on my front steps in a car full of flowers: plumerias and hibiscus and bougainvillea and passion flowers, as proud and hopeful as if he had personally invented love about five minutes before he got behind the wheel. He thought he was the ocean and I was some dune beach he would wear away and rearrange; he didn't know he was splashing against pure hard rock.

As my father didn't know, but was the first to find out. My father had long skinny legs so his pants flopped when he walked. I teased him about it and he slapped me, then he cried in his guilt for hitting his daughter. I learned from that, I can tell you. He could have beat me and I wouldn't have stopped teasing him, I don't know why. But I learned how to manipulate him. In a way it was like learning the whole encyclopedia to have one fact at your fingertips. What I learned about my parents, I mean. I was born fully formed, popped out of the hot water ready for action. Poor parents, what could they do?

I bled the first time during one of my mother's teas when I was eleven. I came down the stairs, my hands dripping red, walked into the parlor and said, Mother, look at this awful mess. She rose crying—all the other ladies sympathetic, ah-ing, reaching for tears—crossed the room and hugged me. I said, Mama stop it; this is ridiculous, all my white things will be ruined. She wanted to take me upstairs, she tried to begin a long talk about what was happening in my body, about how I was a woman—it was very moving to her I could see, but I shushed her, went into the kitchen and washed myself with a rag at the sink. She didn't know I wasn't even a virgin; two years before I had let Jemson Puckett fuck me with his little pencil-thin dick on the white tile floor of my bathroom just to see what it would feel like. It hurt so much I wanted to scream, and I bled then also. I thought a baby would spring out of me overnight—I didn't care if it did, but I wanted to be surprised. I didn't tell that to my mother as she stood behind me at the sink, her fingers flicking at my shoulder like she didn't know whether to hug me or run away, and I remember that out in the yard where the spring was shoveling a new green life into Charleston, I saw two little boys pushing a huge beachball back and forth. It must have been four feet across, the ball was, and striped yellow and red. I had never seen the boys before anywhere in Charleston; they were, I am sure now, angels, blond-headed with skin so white it shone, come to let me know I was free to live. I climbed up on the sink, my behind dripping red, threw open the window and yelled at them to go on about their business now; I raised my sweet sticky hand to show them everything was all right.

Both my parents were tall and they both had eagle eyes, but only my father could foretell the future. The gift made him excitable and diffident and conservative. One night as we walked along the Battery, he said to me, With each gift we are given its opposite, equal for equal; the brighter the candle, the darker the darkness. He could see the future, but he was haunted by the past. In the past he saw the death of dreams, the fallen moments when the arc of beauty frayed and began to falter. It made him want to preserve rather than extend. He saw happiness surely, but he also saw shadows move across the faces of the people he loved, and I am sure that he knew my mother was going to die. He saw her life snap like a twig and the white petals of it flutter down through the branches. He saw me soaring on my white wings.

When I was eight I wrote to the President and told him to pack up his things and go home. He wrote me back on stationery embossed with a red-tinted picture of the White House. He said, "It numbs me that someone your age would say this to me, though I admit the thought has crossed my mind more than once. I was born in a two-room house in a little town at the edge of the Iowa prairie. My father was a blacksmith who died when I was just a boy. My mother didn't long survive him, and after that I moved from relative to relative, leaving Iowa finally for the West. I made a fortune in the West as a mining engineer, but it was never my home. If I were to leave now the only place I would like to return to is Iowa. When I was very small I would peer through the paling of the fence at the back of our little cottage at the prairie which began at the foot of the hill. The wind had a way of punching at the field that made it seem as if a big hand were testing and judging the grass. I thought that hand would do the same to me, that if I didn't prove to be worthy, it would press me down into the earth. Believing that, I became what I have become. I too am afraid that before power like that, it is not enough."

The funniest thing my husband ever said to me was when, after the first month together in my cottage above Pearl Harbor, I asked him how he liked being with me and he grinned and said, "Babe, it's like loving dynamite." We both roared.

I love to touch all the creatures that live in the sea. When I was a child you could take a boat out to the barrier islands and gather scallops in the shallow water near the marshes. Now there are no scallops, as soon there will be no oysters. Folly Beach used to be littered with sponges. They are stiff and coarse as shredded canvas when dry and soft as a baby's skin when you wet them, On the island beaches I found the blue glass balls covered in hemp netting that the Japanese used as fishing buoys; they had floated half-way around the world. I imagined setting out holding one or two, floating off into the sea to some paradise country that existed on no known map.

I remember all this, the way the shore was, the glistening lapis lazuli glass of the floats, but I do not rake down through an ugly present to reach it. In magazines they talk about the disappearing wilderness, they say the wild animals are dying out, we will be alone with pavement before long. I know this isn't true. The fact is we must work constantly not to be overrun by wildness. I have seen a raccoon step into the headlights on a street in Charleston, a city founded in 1650 A.D. Into the backyards of all these houses in all these little towns creep at night the savage creatures. They lie in the grass watching us move about our well-lit rooms. They will be there when the last tycoon has been pounded into the dust. Delight laughs when anyone asks him where the wild game is. The animals are only biding their time, he says, they're waiting.

And more than that, I mean more than that: I sneer at the silly cringing folk who are afraid to love the life in front of them. The only possibility of happiness is to take the bitter with the sweet. To love them both the same. Jack loves his fine music but I have seen him plunge his hands into the innards of a slaughtered hog and marvel at the colors. I never saw purple until I saw the torn breast of a dove.

Delight and I went out to the coon dog trial near Fayton. They put a coon in a sack and dragged it behind a tractor around the pond as a pack of hounds raced after. The sack was slung over the low branch of a water oak and the hounds, skidding in the loose mud, rounded the dam and launched themselves into air. One was faster, better leaper, fiercer teeth, and hurtled into the air snapping, becoming, for that coon, the accurate angel that would tear it to pieces—but the sack was too high. The coon was taken down and chained into an apple box, set on a pole at water level in the center of the pond and the dogs were sent out swimming, two by two, to bring the little bastard in. Then you could see the heart of the hound: the long swim in the cold, the bitter welcome, nothing that wanted to come lightly. But one, a saddle-shouldered bluetick hauled up from Florida in a wire cage in the back of a pickup, starved and whipped and cringing around the hips before its master, scarred along the jawline and across the shoulders, a full hand taller than any other dog, swam toward the coon, its shovel head gliding along the surface, black eyes fixed and gleaming. The coon washed its little monkey paws, reared on high legs and fell back tugging on the chain. It clicked to itself, making the small noises of an old woman shooing away the dark. As the bluetick reached the crate the coon leaned forward and raked blood into the flesh below the dog's right eye. As the dog came on anyway the coon bit, three quick times, stitching perfect holes into the red ragged lip, attempted to leap over the rising, forward wrenching shoulders, was caught, its white breast clamped between the gulping slathering jaws; the winged wall of ribs cracked and, for an instant, its heart beat live and open inside the dog's mouth before the whole front of its body was torn loose. The dog writhed in the well of blood, scrambling halfway into the box, disemboweling, tearing out the throat, bursting the eyes, cracking bone on bone, devouring, scrabbling deep into the body, through the body, into the ghost behind the body, on and on, until . . . until it heard finally the man's voice calling over the water and, awakening, fell away and swam slowly back to shore, kneading the thin taste of blood in its mouth.

I sit on the blue velvet hassock before the streaked mirror turning a knife in my hands. I press the flat of the cool blade against my cheek, draw it closely downward to my jawline. There I level the blade until the edge bites barely into my skin. I press until in the mirror I see the beaded line of blood rise. This is not mutilation, nor is it provocation; it is an assay, a weighing of possibility, of possibility and hope, a peering into the dark dream I will some-day inhabit. My death comes to me like a cloud in the night, I feel myself easing down into the softness of it, the sibilant caress of it, the warmth and the mystery of it. It must be better since we keep it for so long. I will one day sink into the sky of my death, I will ride the long even swells, I will be alone but not lonely, bodiless, thoughtless, dreamless. I feel as if the edges of my body are fraying and dissolving, as if, like those blank days at the edge of the ocean when the sky and the sea are the same color, I am becoming one with the air around me; I am the scent of tea olive wafting through the open windows, I am the buzz and rattle of a bluebottle fly beating against the sill, I am the lick and start and caress of the wind itself, the river tarry and roiled, groping its way along the margins of the land, petting and caressing and calling the trod-upon earth. I am the bitter taste of a camphor leaf, I am the yellow sweetness of the tulip tree blossom; I am the gouging fin of the catfish, I am the soft gray body of the slate-shelled mussel; I am the decoder of mysteries, the detective of the high and low notes, the mystery rider, the one who is known to all. I am the Christ and I am Judas, the murderer and the broken body. I am every feeling that has ever been felt, every thought, every gleam of light shining through the crooked branches of the live oak and I am the eye that perceives the light. I am the darkness and the endless anguished cry of the broken heart, the mother weeping over her drowned child, the father fumbling through his tears to touch the cold face of his dead son. I am the daughter who died, the daughter who lived, I am the inconsolable one, I am the song of mourning and of hope; I am the mystery of birth, I am the baby's cry, I am the gasp and croak in the throat of the dying patriarch. I am among the bodies piled under the willow trees awaiting burning, I thrust my pitchfork into the heart of a crying child.

There is only a thin line of blood separating me . . .

CONVERSATION

Mattie: Don't you think you can sit still long enough to shell a
bushel of butterbeans?

Elizabeth: I don't know; I'm not sure that I can.

M: You'd better learn to still your heart.

E: If I did that I'd die.

M: If you did that you'd learn something about yourself, which
I can't see happening the way you live.

E: How do I live?

M: Like you're trying to catch a fast horse.

E: I think you're talking about my husband.

M: I'm talking about you.

E: You don't understand me.

M (Laughter): You're not that hard to follow.

E: So what is it I am?

M: Spoiled.

E: That's all?

M: In your case that's enough. It hasn't crossed your mind yet
that there are other human beings walking around on this
planet.

E: I see the people. I spend my life looking at the people.

M: You look at people as if they are animals in a zoo. Once in
a while one's cuddly enough for you to want to take it home.

E: I can't be bothered.

M: And that is what you hold to, darling, that nothing can
bother you.

E: If anything could, I'd change.

M: The only chance we have for satisfaction in this life is by
being of service.

E: I am of service.

M: To who?

E (Laughter): To my own hot heart.

M: That's not enough.

E: It'll have to do.

I am an example, I am the woman in long skirts tied around her waist leaning down to pluck a Jupiter shell from the shallow water of Apalachee Bay. I raise my head and see Delight on the beach striking fire into a pile of myrtle sticks. He works intently, finding satisfaction in the small change of dailiness. Delight knows the tracks, he knows the spoor of every creature running in the woods. At night, in his sleep, he calls out in the voices of doves and wood thrushes, he hisses like an otter. I am fascinated by the deftness of his large hands, the way he can quickly braid twine into rope, weave a snare. I bring him my fair body as a gift, as I have brought it to all my lovers, in exchange. We lie together in the cold moonlight; our voices are so small under the immensity of this Gulf sky. I am often so tiny, a grain. The only thing I never am is nothing.

On the afternoons my mother went out to meet her lover she dried her washed and wrung out handkerchief by pressing it against the mirror in her bathroom. The handkerchief looked like a large white lace postage stamp affixed to the corner of a silver envelope. In the mirror my mother's stately beauty was reflected, as if the still perfection of herself was what she was sending trapped and permanent to her waiting lover.

I remember the way we sweated, that night dancing on the pier at Isle of Pines, the way our slick faces seemed to have become parts of the same lovely machine, touching and sliding and glistening. I kissed the salt of him, the bitter stink of his lust.

When Haven's mother died he called me weeping. "I held her head up," he said. "She was drowning in her phlegm and I held her head up, just like she was trying to slip away underwater." My husband and I attended the funeral. She was buried in the family cemetery at Willows near the stand of red cedars her father had planted to remind him of the Cedars of Lebanon. Haven has never been the same since his mother died. He wastes away, a

238

wraith on his farm, riding out every day to put flowers on her grave. I went to visit him and he said, I see black ships, I hear the call of the captains, I have never been able to save anything worth saving in my whole life. I asked him who had ever done that, saved anything, anyone. He looked at me as if I had cursed him and walked away under the flowering water maples.

Sometimes in the night when I hear singing coming from the graveyard of the Burdettes, from the banks of Yellow Spring Course, from this tarry river, I think it is Haven, the elegant boy he once was, diffident and gracious, at sufferance to his lovely courtliness, his endless courtesy, and I want to rise up and run to the window to call out to him, to speak some soothing prayer into the darkness, to lure him into my arms, to feel again his delicate strong fingers caressing my breasts, trailing into my secret hair, finding me, converting me to fire.

Dear God, I'm going to eat you alive.

In the garden of my mother's house: the clown faces of hydrangeas; the sweet yellow ovoids of the mock banana, like the eyes of ghosts; the lacy, fragile blossoms of azaleas; the tender white easily bruised flesh of gardenias; day lilies, the pods of which my friends and I ate at tea parties on the dirt-floored carriage house; morning glory, mother of the five-pointed star; moonvine, blooming only at night; iris like prostitutes in tissue petticoats; Japanese magnolias, the sweet-smelling early blooming flowers as pale as if worn out and wan from their long winter trek; mimosa; althea; amaryllis.

The maid said, "You had better do what I tell you because I am speaking for yo' Mama," and I said, "Nobody speaks for my Mama, even my Mama," and I punched her in the belly, the first time I ever used physical force against anyone. I was eight years old and I could smell the bay which smelled like all the sumps in the world, and already men were a mystery to me, the long muscles in the legs of my teenage cousin that haunted my dreams, my father squatting next to the pool so that I could see his testicles bulged against the khaki pants, the brawniness of his forearms which reminded me of the legs of crabs, the way the hair bristled at the back of his neck—J.C., dressed in white, climbed the steps with flowers in his arms; he said, "You will probably destroy me," and I said, "You will handle that chore yourself, I'm afraid," and then he looked at me as if he were disappointed.

I am not turned away from the town ladies, as men would think, because I find their talk too simpering sweet; I find their talk anything but sweet; it is instead raucous, violent, aggressive and accusatory; it frightens me.

My father, the admiral's son, would not know me, though he lives, puttering about the Reservation that is Charleston, whirling checks through his tills. Sometimes when I was a child and the phone would ring, I would pick up the receiver and gurgle and shriek into it, making noises from the night and from the woods, broken, lost, creature noises, just to give whoever sat silent at the other end of the line the quick knowledge that the world was still untamed. (As I would tell you now that the world lies wild and rolling at my feet, as I would ask you why this is—I look out my bedroom window past the angle of porch at the wind shaking the tops of the live oaks across the river the way a mother would shake an intractable child; I see the martins whirling around the gourd house, flown in just this morning from Saskatchewan; I hear the splash of a beaver's tail, the hollow, questioning cry of a barn owl; I lie down on my soft bed and the room fills with dreams, the white moments, music that has traveled over the great empty spaces of the world to reach me; I heard Schumann and Bach, the majestic questerings of Brahms; I see the shadows rise up the wall, they are friends or corpses, I can't tell which, they do not stagger but move slowly, there is, in the sky, a whole fleet of clouds that look like gentlemen shaking the rain from their coats;

240

across the river, I know this, the white trunks of the sycamores are dirty at the bottoms like the muddy legs of horses; the leap of a bass makes a heavy flapping sound like the wing of an eagle beating the smooth black water; across the stillness of the evening I can hear every sound; I lie lazy in the arms of the world, a child still, wondering, amazed . . .)

Years ago I saw a solar eclipse. All the shadows went out of focus. The bitten sun shining through the tree leaves threw clusters of white brush strokes on the ground, each mirrored and held by its equivalent dark stroke. I held my hand out and the shadow was out of focus; along the length of my shadow fingers the sun made a creation: the lower knuckle dark, the middle knuckle lighter, the tips all light, white and shining.

In a diary dated August 12, 1887, my grandmother wrote: "I have seen him walking on the road when there was no one there, and I cannot understand how I smell the scent of tea olive, I feel the red dust on my wrist, I taste the sweetness of a peach, and he is nothing."

Grown old, she traveled from town to town carrying, like an antique brooch, the faint and singular hope that he might be living there, unnoticed and uncared for among the rise and fall of other people's lives.

My son thinks he will be a painter. I see already the picture he will paint of me: I stand with my arms open, screaming, there is blood on my dress; behind me a figure, sexless and defeated, lies across a bed. I will be the demon who prevents rescue, that will be the role I play in his desperate art.

When I left for Washington in 1937, I know my father cried. He came down the long stairs wearing a white shirt and white trousers. It was Monday morning and I could hear the fish sellers crying their wares in the park. His eyes were red though his face

241

was wiped clean. He said, "Lizzie, Lizzie," in a soft voice and then stood very still looking at me. I could hear the fronds of the cabbage palms ticking against the living room windows and out on the gallery the maid swept away the dew. I knew he would come the rest of the way down the stairs, that he would step through the narrow rectangle of golden sunlight soaking the old carpet and take me in his arms. I knew he would do this and I knew I would not resist him as I had spent all the years doing. He raised his hand, it was as if it drifted up; it stroked the air; I thought, He is caressing me before he gets to me, he is touching already the memory of me. When I drove the car into the river he said nothing, he never spoke of it. I told him that I had seen angels in the trees and he looked at me a long time and his hand rose in the same manner, shaping a form in the air between us and then falling, as it did then, that morning before I left. I took a single step toward him and the thing that held him broke; he stumbled down the stairs and took me in his arms and kissed me, full on the lips. It was one more moment when time stopped, when I held the still heart of the world in my hands.

In the early morning I rose, went out and swam in the pool. The water was the color of young limes. The big curved iron pipe with the little spin wheel on top that fed the pool always looked to me like a penis. I would touch it and a shiver would run through my body. It was very early, I think before six. The eastern sky which I could just see beyond the buildings of the Exchange was rose. As I swam, slowly on my back, I saw a man come into the lane. He wore a shirt of striped colors, a garment like something torn from the back of a clown, and he walked with a slight limp, his head held high as if he were watching birds. I swam to the edge of the pool and watched him come on. He stopped at the lane gate and looked across the yard at me. He had the face of a child under wild gold hair tossed around his head, though his body was old, shrunken under the long shirt. I started to speak, but something said don't break the silence. He said, "The world is a paradise," and smiled. It was the sweetest smile I ever saw. I dove, and when I came up he was gone. I called out, but no voice called back. Then I heard the singing for the first time, inside of me, but large, filling the world, And then the silence came again. I thought, Ghost or Lord, I will follow you. That is what I have done.

The world is a paradise.

FROM

North Gladiola

JAMES WILCOX

For Manon, Louisiana was the end of the world, France's Sibe-
ria, and so, on some days, did it also seem to Mrs. Coco, who
fancied herself an exile of sorts, even though Brookhaven, Mississippi, where she was born and where her brother and sister still
lived, was only an hour's drive north. Denmark and Quailie, the
brother and sister, had never really forgiven her for eloping with
The Italian, which is how they referred to Mr. Coco, who was in
fact about as Italian as the Queen Mother. Oh, he had Italian
blood in him, all right, on both sides, and his grandfather never
did learn English. But it was a rarefied North Italian blood,
which gave him the temperament, she soon discovered once the
fever of the elopement had subsided, of a Victorian dowager. For
a few years she managed to stay in love with him, fervently im-
itating his tight-lipped restraint while adopting a nunlike ward-
robe of ill-fitting blacks and browns. After the first two children
love waned to devotion; with number three, devotion dimmed
until, after four, five, and six, all that remained was a vague sense
of duty. With the last child away from home—in New York City,
studying nutrition at Columbia Teachers College—Mrs. Coco
found herself daydreaming about Mississippi, wondering what it
would have been like if that foolish seventeen-year-old hadn't
fallen in love with The Italian, if she had stayed where she was

244

loved and understood, among her own people, good Baptists who would have killed for her. Would life seem such a burden in Mississippi? No, there was something about Louisiana, something oppressive that she felt every time she crossed the state line on her way back from the mall in Mississippi, where everyone in Tula Springs, Louisiana, did their serious shopping. The nice divider that Mississippi had in its highway, planted with azaleas and camellias, suddenly disappeared in Louisiana, leaving a two-lane that bumped up and down rises that weren't really hills, past rough pastures or meadows—it was hard to tell what was farm or wild in Louisiana, everything was so untidy—and clumps of starved-looking pines that didn't really qualify as woods. Perhaps Manon was lucky, after all, to have died young and escaped growing old in such a place.

Of course, Mrs. Coco never mentioned any of this to her husband, who held Mississippi in the greatest disdain. To him it was a land of boors and rednecks, from which she had been rescued in the nick of time, giving him a chance to do a little molding before she hardened into a mature adult; indeed, whenever Mr. Coco was displeased with something she said, his comment would be, "That sounds like Mississippi talking." Early in the marriage, hoping to smother any trace of Mississippi, the former Ethyl Mae Bickford had immersed herself in culture, studying French with a retired lady professor who, during a field trip to the opera in New Orleans, ate an innocent-looking oyster that led, via several complications, to her demise.

Along with French, Mrs. Coco had taken up the violin, but after several years of struggle, when her eight-year-old son's technique began to outstrip her own, she switched to the cello. Mr. Coco never did approve of this instrument because of the way a lady had to sit; he tried to persuade his wife to play sidesaddle. But Mrs. Coco stuck to her guns. She was enamored of the bass clef, the way the thick G and thicker C strings made her body resonate with a furtive masculine warmth. Such was her dedication that after five years of practicing two to three hours a day she discovered a lump where the varnished maple pressed against her left breast. In a panic Mr. Coco made a special novena for the lump, which turned out to be only a benign cyst. The scar from the operation—Mrs. Coco's only regret was that it was not larger—did not fade with time, but remained livid enough to make Mr. Coco a little uncomfortable when, with that peculiar moan of his, he would fumble with the frogs of her nightgown while she feigned sleep.

On her fifty-seventh birthday Mrs. Coco had an early dinner at home with her husband, who was always depressed on her birthday because his—and this would be his seventy-first—was just a week later. She did not have time for cake and ice cream, since she was due at Tula Springs' new BurgerMat, where her string quartet, the Pro Arts, was engaged for the Grand Opening ceremonies. After hurriedly pecking Mr. Coco on the eyebrow and thanking him for the present—a book that trained you to look on the bright side of life—she lugged her shabby pasteboard cello case to the car. She was saving up for a decent-looking fiberglass case with the money the quartet earned, but this was a slow process since, number one, the quartet didn't have all that many engagements, and number two, not everyone paid their bills. Jack Fairs of Baton Rouge, for instance, still hadn't coughed up a cent for the redfish rodeo that the quartet had played for back in September. All they had gotten out of Jack was a case of Butch Wax Control Stick, which Mrs. Coco had tried in vain to sell to the Tiger Unisex Hair Styling Salon across the street from her house.

As she pulled into the BurgerMat parking lot, the headlights swept over George Henry, who was lounging against the red, white, and blue bunting draped over the drive-in's glass doors. Her third child, George Henry lived in Baton Rouge, where he taught high-school civics and repaired computers on the side. Beer, two six-packs a day, had swollen him up to a hefty two-twenty, and that, along with his being nearly bald—except for a tonsure of frizzy gray hair—made him appear much older than thirty-seven. Indeed, his mother, who was petite and svelte, with only a touch of gray, had a difficult time thinking of him as her son. Could she really be responsible for anything that big and old?

"Look at your fiddle," she said as she got out of the car. George Henry, the first violin in the quartet, did not look as his mother picked the violin up off a newspaper vending machine.

"It was going to fall," she said and then added quickly, "How are you, sug? You look nice." He was wearing scuffed work boots with his tuxedo, but she decided to overlook this for now. "You're smoking," she observed instead.

"Mmm," George Henry said, the same George Henry who had sent her a Hallmark card the other day saying that for her birthday he was going to give up smoking.

"I thought you promised to give up smoking?"

He shrugged and flicked the ashes.

"Then why are you smoking?"

"Your birthday was yesterday. I didn't smoke yesterday."

Mrs. Coco sighed; she should have known it was too good to be true. "For your information, my birthday is today."

"Oh."

Her lips pursed, she went over to try the BurgerMat door and, finding it locked, rapped with her car keys on the glass. "Where *is* that man?" She had told the manager, Mr. Qumquist, that the Pro Arts would need an hour to warm up and test the acoustics, but here it was nearly seven and there weren't even any lights on inside, except for a dull red glow behind the stainless steel counter.

"George Henry, go round back and see if—"

"There's no one here, Ma."

In the lot next door, the site of a defunct insect museum that was going to be turned into a 7 Eleven, a goat tethered to a gas pump gave out a vague bleat that sounded like a car braking. Checking her cropped blond hair in the reflection of the glass door, Mrs. Coco muttered, "Well, it's about time," then turned and realized, as the goat bleated again, her mistake. This, on top of George Henry's smoking and the fact that one of the beads had come loose on the collar of her ankle-length black jersey dress, made her mention something she had promised herself not to bring up this evening: "George Henry, I'm not going to your wedding."

She had planned to write and explain her views to him in a thoughtful, rational discourse on the sacrament of marriage, which, as a convert from the days of Pius XII, Mrs. Coco took quite seriously. Already she had compromised herself by attending the wedding, a second marriage, of Larry, her oldest son, back in February. She had even shelled out two hundred dollars from her cello case fund for a rehearsal supper at the Ramada Inn, something the bride never did thank her for, acting as if it were her due. Then there was Nancy, the baby of the family, barely twenty-four years old and already divorced. Mrs. Coco felt she had to put her foot down somewhere; either she was a Catholic or she wasn't. If she wasn't, why, then there was no reason for her sister, Quailie, to be furious at her for quitting the Baptists.

"Did you hear me?" she said as George Henry gazed vacantly at the museum.

"Yeah, Ma, I heard." He struck a match and deftly applied it to the cigarette hanging from his lower lip. "Larry gets a reception, a new car, a trip to Disney World, and me, you won't even—"

"Larry is going to pay your father back for the car."

"Sure."

"And it was the Cahills who sent them to Orlando." She discreetly removed a small bug that had darted into her mouth before continuing: "Anyway, this is all beside the point. The point is, in the eyes of the Church, you're still married to Connie, who, by the way, sent me a lovely philodendron for my birthday."

"Is it because she sells hot tubs? Is that why you won't meet her?"

"I don't care if Heidi sells bananas," Mrs. Coco said, not quite truthfully, for it did disturb her that Heidi, George Henry's fiancée, sold hot tubs. No one who thought right would sell hot tubs.

"Ma, I love her. Doesn't that mean anything?"

"Oh, love—what do you know about love?" Mrs. Coco waved away some nonexistent smoke; her son was careful to turn his head when he exhaled. "I don't see why you two can't simply live together like everyone else nowadays. Why must you get married?"

"Heidi just happens to have certain principles, and I respect them."

Finding herself on the wrong side of the argument, Mrs. Coco countered with a sudden offensive: "You shouldn't drink so much."

"What?"

"It's ruining your looks."

"Ma, what are you . . . I'm trying to . . ."

"Oh, here's Duk-Soo," she said, waving at the orange motor scooter that had just pulled in off the highway.

Duk-Soo Yoon, the second violin in the Pro Arts, was under tremendous pressure this week, engaged as he was in completing an approved bibliography for his dissertation on tourism, at St. Jude State College in Ozone. Though forty-nine years old, Duk-Soo had the sensitivity of a teenager, making it something of a chore for Mrs. Coco to correct him when he played flat, which was often, or sharp, which was even more often. He took everything to heart, his full, fleshy face contracting with pain at the slightest hint of criticism. Unlike George Henry, who always found an excuse not to practice, Duk-Soo ground out his scales and arpeggios every day, bibliography or no bibliography, and yet he never improved. Several times in the past year Mrs. Coco had resolved to ease him out, turning the quartet into a trio, which meant everyone would earn a little more per concert. But every time she broached the topic, a look of such distress clouded the Korean's lovely dark eyes that she hadn't the heart to continue.

249

After unstrapping his violin from the basket in back, Duk-Soo, a stolid gentleman whose silver hair was obscured by a bulbous yellow helmet, stooped to chain the scooter to a lamppost before joining Mrs. Coco and her son beneath the smiling hamburger that beckoned motorists to the drive-in.

"How can you see out of that thing?" Mrs. Coco fussed as she wiped the helmet's visor with a tissue. Rain had been falling off and on since early morning, bringing no relief, though, to the summerlike spring, one day hotter, more oppressive, than the next. Seeing what looked like the rental stub attached to the lapel of Duk-Soo's baby-blue dinner jacket, she unpinned it while he lifted off the helmet.

"No, please," the Korean said as she tossed the stub and the tissue into a nearby garbage can.

It was a note to himself, he explained. Something he must not forget before going back to St. Jude.

"Duk-Soo, what . . . Get out of there," Mrs. Coco said as he rooted in the garbage can.

"Mother," George Henry said.

"Look what he's doing to his jacket."

"Leave him alone."

Inside the BurgerMat the large white globes hanging from the ceiling flicked on and off, then on again as Mr. Qumquist and two black teenagers walked out from behind the stainless steel counter. Seeing the musicians outside, he unlocked the front door and asked them to stop messing around with his sanitary receptacles.

More teenagers arrived—three large white girls crammed into the front seat of a compact pickup and a lone boy dropped off by his mother—as George Henry and Mrs. Coco hauled in the music stands from the trunk of the car. While they arranged these on a small dais near the french frier, Mr. Qumquist handed out mums to the teenagers, who were slipping beige tunics over their T-shirts and blouses. "Stick them on your *left* side," he said, thrusting four mums at Duk-Soo, who was just standing there, getting in everyone's way.

A few legitimate guests had already begun to trickle in—would-be customers were turned away at the door—and still there was so sign of the viola. Using a pay phone, Mrs. Coco got in touch with the viola's husband, who told her that Myrtice had left the house an hour ago, and no, he had no idea why she hadn't shown up yet. Mrs. Coco's left eye was twitching by the time she got off the phone, and it continued to twitch throughout a protracted welcoming speech delivered by Mayor Binwanger, who, some twenty years ago, had carried on a notorious adulterous affair with Helen Ann, Mrs. Coco's oldest girl, who was then only a college student. Mrs. Coco had nearly died of shame that summer, quitting her volunteer job as a fourth-grade catechism teacher and switching from the A&P to the Jitney Jungle, which had higher prices but fewer shoppers who recognized her. Yet here she was, forced to listen to Mayor Binwanger rattle on about the 'gator bug his grandson had tied a string around and flown like a kite—as if anyone cared. She had often wondered if it were possible to attend a public function, a party, even a movie, without seeing him, but like the psalmist who once asked, "Whither shall I flee from thy presence?" Mrs. Coco knew deep down that the question was only rhetorical.

"All right, boys," she said when the mayor had finally finished his speech. Duk-Soo and George Henry had squeezed themselves onto the wooden dais and were tuning to the A of Duk-Soo's tuning fork. "We'll start with the slow movement of the Haydn, then the Mozart and the Boccherini, and after Mr. Qumquist makes his speech, we'll do the medley from *Cats*. George Henry, are you listening?"

"Hm?"

"Oh, where is that woman?" Mrs. Coco muttered as she gouged a hole in the dais with her jackknife. "I could crown her. Now, after *Cats*," she went on, placing the steel peg of her cello

251

securely in the hole she had dug, "I'm going to say a few words to introduce the next—"

"Ma, no."

"Quiet, heart. Let me think."

"No. I'm not going to play if you give a talk." George Henry's bloodshot eyes gazed sullenly at a shapely redhead who was showing her invitation to Mr. Qumquist at the door. "There's no reason you got to talk. What the hell do you know about hamburgers?"

"I'm not going to talk about hamburgers."

"Then can it. No one wants to be lectured about music tonight. And your jokes aren't funny anyway."

"I disagree," Duk-Soo said, glancing warily at her. "Last week at the Tomato Festival they laughed at her anecdote about the three B's."

"Hey, Duk, give me a break," George Henry said.

Mr. Qumquist, whose left ear, because of a birth defect, was nothing but a pinkish nub, walked over to the dais to inquire when they were going to begin. The teenagers were already serving hors d'oeuvres and drinks as the BurgerMat filled with the first citizens of Tula Springs and Eutaw, the town across the state line in Mississippi where they had the mall.

"Well actually," Mrs. Coco said, "we're waiting on—"

"For Christ's sakes," George Henry muttered. "We don't need her. Let's get this thing over with."

"By the way," Mr. Qumquist said, turning his good ear to her while keeping an eye on the crowd, "were you really Miss Mississippi once? There's a fella from Eutaw told me he recognized you."

Mrs. Coco went red all over. She had never actually been crowned Miss Mississippi, but two years in a row she had won the swimsuit category, an appalling thought to her now. To think that she had ever paraded half-naked in front of all those people, including her future husband.

"Y'all play nice," Mr. Qumquist said; then, turning to a sul-

252

len-looking girl with a purple streak in her hair, he snapped, "Robinette, where's them pigs in a blanket?"

As they launched into the Haydn, minus the viola, Mrs. Coco could tell right away that her son hadn't been practicing. When he was twelve, George Henry used to put in three, four hours a day on the violin, which had paid off when he won the Music Teachers National Association regional auditions. What dreams she had for him then: Juilliard, a Carnegie Hall debut, European concert tours—nothing was too good for her boy. But in his teens George Henry not only lost interest in the violin, he actually became ashamed of it, thanks to his brother Larry. Two years older than George Henry, Larry had gotten nowhere with music, even though he practiced the trombone every other day until he got too big for his mother's whippings to have much effect, other than to make him laugh. By conscientiously teasing his brother at least twice a week Larry had finally succeeded in making George Henry despise music. As for the other children, Mrs. Coco had spent a small fortune on various instruments, from the bassoon— an infatuation of Nancy's that lasted about as long as her marriage—to Helen Ann's brief flirtation with a build-it-yourself harpsichord, which never got built, much less played. It was a bitter pill for Mrs. Coco, this feckless waste of time and money. She had always hoped for gifted children, slightly disabled by artistic genius which she would nourish and protect. Instead, what she wound up with was one child, George Henry, who returned to the violin as a hobby when he began to drink too much.

In the middle of the Mozart the microphone on a second dais loaded with dyed carnations squeaked loudly. Holding up his hand at the musicians like a cop at an intersection, Mr. Qumquist rewelcomed the guests with a joke about a young lady who walked out into the woods at the Bogue Falaya State Park and got chased by a bear, but the park ranger wouldn't let her hop back into the tour bus because Louisiana state law doesn't allow ladies aboard public transportation with a bear behind them. Then, getting serious, Mr. Qumquist extolled the Tula Springs Chamber of Commerce and the tremendous vitality that he was certain the BurgerMat Corporation would infuse into the economic life of the Florida Parishes. After the applause from the hundred or so guests, some in black tie and long gowns, and a few more words from Mayor Binwanger, Mr. Qumquist stood up again and invited everyone to dance to the fine music of the Pro Arts Quartet.

The globe above Mrs. Coco's head dimmed, blurring the handwritten notes of *Cats*. Duk-Soo had made a fuss last week about playing this medley since he claimed that the arrangement for string quartet, written by a friend of George Henry's, a music major at LSU, was illegal; if ASCAP caught the Pro Arts, they would be severely fined and blacklisted. Mrs. Coco was leaning over, telling him to quit worrying and play, when she felt a little stab in her side. Looking up, she saw it was Myrtice Fitt, the viola.

"Move on over, hon," Myrtice said, poking Duk-Soo with her bow as she edged past Mrs. Coco's cello.

"Where have you been?" Mrs. Coco said coldly. In her eyes Myrtice was nothing but a vain, petty local housewife with all the wrong values in life, and she would have avoided the woman like the plague if she didn't just happen to play the viola surprisingly well and in tune. She was wearing a stylish pale gown that must have cost a fortune, and her auburn hair shone with a rich, lustrous glow that was not at all appropriate for a sixty-year-old.

"You told me McDonald's," Myrtice said with a petulant flick of her gold charm bracelet.

"But there isn't a McDonald's in Tula Springs," Duk-Soo said.

"I know. I went clear to Eutaw looking for one."

"I never said McDonald's," Mrs. Coco said.

"You did so. I have a photogenic memory, Ethyl Mae, so don't try and deny it."

"I did not say McDonald's."

"You probably did, Ma," George Henry put in. "I mean like you told me McDonald's, too. The only reason I knew to come here was because I talked to Dad, and he said—"

"I never, no. Why on earth would I say . . ."

From across the room Mr. Qumquist made a sawing motion at Mrs. Coco, who told everyone they better start playing if they wanted to get paid. It upset her to think that George Henry was taking Myrtice's side, and as a result Mrs. Coco forgot she was in A flat and played D natural all through the medley while pondering how much she was going to dock Myrtice for being late.

Country Blues for Melissa

LEIGH ALLISON WILSON

One night, twenty years ago and in the middle of one of the few really blizzard-like storms that pounce on the mountains of East Tennessee, I awoke from a strange dream—about disembodied but kind hearts, oddly enough, throwing bars of music at me—and felt a very cold draft on my face. My breath came out in wizening white gusts. At first glance I thought my parents, in a fit of instruction, had moved me, bed and all, outside the house into the front yard where I was to learn, through experience my mother would explain, not to oversleep on school days; small children and dogs, she'd say, should be shown, not told. At a second, more desperate glance I stared for a full minute, and as if it were the sole orienting point in a universe run amok, at the broken Timex wristwatch on my nightstand. It read, as it always did, a comforting three-thirty. My meteorite rock sat like a sentinel on the dresser, my picture of the Carter Family (Maybelle on guitar, A.P. at the mike) still hung provocatively over the mirror. All was right, though very cold, with my world.

A proprietary inspection, now sitting straight up in the bed, led to an open, an exceedingly open, window of my bedroom and to the bare feet and white pajama-striped calves of my brother, Alvin, who leaned outside on the sill. Except for a wriggling about the toes, there was no movement at the window, although a trickle of snow and cold air moved quite freely into the room. Across the room and through the bath adjoining our bedrooms I noticed that my brother's window was also open, curtains flapping, an inch-thick accumulation of snow lapping over the sill onto the wooden slats of his floor. At the time, precisely three-thirty in the morning on February 15, 1960, my brother was nine, I was eight. And the two of us, according to a certain blood relative, were the consecutive boy then girl amendments to a flamboyant New Year's resolution made public by our mother at a family Christmas dinner in 1950. It's a pack of lies, she'll say when confronted, however.

"What's going on?" I demanded of the hindquarters upon my windowsill. "What is it, people or what?" From his curious posture a sudden, delightful image of two steel guitarists, a banjoist, an autoharpist, and a fiddler had thrust itself into the blizzard outside and begun to play a rousing version of "Let Old Mother Nature Have Her Way" inside my head. The toes on the sill, pink in the shadows, wriggled a vague response.

My brother, at nine, was one of those levelheaded young men who can with impunity disregard a direct question and then, indirectly, answer it in painful detail much later. Once our father took it upon himself to explain Death to Alvin, apparently because he had watched the funeral of a much-loved grandmother with an impassive, almost bored six-year-old's expression. After a week of what Daddy termed "embarrassingly blank stares," the lessons were reassigned to a more sophisticated period of his child development. Much later though, in the act of rummaging for stray cigars in my mother's sewing basket, Daddy came across a folded 8- by 10-inch piece of notebook paper that purported to be Alvin's last will and testament, signed the day, month, and year of that first funeral. He had bequeathed all seventeen personal pos-. sessions, in their motley entirety, to his deceased grandmother.

"It's cold for goodness' sake, Alvin," I told the left foot, the one closest to my bed. Then, hopefully, "I'll bet it ain't half so cold with all these windows shut. What do you think, Alvin, it's *cold* in here, hey?"

No response, not even a wriggle, not that I expected one, and the wind wheezed more snow onto the floor where it lay in latent dunes, white on black. After eight years of studying my brother, of watching him, rather, like a pensive hawk; reading the books he did or having him read them to me (both of us having acquired this skill at the age of four and a half with the agreement we'd quit when someone ordered us to learn it, which they did, and we didn't); wearing the same clothes right down to the J.C. Penney cowboy boots; eating the same food (exclusive of certain varieties of mixed vegetables, particularly those with yellows and pale greens); and most importantly, falling deeply in love with the same country music heroes and heroines; after years of this concentrated footstep-following, I trusted, with a violent passion, my brother's most eccentric whim. If he walked with a slight stoop like Hank Williams, I did. If he etched scars of mascara onto his face and swaggered into saloons to prove his manhood, I did, too. We had stacks of our parents' 45s and old 78s, taller than we were, and we lovingly played them over and over on a beaten-to-death battery-operated Sears-Roebuck phonograph. We acted out the more dramatic scenes, parting with great sorrow and many tears in the front yard and reuniting, with harrowing joy and many more tears, in the back yard where the phonograph and Hank Locklin squeaked out "Please Help Me I'm Falling" from a strategic point in the grass. On one notable occasion Alvin climbed an oak tree, tied a rope to one of its highest branches, and stopped just short of hanging himself to the tune of "Dang Me."

There were other symptoms of love that presented themselves at peculiar moments. For a while Alvin took to quoting, verbatim and with a look of profound dignity, the words of Hank Williams responding to a reporter's sophomoric question, "What exactly is the *appeal* of country music, Mr. Williams?" "'It can be explained,'" Alvin would quote, abruptly, at, say, a dinner party given by our parents, "'It can be explained in just one word:

Sincerity. When a hillbilly sings a crazy song,' " he'd go on, " 'he *feels* crazy. When he sings, "I Laid My Mother Away," he *sees* her a-laying right there in the coffin. He sings more sincere than most entertainers because the hillbilly was raised rougher than most entertainers.' " Here Alvin began to grin maniacally and deepened his voice to a rough contralto. " 'You got to know a lot about hard work. You got to have smelt a lot of mule manure before you can sing like a hillbilly. The people who has been raised the way a hillbilly has *knows* what he is singing about and appreciates it.' " Then Alvin would more than likely burst into tears, bow with dignity, and leave the room.

"Pagan idolater," Daddy would explain, matter-of-factly, to the horrified dinner guests, so that conversation could resume as usual.

"Alvin!" I yelled in my loudest, quiet whisper, "I'm *dying* in here." That got his attention all right, a face appeared with a nose strikingly lavender in shade.

"Business," said two purple lips, then the spectral-colored face returned outside, as though bent on picking up a few greens and indigo-reds. I noticed, in passing, that Alvin had the phonograph in his hands, was therefore in the process of doing Something Important, and so resolved at once to keep my mouth shut and my head under the bedcovers.

It might be noted here that our family lived, literally, out in the middle of nowhere. Our father, once a corporate lawyer in At- lanta, moved—with alacrity, he'd point out—kit and caboodle and new wife to Carter Valley, Tennessee, where he staked out several hundred acres and became a devout thinker-*cum*-va- grant-*cum*-teller of tall tales, and gentleman farmer. Mama, by virtue of having loved such a madman, did what she always does. She made do. And she made it well, single-handedly pulling what soon became a family of four through six lean, positively ema- ciated years. Alvin and I, too, from the moment we could walk, pitched our efforts into the farm with a mighty gusto and an abso- lute lack of talent. To this day Mama remembers a manly two-year-old Alvin, half-drowned and surrounded by sorrowful thirsty cows, struggling valiantly out of a water trough he'd just filled.

The nearest city was Bull's Gap, ten miles away, a bustling little urban area approximately the size of a city block in Queens, containing, among a few other things, an elementary school, a hardware and farm equipment store, a Cas Walker grocery store, and eight extremely social Protestant churches, each of which slipped a phrase with "God" or "Jesus" or "Holy" into its title, boasted a congregation of at least a dozen, and chattily proselytized among the other churches for lack of an outside audience. "The Holy Icon Churches of God and Jesus His Son the Only Beleaguered Redeemer," Alvin called them, as well as "Those it-won't-hurt-a-bit salvation places."

The nearest house, though, was a ramshackle wooden structure only two hundred yards down the road and inhabited by a remarkably insane old woman, Miss Mildred. Above all else Miss Mildred loved to sit on her porch and take imaginary potshots at the appendages of unwitting trespassers against her, and she just sat there, decked out with a fine black silk dress, a string of cultured pearls, and a highly-polished and unloaded twelve-gauge shotgun, sat there all day long. Alvin, of course, was the only human being allowed inside her house, except that on certain occasions, when all winds and stars and shotguns were in collusion, I—that *other* young-un—would be allowed to sit, very quietly, on the porch, while they went inside and Miss Mildred taught Alvin how to play her big D28 Martin, a guitar mail-ordered, mysteriously, from Nashville. Sitting on that porch where Miss Mildred sat, with the Smoky Mountains just blue wisps in the distance, with Miss Mildred crying "Feeling now, boy, with *feeling!*" and Alvin strumming madly away with feeling, I felt, as I've rarely felt since, that the world was as beautiful and as serious, as perfect and complex and eminently handleable, as a highly-polished and forever unloaded twelve-gauge shotgun.

To return to that "out of the middle of nowhere" business; it's a lie. We were a family profoundly Somewhere, and we each of us clung like cornstalks to the soil and air and hills of East Tennessee. If we told stories or read stories aloud, we did so in our natural and unabashed hick idiom—sounds not excluding Shakespeare's "The Tamin of the Shrew" and "Much Do Bout Nothin"—because it *felt* right. If we fought like monkeys, and we did with real pleasure, if we fought and argued and picked at our faults in exacting detail, we did so because we *felt* like it and loved each other, not because we had ulterior motives or ulterior reasons or, Lord knows, exterior *goals*. We were honest-to-God, hoedowning, shitkicking, life-loving hillbillies, and we were smack in the middle of an overpowering somewhere.

To all irregionalists everywhere, to all mainstreaming, trend-following, media-addicted, suburban intellectual-mystic peoples everywhere, we ask you, from the bottom of our hearts, we ask you: From whence come *your* words?

Alvin once told me, on one of his more despairing days, that the essence of modern language and its slow death could be traced to a convalescent home in New Jersey, where the original movie Tarzan was moved unceremoniously to a private suite because of his "repeated and disruptive elephant yells." We need every goddamn elephant yell we can get, he'd said, and we need them shoved into every available nook, cranny, and sphincter among us, he'd said. Alvin, even on his good days, was quite an elephant yeller himself. Sometimes you could hear his elephant yodel for miles and miles before he even opened his mouth.

When Richard Nixon was resigning in 1973, Alvin and I both happened to be home from our respective, if not wholly respected, northeastern colleges. We sat in the living room, ears poised toward the radio, and heard an ex-two-time president address the nation that voted for him and was listening to him for perhaps the last time. The muted flutter of the presidential helicopter sounded like static in the background. When he got to the part about Rose Kennedy, about how *his* mother would never have a biography written about *her* as Rose Kennedy had, Alvin

261

jerked sharply upright, into his Lester Flatt G-run listening position. Then, when Nixon choked off the part about his mother
and went tearfully on into the part about how the nation had to
utilize and unify and rise ever onward over every obstacle, I
looked up into Alvin's face. His eyes were teary, and Alvin's eyes,
to the subjective observer, alternated between reflections of the
sheerest sincerity and instruments of the most exposed torture.
"He doesn't have the words, he doesn't have the *words*," he kept
saying and sobbing, "Lord help us, we don't even have the *words*
for our own goddamn tragedies!"

I woke up to find Alvin's pale blue face peering under the covers into my eyes. He might have been that Sam McGee from
Tennessee in sore and poetic need of a healthy cremation. "Shut
the *door*," I told him, as if he were intruding on a private conversation; I sleep the big sleep when I sleep. "Hug this," Alvin said.
He then thrust under the covers what was effectively a frozen
solid phonograph with an old Roy Acuff 78, "The Great Speckled
Bird," iced over on top of it. Snow was melting rapidly, lux-
uriously, onto my green polka-dot percale sheets. "C'mon, warm
it up," Alvin said. "Give it a hug." He bounced from the ball of
one foot onto the other and back again, smacking his palms and
smacking his lips, warming up, looking for all the world like a
rabid football coach with an exotic skin disease. "Jesus damnit!
Alvin," I cried, "it's going all over my bed!" "Right," he said
enthusiastically. "Froze up on me, needs warmth."

When Alvin became enthusiastic there was nothing to do but
relax and hug a frozen phonograph.

"That's the idea," he said. "Just hold on for a minute and I'll go
downstairs and get the heating pad and be right back."

The heating pad in question was *the* heating pad, a 12- by 12-
inch square of pink cotton material, flecked with maroon stars
and stuffed with electrical circuits, used by our mother as a sub-
stitute bottle of aspirin, comforter of depressions, dryer of tears,
and divine cure-all of endless childhood diseases. Once she
nearly and lovingly suffocated Alvin during the treatment of a

cold sore. Our father, on the other hand, who was never sick a day of his adult life—whenever either or both of us were "indisposed" (his word) by a violent case of measles or mumps—didn't know what the hell to make of us *or* the heating pad and generally retired to his ever-healthy cattle. One incident, though, does deserve mention. I remember Daddy entering my sickroom, on tiptoe no less, during a virulent case of chicken pox wherein even my tongue itched like fifty devils. "Thought you might like some entertainment," he had said, humbly, then he proceeded to read for seven uninterrupted hours the entire contents of Flannery O'Connor's *A Good Man Is Hard to Find*. Suffice it to say, he cured me of a great many things, except the chicken pox, during that session.

"Let's see what the story is," Alvin said, peeking under the blankets where the phonograph and I lay, arm to arm, in cold water. "Looking better," he said authoritatively, man-to-man with the phonograph. "Grippy, though, a little grippy." He all but took its pulse, lifting this, twirling that, sliding the record, blowing on the needle. At last he took it out and set it on the floor, plugged in the heating pad, and placed it gingerly over the phonograph.

"Wait see is what we do now," he told me, and nodded sagely. He sat cross-legged on the floor, a consoling hand on top of the heating pad, his eyes a troubled mixture of colors. Around the edges of his face there showed remnants of blue, but for the most part the skin had undergone a reversal, was pale, bloodless.

"Nothing personal, it ain't that," I said, "but what are you doing, Alvin?"

"I'm melting snow," said Alvin.

"I know, but what are you *doing*?" The water on my sheets was growing warmer by the minute, but it felt none too interesting.

"You know that verse in the Bible, that one that's the nine verse, twelve chapter somewhere?" I said, no, that I didn't, but that I would be very interested to hear it. "It went like this: 'Mine heritage is unto me as a speckled bird, the birds round about are against her.'"

263

Alvin could quote, at nine and at will, smidgens of songs, books, advertisements, movies, gossip, and even bird songs; he *attracted* all the good quotes.

"But that's Roy Acuff," I said. "That's that song right there, 'The Great Speckled Bird.'" I pointed elaborately in the direction of the heating pad.

"Bible did it first." He uncovered the phonograph for an experimental poke or two, then covered it back up. "Can't tell, though, who *really* said it, somebody just passing through. Heard it at the Church of God down to town."

"But what's it mean?" For all the cold air and open windows and wet sheets I was getting hot, hot and bothered. My brother was born with a knack, a sleight of imagination, for unconscious dramatic suspense, almost as though it might kill him, or kill something in him, if he ever got right to the point. I was getting hot and bothered.

"It's this bird," he explained. With the consoling hand he felt the phonograph, then screwed his face into a concentrated expression, considering its temperature. "Very better," he announced finally. Then slowly, painfully slowly, he unveiled the phonograph and after some cautious negotiation switched it on. Old Roy Acuff sang out with fuzzy, plaintive sincerity. His voice, at least, created no unsettling gusts of white air in the room; no cold words from old Roy.

"Business," said Alvin. He stood up and backed his way toward the window, phonograph in tow. Already the snow had drifted across the floor due to wind currents, although it had stopped snowing outside, and I stared blankly, fixedly, a veritable Robinson Crusoe in Nightgown, at Alvin's footprints on the floor. Alvin was back up on the sill, singing now, singing along with Roy Acuff.

"It's really weird to me," I said, grim as a soldier, "that whenever something important happens around here, I don't know what it is." Alvin reared back, teetering on the sill, and cast an appraising look in my direction.

LEIGH ALLISON WILSON

"All right then," said Alvin. "Come on up and help me sing."

It was a hearty "Welcome Aboard" and I jumped out of bed, nightgown flapping, and joined Alvin on the catwalk of the sill. It was spectacularly cold up there, too cold for East Tennessee and so cold it might have been warmer than anything I'd ever known. Outside the moon shone forth in a sedate light and the snow, moon-silvered, had turned our farm to stone. The fenceposts around the cattle yard were entirely gone, disappeared, as though the very earth had surged upward to swallow all feeble boundaries. The cornfield, prickly with last year's stubble, was now a slab of solid marble. Through the trees that stood in funereal black procession across the back yard, I know I saw Jimmie Rodgers, thinner than a sapling, dancing with his Boston terrier, Mickey, prancing between the oaks of our farm. "Play that thing, boy!" he sang. And way off in the distance a single yellow square of light testified to a night of insomnia, of waiting and watching, at Miss Mildred's house.

"Don't be afraid," Alvin said. "Sing!"

In his eyes was the ecstatic glint of a madman, of someone very far away and irretrievably gone. So I sang, quietly at first, then louder, then louder still, until the world of stone outside cracked and gave way to country music. We sang in harmony, Roy and Alvin and I, and when Roy quit, Alvin started him up again. After an hour, though, hoarse and chilled, I said I'd had enough, that I'd give moral support from my bed but to bed I was going.

"Don't you want to know what we're doing?" Already in bed I said yes, yes, *yes* for goodness' sake.

"It's this bird," he said and pointed outside. I got out of bed and walked, rather impertinently, to the window.

"I don't see anything, Alvin, nothing. This isn't one of your games, is it? I want to know that right now. I want to know what's going on, it dark and cold and me not knowing what's going on. I'd like to know right now what's going on. It's *weird* is what it is." I had a good hold on Alvin's arm and jerked the sleeve of his pajamas for emphasis.

265

"Don't you see it? It's a bird down there." By leaning over the sill I could make out what looked like a black patent-leather woman's purse, spraddled messily on top of the snow.

"Is it alive?"

"Crippled," said Alvin.

"Why?"

"Flew into my window, never saw it, just flew around in the storm into my window and never saw it. Like a gunshot it sounded, like a snare drum." He paused, frowning, as if to remember how the lyrics went. "Then it crawled around the house over here and I figured maybe it could use some songs. Crippled itself and don't have no home it can go to. It'll be froze tomorrow and the others'll peck at it—that's the way birds do, peck and all."

I went back to bed and Alvin stayed put, singing. Before I fell asleep, in the back of my mind I wondered whether a tear, dropped from a height of two stories in near-zero weather, wouldn't freeze before it hit the ground.

At sunrise Alvin woke me and told me to get dressed, we would go see the bird together. He hadn't slept and his eyes blazed, kindling some kind of desperate fever. In the back yard we crouched over the bird, didn't touch it; it was an ebony-glossed crow with one small speck of bright red blood on the yellow beak, and its legs stuck out rigidly to the side, like broken twigs. It certainly wasn't going anywhere anymore and I said as much and stood up, washing my hands of the whole business with a palmful of snow. Alvin, too, stood up. "Dead," he said sadly. "Old dead crow," he said, more sadly, then he smiled brightly, maniacally, and stamped his foot squarely onto the bird. It slid deep inside the snow and disappeared. He looked at me with that smile on his face. "I hope . . ." he began, but he never finished the sentence.

A special license of country music, and one I highly recommend, is the manipulation of anonymity. If not God, goes the license, then by God *pretend* to be. Take that thing by its horns and wrestle it, like St. Michael, to Kingdom Come and Back, before it hits the newspapers. As Alvin said to me one rainy Sunday morning, over the Bull's Gap *Review* comics section: "You've got to sing the words for everybody, and if you leave somebody out, you've got to make damn sure they'll at least hum the tune for the rest of their life." He meant, I think, that the country musician has to distill himself down to a cellular particle approximately the size and shape of a human mouth in the act of kissing Death.

With license in my back pocket, I accordingly whittle the past from twenty years ago into a smaller, more compact, four. What follows is not my story; it is, of course, my brother's. Before he went gallivanting, with all utter seriousness, southward, he told me this story in hiccupping, daily installments. Alvin was not one for sordid detail, and even less for making points, drawing conclusions, declaring an overt meaning, and his stories follow the solid oral tradition of painless instruction. One is hit in the head, repeatedly as a matter of fact, before one feels it, a psychological effect closely akin to an aural placebo. What I'm trying, awkwardly, to point out is for me the awful magnitude of taking this particular thing by its particular horns and wrestling the particular life out of it.

The time, to be precise to the point of disinterest, will be exactly ten o'clock in the morning on May 18, 1976, and the young man with the black beret, to be precise with considerably more interest, will be my brother, twenty-five and traveling incognito. As his sister and the stealer of his story, I interrupt here, or better yet, I hereby *nip in the bud* the flow of this narration to say one thing: I am a barefaced liar, as any member of my family, and especially my brother, would be the first to admit; don't trust me, and I mean it. Any lover of country music will understand this statement, will even forgive the self-consciousness of this and any ensuing interruption, because soon, very soon, this lover understands, the story must continue and, finally, end, regardless of my dishonesty—*in spite* of it, actually. For at the core of any good country music lover beats the heart of a believer, beats the heart of an inveterate truth seeker who, deep down, believes that

267

every word is at best a pack of decent lies and at worst a matter of opinion, and that the real truth is in the melody. The *twang* so to speak, of the beloved.

Melissa: wherever you are out there, whatever you're doing, *I know you can hear this.* Listen.

One mugging, two pocket-pickings, and one attempted rape occurred during the young man's three-hour layover in the Washington Trailways station. He wore a black beret and carried a guitar case and had seen or overheard each of the four unrelated incidents with a facial expression of the keenest interest. Had it not been for his eyes—round, gray-brown, openly innocent eyes, the kind of eyes that are the confession of a whole face—but for those eyes he might have been mistaken for the gloating mastermind behind all four criminal acts. Nevertheless, as his eyes suggested, or rather, shouted, the young man with the black beret had merely been very interested: two days before in Port Authority he was robbed of every piece of luggage, every cent, and a carton of Marlboro cigarettes, by a roving lunatic with a switchblade. He had saved the guitar, though, telling the switchblade that, thank you, it would just have to kill him to get it and the switchblade, made a little awkward by the bulk of its spoils, had relented and rapidly withdrawn.

He stood on the boarding platform, guitar in hand, beret cocked like a trigger on the back of his head, and leaned in a quiet, neutral position against a concrete pillar. A decade before, he would have been a political caricature of himself, a stereotypic young man with a black beret, fresh, in the loose sense of the word, from New York. A decade before, he looked like the type of young man who might *give* everything he owned to a roving lunatic without a switchblade. Times change; no one looks like that any more. All decadent stereotypes had changed clothes, stiffened their upper lips, and risen ever onward toward the vicinity of Wall Street. Now they played their guitars for small social groups, cultivated interesting hobbies, met interesting people, and coolly observed the course of world and national affairs over green bottles of interesting bubbly-water. They were all very healthy in this decade, health apparently a first bastion of self-control, self-control apparently the sole bastion of utility. Any traveling young man with a black beret and a worn guitar was immediately suspect as a chic punk or a redneck who didn't know any better. This particular young man fell, plummeted, into the latter suspicion.

The young man coveted his health no more and no less than he trusted the weather. In fact he knew of at least nine latent cancers all over his body and yet he smoked, with relish, over a pack of cigarettes a day. He had jogged once, on impulse, down Fifth Avenue in order to skirt a group of small boys who were throwing water balloons at passersby. One, a blue one, hit him on the back of the head.

In truth he was not even from New York, had lived two years in a cat-infested fourth floor walk-up on East Seventh Street, which qualified him as an overstayed tourist in that city. Of the eight million possible accents there, his, he had felt, was the least acceptable. And although he tried to control it, temper it, beat it to death, the only surefire method of communication he'd hit upon was an extremely difficult maneuver, involving the placement of his tongue firmly against the inside of his cheek plus a sundry repertoire of hand gesticulations. In this manner, tiresome though it was, he might attempt the rudiments of accentless communication—hailing taxis, cashing checks, ordering food, "Please," "Thank you"—without wearing a "Whar you-all frahm, Sahnny?" In a Brooklyn accent. In a Brooklyn accent pleased as punch with itself and overcome with the pride of a voice that knows it can do a pretty good imitation or two. He had met each and every Italian, Jew, Dalmatian, high and low Bostonian, vegetarian, and Republican streetside mimic in New York City.

In this decade, however, he was headed home, to the Great State of Tennessee, and more particularly to Nashville where he would, without a doubt, become the greatest country music singer of his generation. Such were the ambitions of the times.

The express to Dallas, his connection, already hemmed and

hawed at the gate, its unlit headlights staring at him, stupidly, right between the eyes. The bus reminded him, uncomfortably, of the cornbore caterpillars he used to mash on his family's farm. In thousands the caterpillars would devour sweet corn with a rapidity that seemed to come from an ugly grudge of a personal nature. An accident had occurred in his presence many years before. At an intersection called Bean Station, far from any town in East Tennessee, a tractor trailer rammed, almost nonchalantly, into a Greyhound bus. People flittered all over the pavement. And his only thought was: it looks like a caterpillar and they look like sweet corn. Afterwards, that very night, he went home and ate thirty-nine cornbore caterpillars, chewing well and swallowing; it had been only fair.

The young man accosted a rabid-looking man in fat trousers and asked for a cigarette, keeping an eye on the guitar in his hand as if it were a child, an unruly child that any minute might break free to inspect the gumball machines. The rabid man paused with a look of horror on his face, thrust an entire pack of cigarettes into the young man's hand, and muttered, "Missing my goddamn't bus, buddy," before waddling quickly on. Inside the man's mouth, he couldn't help noticing, only three yellow teeth had disrupted the empty symmetry. Briefly, but powerfully, the young man wanted to chase after the rabid man and pat his hollow cheek and maybe tell him a sadder story than the ones he already knew. Recently he had taken a turn for the worse, wanted to accost strangers in phone booths and shake their hands, wanted to attend the funerals of people he'd never known and weep, wanted to set the newspapers to music and sing of lives made black and white. He thought he might be crazy and almost, though not wholeheartedly, wished to hell he was. But deep down he knew he had never been saner.

"Thank you," he said, to no one in particular. By way of answer the sun rose over the metal horizon of the bus and blinded him for several seconds.

"Everbody get on board," said the driver to Dallas, in a surly baritone voice. The driver wielded, and wielded well, the impersonation of a bouncer in a hard-bitten country bar, intimating that he, by God, could take on any man boarding *his* bus. The sleeves of his regulation white shirt rolled back in neat creases above the elbow, clung tightly to the muscles there, and added a distinguished touch of elegance to the impression of scarcely suppressed violence. With a mouth wizened into distaste he assisted a woman and child up the steps by using their elbows as fulcrums and literally levering them into the bus. The young man scanned his ticket, a trifle desperately, to make sure all was without a doubt in order, and then handed it, rheumatically, over to the driver.

"What we got there," the driver said, grim as Death. His baritone was an instrument uniquely capable of rendering the shortest declarative sentence into a physical threat, and he stared with idle interest at the young man's ticket.

"I believe we've got a ticket," said the young man, grinning desperately. He had a sudden urge to explain in detail that he was just a conspicuous nitwit, passing through.

"Funny boy, huh." The driver glanced at him with a sweet grimace of introspection on his mouth. It was a short, indifferent once-over, as though he contemplated an open invitation to step back of the bus and discuss some things and maybe break somebody's neck.

"Nosir, honest to God, I haven't been funny for years." In a second, equally sudden urge, the young man wanted to point out that he was very likely the next Hank Williams and would probably need his body, in its entirety, in the near future.

"You know, funny boy," the driver said wistfully, "I could wipe that smile off four a you."

"I know, really, twenty, no kidding, thirty at least. I know you could do it, sir."

"All right then." With real finesse the driver hitched the sides of his trousers, like six-shooters, a little higher onto his waist. In the process he mutilated the young man's ticket. "We got luggage compartments for that'ere music."

"I know you do, I've known it for a hell of a long time, I can

271

tell you that, sir. The thing is, this guitar and me, we're almost kin, that's the thing. You wouldn't put your sister under a bus, would you?"

The driver stared at him.

"I don't like you," he said, finally, with an impressive and ominous control. "Nor none of your kind, nor your hat neither. Get your butt on the bus, bud."

"Right," said the young man. "Will do. Bud on the bus right away." He leapt like a drowning man for the steps, stumbled on the second one, overturned a fire extinguisher with the guitar, then got back to his feet. A large knurl of chewing gum adhered to the side of the guitar case. "Bud's butt is on the bus," he told the gum, confidentially.

"Hey, funny boy." Down on the street the driver stood with his arm upraised; had he held a gun it would have been point-blank range. "Your ticket."

"Right," said the young man and he thrust out a hand that looked, strangely enough, like a branch in a gale-force wind. Into it the driver dropped a wad of paper approximately the size of a quarter.

"Thank you," the young man said.

"Just you sit in the back," said the driver with infinite patience, "or I might just lose my temper."

"Right," the young man agreed. "Way back, back to Methuselah."

Once the young man had seen Johnny Cash in concert, more live than life on the stage, and accompanied by June Carter who sang quite pleasantly at his left hand. During the refrain of "A Boy Named Sue" he was knocked unconscious from behind by an overexcited fan with a beer bottle just as Charlie Pride came onstage to join in on the fun. He had regretted that four-hour blackout ever since. Even now he felt a little faint, the recurrence of a possibly serious malady.

Down the aisle of the bus tier upon gray tier of inquisitorial faces watched him suspiciously as he negotiated himself and his guitar toward the rear. Those were the gray faces, he knew, that would form the juries of the future, that might follow the lead of yesteryear's decadent stereotypes and sentence the country to a status quo no longer handleable. Faceless and wordless they would sit and knit beside the guillotines of their own sons and daughters, fighting only for the right to front-row seats. And the hell of it was, a hell the young man had known from the day he picked up a guitar that belonged to a crazy old woman out in the middle of somewhere, the hell of it was that at the heart of every gray juror and every gray judge was a melody, as elusive as the character of America itself, and it was undeniably, ineradicably, a country melody of salvation. "For my next song," he wanted to say and wink engagingly at his audience, "something more on the upbeat side of things." Instead he proceeded, guitar foremost, toward the rear.

He passed, on his right, the woman and child who had been teeter-tottered into the bus, and he noticed that—although her magenta-colored hair was a little worse for wear and her pancake makeup had begun to scale off around the nose—the woman was lovely. The child sat primly on the seat next to the aisle, her little patent-leathered feet crossed neatly at the ankles, six inches above the floor, and her little lap obscured by a large unopened book entitled *Patterns of Grace*. She looked up and nodded officiously as he passed; he looked down and nodded officiously, if not zealously, back. Hers was the first unsolicited benign nod he'd received in two years.

He took the seats directly behind the woman and child, arranged his guitar with the care due an invalid on the plastic upholstery, then sat down beside the window. Outside the sun wreaked an interesting havoc on the neon signs of the strip joints across the street, and he lit a cigarette, observing that every man who entered a strip joint wore a polyester overcoat. He wondered whether polyester overcoats reflected a Washington style preference or whether they represented a secret rite of passage, like credit cards, into the realm of striptease. After a while the driver revved his bus into gear, gave a hearty deafening blast of the horn to several old men on the boarding platform (one of whom put a palm to his ear, as if he didn't quite catch the drift of the conversation), and they pulled out of the station, headed south.

The young man finished his cigarette and took out his guitar and, very quietly, began to fiddle around with a few bars of a new tune. For weeks he'd been working on it, refining it, wrestling with it, but something—maybe only a chord or two—was missing. In all honesty, he wanted this tune to sound like nothing short of an elephant giving birth to the continent of Africa, without an anesthetic.

"You need to go from D to A in eighth notes," said a high-pitched voice. It was the child or, rather, the child's head, propped on the seat in front of him. And it was, in fact, exactly what he needed to do. The young man jerked sharply upright.

"How do you know that?"

Invitation enough, the child climbed over, not around, her seat, and settled demurely into the seat beside the young man. She crossed her legs. She rubbed her nose, delicately, as only the polite veteran of many runny noses can do. She adjusted her hair ribbon that held her medium-length red hair in token control. In short, she took her own sweet time.

"I don't believe we've been introduced," she said and extended her left hand.

The young man apologized profusely, shook her hand vigorously, and said that his name was Bud, that he'd come from New York, and that he was headed for Nashville.

"My name is Melissa," she said. "You may call me Melissa. My mother's name is also Melissa, but she's asleep. Buses give her the morning sickness. My father was an unknown factor really." She looked to her right, craned her neck behind them, ascertained that the coast, as it were, was clear and continued, *sotto voce:* "You may have noticed that I'm a genius. At the present moment I am disguised as a perfectly normal eleven-year-old child, but I'm really twenty-two. I've been tested. Five times. I would appreciate

274

your silence." She directed a penetrating look, with eyes no larger than dimes, toward the young man who promptly assured her that, as far as he was concerned, mum was the word.

"You're not, I hope, a *pop*ular singer?" She stressed the word "popular" with an unmistakable, but very pretty, groan. Then she asked for a cigarette and recrossed her legs. When the young man suggested, solicitously, that perhaps a cigarette would be bad for her health, Melissa gave a much less pretty groan and produced, from her back pocket, a pack of Marlboro cigarettes. The young man lit her cigarette, not out of courtesy, but because he was becoming, more or less, quite afraid of her.

"My life expectancy," she said, inhaling, "is endless really. Are you a popular singer?"

The young man said, no, he was not, that he played country music, a genre in itself unpopular in most areas, that he had yet to make his mark even in an unpopular genre, and that, in effect, he was absolutely unknown except to blood relatives and an occasional stranger.

"Good," said Melissa. "You should go to Central America then."

He readily agreed, would have agreed at this point to go almost anywhere she saw fit to tell him to go, then, come to think of it, he asked: "Why?" She cast an appraising look at him, rubbed her nose, and settled more comfortably against her seat. She blew out a perfect ring of smoke and watched it float off toward the front of the bus.

"You'll have to learn Spanish," she decided. "And you'll have to travel light. Do you speak Spanish? I'm fluent really, know around four hundred and thirty-three words, not including numbers. Any child could do the numbers."

"But why," said the young man, "should I go to Central America?" In his excitement he burned his elbow on the cigarette Melissa held in her left hand.

After a flurry of apologies, mostly from the young man, Melissa sighed and leaned forward. "Because," she said. "It needs

275

to be heard. I'm going there myself, when I come of age. That'll be in about seventy-two months."

At this she stubbed out her cigarette and stood up, explaining that her mother disliked to wake up alone. Her mother was the "clinging type," she said, "and worried about every little thing," whereupon she performed a curtsy, on top of the seat, and climbed over the ramparts to where her mother slept. For the rest of the day and all night she didn't say another word to the young man.

Early the next morning he woke to the smell of coffee and, squinting his eyes, found Melissa in the seat beside him; she sat there and read her book and held a Styrofoam cup of coffee in one hand. From the vantage point of eyes that were supposed to be asleep, he tried to size her up, to make sense out of her, to see what she could possibly be. It turned out that she looked like an eleven-year-old child reading a book and drinking a cup of coffee.

"Quit looking at me," she said. "It just so happens that my mother makes snores and this is the only available seat on the whole bus. I thought you could be trusted, that's all. We're almost to Nashville, you know, and I slept very badly. Everybody used up all the air. I'm fit to be tied really."

"Good morning," said the young man. He, too, had slept badly, had not slept well for longer than he cared to remember. It struck him that everybody had been using up his air for quite a while.

"It's a terrible morning," Melissa said. She closed her book. "It's raining and the newspapers at the rest stop said our president fell down again. Off a *plane*. In front of a million cameras. Those men are always falling down somewhere in front of a camera. It's a terrible morning really. Would you care for some coffee?"

"Thank you, yes." The young man took off his beret and placed it in his lap, attempting against all odds to look presentable. Among other things, he was unshaven, unwashed, penniless, unhappy, and fairly uncertain. Things, however, were

276

looking brighter. Melissa exchanged the coffee for the beret, which she placed on top of her head.

"Do you think I'm cute?" she asked, coyly. The young man pointed out that cute was really an understatement.

"My mother was beautiful in her prime. She was a professional woman. We're going to Dallas, Texas, to further her career. She dances, badly enough, but Uncle Burnt—he's her manager, insists I call him Uncle but he isn't really, looks more like a massive murderer to tell the truth—Uncle Burnt says they may not know the difference in Dallas." Melissa took off the beret, punched it several times, stretched it out, punched it again, then returned it to the young man's lap. "I'm one of those bittered children," she said and sighed. "It's made me very religious though. I was an immaculate birth, you know. I'm practicing to be a martyr, but once I punched this girl, Marcia Dinwiddie, in the face for making a sinuous comment on my mother, so I might be disqualified already. Do you believe?"

"In what?" the young man asked. In five minutes he had progressed from a fitful sleep to the very edge of his seat. "I mean believe in what?"

"You do," Melissa said, "I can see you do. Your eyes are a dead giveaway really. I collect eyes, matched pairs only. Once I met this woman that had one green eye and one blue one. Honestly. But what happened was, she used contacts. She *wanted* two different eyes. I really couldn't see that."

The young man nodded. He said he really couldn't see that, either, then he asked her where she came from. He still sat, perched like a pigeon, on the edge of his seat.

"I was born in Okemah, Oklahoma, you know, where that guy Woody Guthrie came from, but I'm pretty flexible. I was only a very young baby then." She paused, rubbing her nose with a poised index finger. "It's not where anyway, it's how. I learned music in Tampa Bay, Florida, and got a sunburn and went to a hospital. I learned Spanish from this man with a finger where his thumb was supposed to be, out in Dracula, Georgia. I had a boyfriend in Washington, D.C., where they tested me for the I.Q., but we left there and I was glad. He had these nitwit canaries at his house and every time you went there he'd go up to those canaries and say 'How are we today?' like he was a canary too, or like they weren't doing terrible in that nitwit cage. Then his mother would come in, she's why I was glad we left, and *she'd* ask them how they were, too, and make us come over and look at them sing. At night they put a blanket over it to shut them up. They were all nitwits, especially the birds. He was my only boyfriend. I adored him a little bit really."

Melissa pulled reflectively on the hem of her skirt.

"I have to be running along," she said. "She'll wake up any minute. She's a very nervous person when she wakes up on buses." She stood up with her book. The young man stood up, awkwardly, one knee on the seat, and said he hoped they'd meet again.

"It's likely," she said, "I get around. Do you ever write unquieted love songs, because if you do, I'll keep my ears open." With her free hand she placed a finger beside her nose, looking up at the young man. "Do you think you could kiss my forehead goodbye?" she asked pensively. "Just a little one, really, is all I want." The young man complied with no hesitation whatsoever, and kissed the place a half an inch below the part of Melissa's hair.

It happened right then, and it happened quickly. First, not two feet away, came an incredibly high-pitched, resounding scream that listed sideways and echoed down the aisle of the bus like a tidal surge. Every face turned around and the bus pulled over to the side of the road. Next, Melissa disappeared and a torsoless head of magenta-colored hair began to bob up and down, screaming "Rape! Rape!" in a voice that, unbelievably, didn't shatter every glass object in a three-mile radius. The young man grabbed hold of his guitar, as if it might prove to be an anchor through the ground swell. It did not. In his approach the driver to

Dallas rolled up his shirtsleeves and, upon arrival in the rear, picked up the young man bodily from his seat by the scruff of the neck, carried him effortlessly, guitar and all, back down the aisle, and tossed him like so much chaff out the door and into the street.

"Preverted motherfucker!" the driver yelled, then he slammed the door shut. Forty faces peered with obvious delight out of six large windows.

The young man picked himself up slowly. He executed a quick double check, found himself to be intact, in his entirety, and found his guitar to be roughed up, though healthy. He watched his connection to Nashville disappear around a stand of forlorn pine trees. And then, for reasons uncertain, but certainly for questions unanswered, he began to spring at a high speed down the road, through the rain, after the bus, into the direction of Dallas, Texas; he was going to follow her, find her—grab on to her, cleave to her—listen to her, ask her—

There is a second license of country music, one often confused for a very different thing, and it concerns the nature of sentimentality. I shall dispose of this matter right now. Back in the thirties when Roy Acuff first recorded, a story floated around asserting that whenever he sang a sad song he wept openly because of a "sentimental" nature; it's a lie. Sentimentality is rose-colored and walks a poodle. What Roy Acuff saw and felt and sang was a different color, and sadder than even a poodle. The second license of country music is, of course, sentimentality standing precariously upon its head. It is a view of the world from the bottom up, blood rushing toward the brain, arms trembling, feet flailing. It wants more than anything in the world to see things right-side up, and it's scared to death it will.

After my brother's death they shipped the guitar with him by steamer and by freight train back home to Carter Valley. He died in Nicaragua, guitar in hand, with a well-aimed sniper's bullet in his head. He died there, for unspeakably good reasons, two years ago. I happen to have his guitar with me, and although I can't play it, still I can sit, very quietly, and look out over the frozen Hudson River, and then I can hear the thing for miles and miles.

Melissa, wherever you are out there, whatever you're doing, I *know* you can hear it, too: Listen—

The Writers

RAYMOND ANDREWS was born in Morgan County, Georgia, the son of a sharecropper, and left home at fifteen to live in Atlanta, where he finished high school while working at jobs as a hospital orderly, bartender, busboy, and dishwasher. After four years in the U.S. Air Force he attended Michigan State University. Andrews is the author of three novels. The first, *Appalachee Red* (1978), won the James Baldwin Prize. *Baby Sweet's*, the third novel in a trilogy set in the fictional Muskhogean County, Georgia, was published in 1983. For many years Andrews lived in New York City. He now lives in Athens, Georgia.

MADISON SMARTT BELL grew up on a farm near Franklin, Tennessee, the son of a country lawyer (now a circuit judge) and a mother who was a Fulbright Fellow. He was educated at Princeton and studied writing at Hollins College. Bell has published stories and articles in magazines such as *Harper's*, the *Hudson Review*, and the *Carolina Quarterly*, and he is the author of three novels: *The Washington Square Ensemble* (1983), *Waiting for the End of the World* (1985), and *Straight Cut* (1986). He lives in Baltimore.

PAM DURBAN was born in Aiken, South Carolina, and grew up there. She has lived in New York, Kentucky, and Ohio for the past ten years, most recently in Athens, Ohio, where she taught at Ohio University. In the fall of 1986 she returned to the South to teach at Georgia State University in Atlanta. Durban's stories have appeared in magazines such as the *Georgia Review*, *Crazyhorse*, and *TriQuarterly*, and her collection of stories *All Set About with Fever Trees* was published by David R. Godine in 1985.

CLYDE EDGERTON lives in Apex, North Carolina, and teaches at St. Andrews Presbyterian College in Laurinburg. He grew up in the small rural community of Bethesda, near Durham, and attended the University of North Carolina. *Raney*, Edgerton's comic novel of the modern South, was published by Algonquin Books of Chapel Hill in 1985 and proved to be a Southern best-seller: it has now gone into six printings. Edgerton is working on his second novel, *Walking Across Egypt*, which is tentatively scheduled for 1987 publication.

RICHARD FORD was born in Jackson, Mississippi, spent his early years in the South, and in 1985 returned to the South to live in the Mississippi Delta. In between he attended Michigan State University, studied writing at the University of California, and lived at various times in Vermont, New York, Montana, and New Jersey. Ford has won fellowships from the National Endowment for the Arts and the Guggenheim Foundation. He is the author of three novels—*A Piece of My Heart* (1976), *The Ultimate Good Luck* (1981), and *The Sportswriter* (1986)—and a collection of his stories is forthcoming.

ELLEN GILCHRIST was born on the Mississippi cotton plantation where she lived as a child, but she has also lived outside the South as well as in Fayetteville, Arkansas, and in New Orleans, the setting of many of her stories. She now makes her home in Jackson, Mississippi. With the publication of *In the Land of Dreamy Dreams* in 1981, Gilchrist moved into the forefront of contemporary short fiction writers. She has since published two other collections of stories, *Victory Over Japan* (1984), which won an American Book Award, and *Drunk with Love* (1986), and a novel, *The Annunciation* (1983).

DONALD HAYS was born in Jacksonville, Florida, where his father, a career enlisted man, was serving in the Navy. When he was seven his father retired to a hill farm in northwest Arkansas. Hays grew up there, went to high school in Van Buren, and attended Southern Arkansas University. In 1982 he received an MFA in creative writing from the University of Arkansas in Fayetteville. His first novel, *The Dixie Association*, was published by Simon & Schuster in 1984. His second, *The Hangman's Children*, is tentatively scheduled for publication in 1987.

MARY HOOD lives in Woodstock, in the foothills of the North Georgia mountains, the locale of her fiction. She was born in Brunswick, on the Georgia coast. Hood's stories have appeared in the *Kenyon Review*, the *Georgia Review*, and other magazines, and her first collection of stories, published by the University of Georgia Press in 1984, was a winner of the Flannery O'Connor Award for Short Fiction. It also won the *Southern Review* Prize as the best first collection of short fiction published that year in this country. Mary Hood's second collection, *And Venus Is Blue*, was published by Ticknor & Fields in 1986.

JOSEPHINE HUMPHREYS has lived all of her life in Charleston, South Carolina. She attended Duke University, Yale, and the University of Texas, and while at Duke studied writing with Reynolds Price and William Blackburn. Humphreys's first novel, *Dreams of Sleep*, published by Viking in 1984, won the Ernest Hemingway Foundation Award. She is now at work on a second novel, and she will be writing her third with the assistance of a Guggenheim Foundation Fellowship recently awarded her.

BEVERLY LOWRY was born in Memphis, Tennessee, and grew up in Greenville, Mississippi. For the past twenty years she has lived in Texas. Her publishing debut came with Doubleday's release of *Come Back, Lolly Ray* (1977), and her second novel, *Emma Blue*, appeared a year later, followed in 1981 by her third, *Daddy's Girl*. Her work has been widely praised and she has been awarded fellowships by the National Endowment for the Arts and the Guggenheim Foundation. Lowry's short stories and articles have appeared in *Vanity Fair, Texas Monthly*, the *Black Warrior Review*, and elsewhere.

JILL MCCORKLE, author of *July 7th* and *The Cheer Leader*, is one of the youngest of these writers. Born in Lumberton, North Carolina, on July 7, 1958, she attended the University of North Carolina and studied writing at Hollins College. The decision of Algonquin Books to publish her two novels in the same 1984 season gave McCorkle's debut added importance, and the reviews of both books amply justified Algonquin's faith in them. Jill McCorkle presently lives in Chapel Hill, where she is a lecturer in creative writing at the university.

BOBBIE ANN MASON was born and grew up in Mayfield, Kentucky, but left the South when she was in her early twenties. For a time she lived in New York City. She now lives in rural Pennsylvania. Her first book of fiction, *Shiloh and Other Stories* (1982), was eagerly awaited by those who had admired her stories in the *Atlantic Monthly* and the *New Yorker*, and won her the Ernest Hemingway Foundation Award. In 1985 Harper & Row brought out her first novel, *In Country*. Some of Mason's stories have appeared in the *Best American Short Stories* volumes.

LEWIS NORDAN was born in Jackson, Mississippi, and grew up in the Mississippi Delta town of Itta Bena. He attended Millsaps College and received advanced degrees from Mississippi State University and Auburn University. Nordan's short stories began

284

to appear in magazines in the 1970s. His first collection of stories, *Welcome to the Arrow-Catcher Fair,* was published by the Louisiana State University Press in 1983. The LSU Press has scheduled publication of his second collection, *The All-Girl Football Team,* for fall 1986. Nordan lives in Pittsburgh.

T. R. PEARSON is a young North Carolina writer who has delighted readers with two novels chronicling the secret and not-so-secret life of a small Southern town that Pearson calls Neely. Sections of his first novel, *A Short History of a Small Place,* originally appeared in the *Virginia Quarterly Review.* Linden Press published the book in 1985, and followed it with *Off for the Sweet Hereafter* (1986). Pearson was born in Winston-Salem in 1956 and now lives in Fuquay-Varina, North Carolina.

JAYNE ANNE PHILLIPS was born and grew up in Buckhannon, West Virginia, and attended West Virginia University, but she has lived outside the South for much of her life, presently in Massachusetts. She also studied at the University of Iowa, and in 1978 was the recipient of a National Endowment for the Arts Fellowship. Two years later she received the Sue Kaufman Award for First Fiction from the American Academy and Institute of Arts and Letters for her collection of stories *Black Tickets.* In 1984 E. P. Dutton/Seymour Lawrence brought out *Machine Dreams,* her first novel.

PADGETT POWELL was born in Gainesville, Florida, where he presently lives, and grew up in Jacksonville, Tallahassee, and Orlando. He went to school in Charleston. Powell's fiction has appeared in the *New Yorker* and he is the author of the 1984 novel *Edisto,* from which the excerpt in this anthology was taken. His second novel, *A Woman Named Drown,* is scheduled to appear in 1987. In the meantime he has a story coming out in *Esquire.* He teaches at the University of Florida.

LOUISE SHIVERS, author of *Here to Get My Baby Out of Jail*, grew up in eastern North Carolina and attended Meredith College in Raleigh. The North Carolina tobacco country is the setting for her novel, which was published in 1983 by Random House and won generous praise from reviewers. Shivers is now at work on her second novel. She has also written poetry and short fiction. She lives in Augusta, Georgia.

CHARLIE SMITH was born and raised in Moultrie, Georgia, and has spent much of his life in the South, but for the last five years has lived mostly in the North, in Iowa City and now in Provincetown, Massachusetts. Smith's novella *Crystal River* won the Aga Khan Prize for Fiction from the *Paris Review* and was subsequently anthologized in the 1985 *Editors' Choice*. In 1984 Simon & Schuster published his first novel, *Canaan*. He also writes poetry, and has a collection coming out from Dutton.

JAMES WILCOX was born in Hammond, Louisiana, and grew up there and in Tallahassee, Florida. He went off to Yale in 1967, but spent summers in Louisiana. His stories began appearing in the *New Yorker* in the early 1980s, and his first novel, *Modern Baptists*, came out in 1983, followed two years later by *North Gladiola*. Wilcox was awarded a Guggenheim Foundation Fellowship in 1986. He is now living in New York City and working on a novel tentatively scheduled for publication by Harper & Row in 1987.

LEIGH ALLISON WILSON, the young Tennessee writer who was one of the early winners of the Flannery O'Connor Award for Short Fiction, now lives in Oswego, New York, where she teaches. Wilson's prizewinning collection of stories *From the Bottom Up* was published by the University of Georgia Press in 1983, and subsequently came out in paperback in the Penguin Contemporary American Fiction Series. Her stories have appeared in *Mademoiselle*, the *Georgia Review*, the *Southern Review*, and, most recently, *Harper's*.

The Editor

Charles East has been editor of the Flannery O'Connor Award for Short Fiction since the series was established by the University of Georgia Press in 1981. He was editor of the short fiction series that was established by the Louisiana State University Press in the 1960s. A native of Mississippi, East began his career in publishing as an editorial assistant on the staff of *Collier's* magazine in the late 1940s. For several years he worked on newspapers before moving into book publishing. From 1962 to 1975 he was with the LSU Press, first as editor and then as director. Later he was assistant director and editor of the University of Georgia Press until he returned to Baton Rouge in 1983.

Charles East's short stories have appeared in the *Southern Review*, *Mademoiselle*, the *Virginia Quarterly Review*, the *Yale Review*, the *Antioch Review*, and other magazines, and he is the author of *Where the Music Was*, a collection of stories published by Harcourt, Brace & World. He has also written articles and reviews as well as two books that grew out of his interest in photographs as historical documents.